BLOCK 4 PERSONAL WORLDS

BLOCK INTRODUCTION

UNIT 12 THE EXPERIENCE OF BEING A PERSON

Prepared for the course team by Richard Stevens

UNIT 13 MAKING SENSE OF SUBJECTIVE EXPERIENCE

Prepared for the course team by Richard Stevens

UNIT 14 DEVELOPMENT AND CHANGE IN PERSONAL LIFE

Prepared for the course team by Richard Stevens

SOCIAL SCIENCES: A THIRD LEVEL COURSE
SOCIAL PSYCHOLOGY: DEVELOPMENT, EXPERIENCE
AND BEHAVIOUR IN A SOCIAL WORLD

THE OPEN UNIVERSITY PRESS

Set Reading

Unit 12
Pages 71–3 of the Set Book (Stevens, 1983)
Unit 14
Pages 76–8 of Set Book (Stevens, 1983)
Chapter 14 of the Set Book (Stevens, 1983)

The Open University
Walton Hall, Milton Keynes
MK7 6AA

First published 1985. Reprinted 1988, 1991

1.3

BLOCK 4 INTRODUCTION

Both you and I are aware that we are *persons*. Being a person is not the same as being a machine, a collection of physiological functions or a set of behavioural reflexes. Each of us inhabits a distinctive world of subjective experiences on which we can reflect; each of us has self-awareness. We are conscious also of being a *particular* person with a particular past and with particular expectations of the future. Alex who lives near me, for example, exists in a world of shadows and sadness. He is fighting cancer, his wife has left him and he is out of work. Only his belief in God has stopped him from trying to end it all. In contrast, for Sally, his next-door neighbour, the future is bright with hope. She has just left school to start work as a hairdresser, which is all she has ever wanted to do. She lives comfortably with her parents, spends most evenings out enjoying herself with her friends and has just got engaged. Two personal worlds which, while they share features in common, are somehow 'owned' by and particular to the people concerned.

Take a few moments to think about your personal world. Focus on how you *experience* it, not on how it might be described by a scientist or an outside observer. What does it seem like to *you*? You might like to note down its more significant features.

This Block sets out to examine the nature of such personal worlds. It looks at the role of psychology in trying to make sense of the subjective experience of being a person and in conceptualizing the pattern of our lives. It also considers the inevitable problems which such investigations involve.

The Block consists of three units:

Unit 12: The Experience of Being a Person   An analysis of some sample glimpses of different personal worlds in Part 1 of Unit 12 suggests some of the general features which they seem to have in common. Part 2 then goes on to explore in greater depth four key features:

(a)   Our experience of *time*, particularly the impact of knowing that at some stage we shall cease to exist.

(b)   Our sense of *agency* (i.e. that we can, if we choose to, make things happen).

(c)   The significance of purpose and *meaningfulness* in our lives.

(d)   The awareness of having a particular *identity*.

Unit 13: Making Sense of Subjective Experience   At the centre of any personal world lies the flow of immediate subjective experience. Unit 13 looks at some of the different ways in which psychologists have tried to make sense of this. It emphasizes that subjective experience is constituted by meanings and discusses the problems involved in studying so elusive a subject.

Unit 14: Development and Change in Personal Life   Personal worlds can also be regarded as a biographical flow from the awakening awareness of self through maturity to old age. Part 1 of Unit 14 looks at how social psychologists have thought about and investigated the *life-cycle*. Part 2 concludes the Block with a discussion of the theoretical, methodological and personal implications of the analysis which has been presented of the experience of being a person and of the changing pattern of personal worlds as we progress through life.

Associated reading

The readings for this Block, which are from the Set Book *Freud and Psychoanalysis* and the Course Reader, are listed in the table below.

	Set	Optional
Unit 12	*Freud and Psychoanalysis:* part of chapter 8 (pp. 71–3)	
Unit 13*		*Freud and Psychoanalysis:* chapter 1 (pp. 3–15)
Unit 14*	*Freud and Psychoanalysis:* part of chapter 8 (pp. 76–8); chapter 14 (pp. 143–8)	Course Reader: article by Sarason (pp. 314–30)

*Also revision work on chapters from *Freud and Psychoanalysis* which were set reading in previous weeks. For Unit 13: chapters 3–5, 6–7 (optional) and 9. For Unit 14: chapter 11.

Associated project

The Interview Project requires you to explore by means of interviews some aspect of another's personal world. In this way, it provides a useful practical complement to the issues discussed in the Block. Working on it should help your understanding of the problems of gaining access to another person's experience and life history and of describing this.

Plan of Block 4

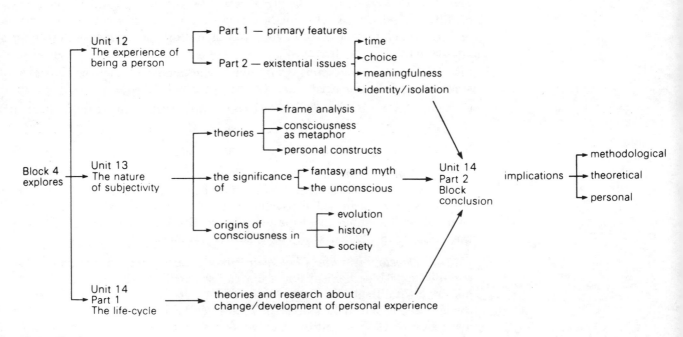

Associated reading — *Freud and Psychoanalysis* (set and optional readings) / Course Reader (optional)

Associated project: Interview (optional)

A note on the approach of the Block

Although we will be looking in this Block at both theories and research, there will be little reference to experimental results and 'hard data'. Our subject-matter is personal experience and the pattern of our lives. It will be argued that these are best regarded as *qualitative*: i.e. they are not effectively reducible to numbers and specific testable hypotheses. (For further discussion of this issue see Unit 14, Part 2 and Metablock Paper 5.) To say that we need to explore our personal worlds as we experience them is not to deny their interdependence with physiological functioning, physical contexts and processes of cognition, but it is to assert that they are not reducible to these. We need to explore them at their own level of analysis too. What interests us are the *meanings* which personal worlds contain. To understand these it is necessary to tease out the pattern and nature of our personal experience and explore its implications, rather than attempting an explanation in terms of specific causes and effects. This goal has been well summarized by Clifford Geertz:

> Toward the end of his recent study of the ideas used by tribal peoples, *La Pensée Sauvage*, the French anthropologist Lévi-Strauss remarks that scientific explanation does not consist, as we have been led to imagine, in the reduction of the complex to the simple. Rather, it consists, he says, in a substitution of a complexity more intelligible for one which is less. So far as the study of man is concerned, one may go even further, I think, and argue that explanation often consists of substituting complex pictures for simple ones while striving to retain the persuasive clarity that went with the simple ones.

> (Geertz, 1975, p. 33)

In terms of the concepts expounded in Paper 2 of Part III of the Metablock, the emphasis in this Block then will be on *differentiation* not testability (i.e. on making sense and stimulating thinking about our subject-matter rather than looking at research involving the testing of specific hypotheses with the aim of establishing general laws about the causes of what we are studying).

Although this emphasis contrasts with much of the work discussed in Unit 10/11, it has characterized several of the theories you have encountered earlier in the course: for example, systems theory (Unit 2), psychoanalysis, Piaget's theory and symbolic interactionism (Unit 4) and personal construct theory (Unit 8). However, one difference between these theories (with the exception of the last one) and this Block is the greater emphasis here on personal, conscious experience – how it feels to be a person, rather than looking at people, as it were, from the outside. In other words, the broad perspective of much of the Block is phenomenological and existential (see Box 1). To some extent, another difference is that in this Block we are more concerned with a person's life experience as a whole (i.e. a *holistic* approach) rather than with some particular aspect such as how they perceive others or who they find attractive and why.

We all experience ourselves as persons but we vary a good deal in how far and in what ways we reflect on that experience. The essential aim of the Block is to stimulate your thinking about the personal worlds of both yourself and other people. It is intended to 'raise consciousness': that is, to suggest aspects of and ways of thinking about your experience of being a person which you may already have some awareness of but have not before articulated explicitly in quite that manner.

phenomenological approach

[handwritten margin note: e.g. dying — can write from personal experience]

existential perspective

[handwritten margin note: but can write about dying from this perspective — as everyone will experience it.]

[handwritten mark: ✱]

Box 1 Phenomenological and existential perspectives in psychology

The core of the phenomenological approach is '. . . the general principle that. . . priority should be given to an analysis of experience from the point of view of those who have the experiences or are able to have them' (Pivcevic, 1975, p. xii).

To adopt an existential perspective is to take as your starting point the experience of existing as a person. Thus there is concern with the problems that each of us confront as human beings: for example, the need to make choices about how we act and the need to confront the fact that eventually we shall die.

The most radical contrast to these perspectives within psychology is, of course, behaviourism. For this stresses the need to look at people from the outside – in terms of what you can observe and measure. It also emphasizes a determinist position – that we are entirely the product of causes outside our conscious control. Thus subjective experience and conscious choice are not considered by behaviourists to be legitimate subject-matter for psychology.

While both phenomenology and existentialism began as philosophical movements, similar approaches have made their appearance throughout the history of psychology and sociology. Early psychologists, like Wundt and James, both placed great store on the importance of introspection and investigating subjective experience. The Gestalt psychologists emphasized in their work on perception and learning the need to work with what people actually experience. Two theories you have already encountered, symbolic interactionism and personal construct theory, also take as their subject-matter the way people experience and make sense of the world. Humanistic psychologists like Maslow and Rogers have emphasized not only the significance of subjective experience but also that we can be to a large extent as we choose to be – a position very much in line with existential thought.

General objectives

After working on the Block, you should be able to discuss in greater depth:

1 The nature of personal worlds and the problems of conceptualizing and investigating them. What kind of knowledge is possible here?

2 Some of the ways in which psychologists have tried to make sense of the subjective experience of being a person.

3 Social psychological research and theories on the changing pattern of life from childhood to old age.

References

GEERTZ, C. (1975) *The Interpretation of Cultures*, London, Hutchinson.

MURPHY, J., JOHN M. and BROWN, H. (eds) (1984) *Dialogues and Debates in Social Psychology*, London, Lawrence Erlbaum (Course Reader).

PIVCEVIC, E. (1975) *Phenomenology and Philosophical Understanding*, Cambridge, Cambridge University Press.

STEVENS, R. (1983) *Freud and psychoanalysis*, Milton Keynes, Open University Press (Set Book).

UNIT 12
THE EXPERIENCE OF BEING A PERSON

Prepared for the course team by Richard Stevens

CONTENTS

'Truth is not that which is demonstrable. Truth is that which cannot be escaped.'
(Antoine de Saint-Exupéry)

Objectives

After having studied this unit you should be able to discuss the following:

1   what is meant by the concept 'personal worlds';

2   some of the primary characteristics of our experience as persons;

3   the nature and significance of the experience of time and finiteness;

4   the sense of ourselves as 'agents' i.e. as capable of initiating actions, and the implications of this;

5   the concept of personal identity;

6   how our awareness of ourselves and of the world is, in part at least, constructed by the social context in which we live.

PART 1: EXPLORING PERSONAL WORLDS

1 WHAT ARE PERSONAL WORLDS?

personal worlds Something of what I mean by the rather curious term 'personal worlds' was sketched in the Block Introduction. Before going further, it might be worth clarifying this a little more.

I have coined the phrase to denote our subjective awareness of ourselves as persons and the overall pattern of our personal life experience. To study personal worlds is not to study people as physiological organisms or information processing machines. It is to study the general features of personal existence as each of us experiences or *can* experience it as a human individual. In Box 1 I try to express something of what this means for me.

Box 1   General characteristics of my personal world

I have a sense of existing at a particular point both in time and space. My personal world is circumscribed by *time*. There is a paradoxical sense of being fixed at a moment of continuous change. I locate my present in terms both of my particular life history and that of the society of which I am part. My present contains within it an awareness of what has happened in the past and also anticipations of the future. I am located too in *space*. As school children sometimes write their addresses, I can think of this in a hierarchy of levels: my position in this room, this room in the house; the house in the district; and so on through town, county, country, world, the universe, etc. I am aware of definite limits and rules which govern my existence in physical space. I cannot walk through the wall nor will I suddenly and unexpectedly find myself in India. In the world of my imagination I may wander both temporally and spatially. I can project myself to far distant, even imaginary, places, and into the past and future. But even then there is a sense in which I know I remain here in the continuously changing and located present.

My personal world is rooted not only in a *body*, but in a *sense of self*, which involves my particular history, an anticipated though vague future, a set of relationships and a social context. This pattern distinguishes me from other people. Although there may be many aspects which we share in common, my personal world is distinct. It is unique in that no-one else experiences quite the same pattern as I do.

I *find* myself in this world which I inhabit. I did not choose it. Its basic characteristics are not of my making. I did not decide when or where I was to be born, whom my parents were to be, the form of my genetic and material inheritance, nor, consciously at least, the way I was brought up. I do not suppose that there is that much that I personally can do to determine the nature of the society in which I live or even (unless I commit suicide) the time and manner of my death. Thus, much of my personal world seems decided for me. Paradoxically though, I also have an almost awesome sense of the possibility for self-direction – that I can choose both what I do and what I shall become. Although I am aware of being caught up in a flow of events and other people's actions, I still assume that I can help create not only my own future but that of the groups in which I play

---

[handwritten margin note: body / sense of self]

11

an active part. To this end, I plan procedures and schedules and work to try to bring things about in the way that I think best.

I am aware of the multiple nature of my personal world. It is peopled by different characters, requirements, joys and frustrations. I am aware too of differences in mood and quality – often it is a mundane taken-for-grantedness, very occasionally a bleak landscape in which I can only resist passively or struggle with fortitude to survive. There are also times of quiet serenity or joyful exhilaration. I am pretty sure that, although they have much in common, the personal worlds of others are not quite the same as mine. The quality of my communication is measured by my capacity to enter other people's personal experience and to share mine with them, though it is difficult to be sure how far I have succeeded in doing so. My everyday social intercourse and relationships demand and provide a constant test of this ability to achieve at least a modicum of shared understanding.

Does this general description also apply to *your* personal world? Check each point against your own experience. Are there any features which do not hold for you? If so, you might like to discuss such differences with one or two other people to see how it is for them.

The term 'personal world' is intentionally loose. To define it more precisely would be to lose the breadth and flexibility it provides. 'Identity' is a part, but a 'personal world' is more than this. It incorporates not just our awareness of our own self but our experience of the world about us. The core of any personal world is an individual sense of being. It involves a *Gestalt* or pattern of perceptions, thoughts, feelings, and an awareness of oneself and of other people and events in the world. It depends on the meanings these have for one at different times, both conscious and unconscious. All this is underpinned by a sense of profound mystery. How did you or I come to inhabit the particular personal world that we do? The coming into being of each of us hangs on an infinite chain of chance events: our parents meeting and their ancestors before them, the precise moment of our conception and on one particular sperm reaching the ovum first, and all the other events which might have been otherwise and yet were not and which make you and I what we are. And how is it that each of us comes to be locked in the particular personal world which is ours and not someone else's? And how might the course of our lives be different had we consciously chosen at certain moments to do differently than we did?

Such wonders you may think are the province of metaphysics. And yet, because they lie at the core of our sense of being, they are surely the concern of psychology too.

1.1 Four windows

At this stage, it would be useful if we could examine some samples of personal worlds. This is not easy to do. Actual experience has a partial, fragmented quality. And when we try to express such experience, it is difficult to communicate the vividness and complexity, the 'feel' of the original. For one thing, such expressions usually take the form of words. But our personal worlds are so much more than can ever be expressed verbally or in print. They are made up of sounds, feelings, sensations, images, meanings – all of which can only be indirectly conveyed.

The four extracts which follow have been selected because they provide varied pictures of personal worlds. Taken together, they also serve to illustrate a good range of the characteristics which all personal worlds seem to have in common. I call them 'windows' because they can inevitably offer us only the barest glimpse of the worlds that lie beyond. But they can still be useful to stimulate our thinking about the nature, form and variety of the subjective experience of persons in a social world.

They are worth reading carefully because they will be used to illustrate the discussion of general characteristics of personal worlds which follows. In particular:

1 Try to get the 'feel' of the personal world which each suggests? What kind of experience is it? How would you describe it?

2 Look for any features or dimensions which these personal worlds may have in common.

Window 1

The first extract, taken from the autobiographical book *Changing* by the Norwegian actress Liv Ullman, gives us a glimpse of her personal world as she experiences it towards the end of a flight from Europe to Los Angeles. Linn is her daughter.

Window 1 Liv

My reality this winter consists of many things. Even this: I wake from a doze. My flight is approaching a city. The sun vanishes behind tall mountains. Far below, lights go on in thousands of windows and street advertisements. For a moment I don't remember where I am going. Cities resemble each other as much as the planes that take me to them. It is disquieting that one's destination should be so unimportant. The same women and men will be standing by the same exits and will exclaim the same words of welcome when they see me. People with flowers and kindness, all in a hurry to pack me into a car and drive me to some luxury hotel, where they can abandon me and go home to their own lives. A suite with sitting room and bedroom, deep armchairs upholstered in silk, big windows looking out onto palms and a swimming pool.

Champagne on ice with the compliments of the management. Flowers and baskets of fruit. Hall porters bowing themselves in and out with my luggage and my letters and my telephone messages. Smiles and politeness and the unreality that surrounds it all.

While I smile enthusiastically and thank them.

My reality is also this:

The airplane is circling above a city. There is expectancy in me as I look out into the night. I know it is hot. No need to think of Norwegian homespun and boots for a few days . . . air that calls for no more than a thin blouse.

I shall be awake when everyone at home is asleep.

The stewardesses are busy clearing up after their long trip. They are eager and bustling; we are all infected with the same anticipation.

It has been a long flight. There has been a film and breakfast and lunch and dinner. Trolleys have been trundled in and out with food and fruit, ice-cold drinks, and a woollen blanket to put round me when I want to sleep.

I try to arrange my hair, glad that Hollywood has accepted my 'natural look'.

At home people will soon be waking up to a dark winter's morning and their feet and bottoms will be freezing, while I am sitting in the shade of a palm, and the feel of the evening air will be sensual, as it never is in Oslo. I shall sleep in a broad, soft bed. Be woken in the morning by a waiter who knows me from earlier visits. He will draw the curtains and let the sun flood into the room, push in a table with breakfast and fresh orange juice. Then he will ask after Linn. Give me a newspaper of a hundred pages and wish me a good day.

It's easy to make me feel secure and happy for a short while. I don't need to be near the man I love. Or Linn. Sometimes the sense of security is within myself.

(Ullman, 1976, pp. 9–10)

Before reading on, stop and jot down any points which this passage may have brought to your mind about the general nature of personal worlds. What are the key features which characterize this one? How well do they match the description in Box 1?

You might like to make similar notes at the end of each extract before reading the commentary which follows each one. There I indicate aspects which seem relevant to me. (NB These are points to which I want to draw your attention. They are not meant to suggest that this is necessarily what *you* should have put.)

Notes

1   There is a focal point in this account – the *conscious awareness* of Liv.

2   This is located in *space* (in an aeroplane and a Hollywood hotel, etc.), though sometimes (e.g. as she awakes from dozing) it may require an effort for her to recall where she is.

3   This personal world is located in *time* also, and in a narrative of events governed by implicit order and expectations as to what is possible and probable.

4   In a sense, it is possible for Liv, while remaining physically located in time and space, to *transcend* these. Thus she can envision what will happen to her later at the hotel and how everyone at home in Norway will wake up shortly to a dark winter morning.

5   There is location in a *physical environment of a particular quality* – sensual evening air, soft bed, freezing cold. The objects (like champagne and flowers) carry meaning, suggesting a particular style of life, a particular kind of person and social context.

6   *People* clearly form part of Liv's personal world. They assume varying degrees of relationship. Some are hardly more than background figures – though even here there is a sense of interlocking with the personal worlds of other people (the supporting characters are seen as going 'home to their own lives'). People who are special in her life like her daughter Linn are still thought about and so form part of the world of her experience even though they are far away.

7   This personal world has a particular *emotional tone* – positive and comfortable though perhaps rather bland and with just a suggestion of underlying insecurity.

8   Finally, an interesting aspect is the hints ('My reality . . . consists of many things' and later 'My reality is also this') that her personal world does not just exist in one form but has *multiple aspects*; and also that Liv is capable of construing her personal experience in rather different ways.

Window 2

The second excerpt is part of an interview with an old gardener. It comes from a collection of interviews by Ronald Blythe with people living in the Norfolk village of Akenfield.

Window 2   Christopher

I went to Lordship's when I was fourteen and stayed for fourteen years. There were seven gardeners and goodness knows how many servants in the house. It was a frightening experience for a boy. Lord and Ladyship were very, very Victorian and very domineering. It was 'swing your arms' every time they saw us. Ladyship would appear suddenly from nowhere when one of us boys were walking off to fetch something. 'Swing your arms!' she would shout. We wore green baize aprons and collars and ties, no matter how hot it was, and whatever we had to do had to be done on the dot. Nobody was allowed to smoke. A gardener was immediately sacked if he was caught smoking, no matter how long he had worked there.

We must never be seen from the house; it was forbidden. And if people were sitting on the terrace or on the lawn, and you had a great barrow-load of weeds, you might have to push it as much as a mile to keep out of view. If you were seen you were always told about it and warned, and as you walked away Ladyship would call after you, 'Swing your arms!' It was terrible. You felt like somebody with a disease.

The boy under-gardeners had to help arrange the flowers in the house. These were done every day. We had to creep in early in the morning before breakfast and replace great banks of flowers in the main rooms. Lordship and Ladyship must never hear or see you doing it . . .

As the years went by, we young men found ourselves being able to talk to Lordship and Ladyship. 'Never speak to them – not one word and no matter how urgent – until they speak to you,' the head-gardener told me on my first day. Ladyship drove about the grounds in a motor-chair and would have run us over rather than have to say, 'get out the way'. We must never look at her and she never looked at us. It was the same in the house. If a maid was in a passage and Lordship or Ladyship happened to come along, she would have to face the wall and stand perfectly still until they had passed. I wouldn't think that they felt anything about their servants. We were just there because we were necessary, like water from the tap. We had to listen for voices. If we heard them in a certain walk, we had to make a detour, if not it was, 'But why weren't you listening?' and 'Be alert, boy!' and, when you had been dismissed, 'Swing your arms!'

The garden was huge. The pleasure grounds alone, and not including the park, covered seven acres. The kind of gardening we did there is not seen nowadays. It was a perfect art. Topiary, there was a lot of that. It was a very responsible job. You had only to make one bad clip and a pheasant became a duck. The gardeners usually made up these creatures themselves. We were tempted to cut out something terrible sometimes, so that it grew and grew . . . but of course we never did. . .

There were so many things which really had no need to be done but which we did out of a kind of obstinate pleasure. The asparagus beds in winter were an example. We'd spend hours getting the sides of the clamps absolutely flat and absolutely at a 45° angle, although an ordinary heap of earth would have done just as well.

None of the village people were allowed into the garden. Definitely not. Trades-people came to their door and never saw the main gardens. Work in front of the house had to be done secretly. About seven in the morning we would tiptoe about the terrace, sweeping the leaves, tying things up, never making a sound, so that nobody in the bedrooms could hear the work being done. This is what luxury means – perfect consideration. We gave, they took. It was the complete arrangement. This is luxury.

Of course, they spent a terrific amount of money on the house and garden. It was the machinery they had to have in order to live. So they kept it going, as you might say. A bad servant was just a bad part and was exchanged for a good part as soon as possible. I thought of this when I was doing my National Service as a fitter in the R.A.C. It made sense. Yet I got so that I didn't know quite what to think about it all. It was obviously wrong, yet because Lordship and Ladyship were old and had never known any other kind of life, I suppose I felt sorry for them. I always had to give more than was necessary. I couldn't resist it. It was exciting somehow. But when I got home I would be angry with myself. the butler would sometimes come to the pub and imitate them. Laugh – you should have heard us! But I would feel strange inside, pitying and hating at the same time.

It was strange coming back to the big house after the R.A.C. I was married now and we had an estate cottage without inside water, a bath or electricity, although it was very pretty and we were very happy. At first, that is. Until Ladyship said that my wife must work in the big house. My wife didn't understand what it would mean. She came from Ilford and had never seen anything like it. She got worried and then she got migraine. The doctor told her that she must leave her work at the big house because it was making her anxious and ill. I told Ladyship, who said, 'But she must come'. I told her what the doctor had said but she just drove to the cottage and told my wife, 'You must come back to the kitchen – do you understand? You *must*.' So that is why we went away. I felt sorry for my wife and for Ladyship; they had no way of knowing each other.

(Blythe, 1969, pp. 103–5)

After reading this extract, are there any general points about the nature of personal worlds which you want to confirm or add to those you already have?

Notes

1 The overall pattern of Christopher's life has a distinctively different feel from that of Liv. It suggests a very different life-style and a different *sense of self*. As merely one example, it would be framed by an implicit awareness of being male rather than female.

2 Christopher expresses his personal world in the form of a *biographical narrative*. He begins his working life in one situation but eventually the war comes and there is change. The flow of his life centres round areas such as home life, marriage and especially work.

3 We catch glimpses of the very different personal worlds of the owners of the big house. The differences and the fact that 'they had no way of knowing each other' emphasize the often *private nature* of a personal world. It is by no means always possible for one person to penetrate another person's experience.

4 What comes across clearly in this account is how so much of our personal worlds can be *defined by other people and by the social context*. Christopher's life

is dominated by the needs and demands of others rather than himself. Interestingly, this power is exercised not through physical constraint or even control of resources (e.g. wages), but by the fact that 'reality' for Christopher and his fellow workers is defined in their employers' terms. Christopher's ability to rebel comes about only after he has experienced the very different social context of the army.

moral evaluation

5 There is an implicit sense of *moral evaluation*. There are 'right' and 'wrong' ways to behave. When these are transgressed, Christopher may be reprimanded or may even feel some guilt.

legitimation

6 Points 4 and 5 raise the question of *legitimation*. Personal worlds are enmeshed in a social reality where the demands and experiences of some are given precedence over (and are seen perhaps as morally superior to) those of others.

power

7 Although Christopher's world is for a long time dominated and defined by others, eventually he reacts by leaving his work. Even in a situation as constrained as this one, people have some power of *agency* – they can initiate change by their actions.

humour

8 In the account we also become aware of the possible disparity between outward actions and the *inner world of thought and imagination* ('we were tempted to cut out something terrible sometimes . . .'). We perhaps also see here the way humour can be used to help a person cope with negative feelings.

metaphors

9 Finally, it is worth noting Christopher's use of *metaphor* as a means of making sense of his experience, as when he describes his employers' view of the servants as replacement parts in the machinery of the house. The fact that Christopher has been a fitter in the RAC also suggests that social context may provide an important source of the metaphors we use.

Window 3

Our third account is taken from Oliver Sacks' clinical studies (Sacks, 1976) of the effects of administering the drug L-Dopa to patients suffering a special form of Parkinsonism incurred as a result of having had sleeping-sickness (*encephalitis lethargica*). This condition is characterized by shaking, stiffness, and often a feeling of being driven or hurried ('festination'). The 'post-encephalitic' patients whom Sacks describes, including Leonard, had been in a comatose state for many years before they were given L-Dopa (a so-called 'miracle' drug found to be generally effective in treating Parkinsonism). Although Leonard's personal world is an unusual one, as you read try, as with the other accounts, to empathize with him and get into his world as he experiences it.

Window 3   Leonard

I first saw Leonard L. in the spring of 1966. At this time Mr L. was in his forty-sixth year, completely speechless and completely without voluntary motion except for minute movements of the right hand. With these he could spell out messages on a small letter-board – this had been his only mode of communication for fifteen years and continued to be his only mode of communication until he was given L-DOPA in the spring of 1969. Despite his almost incredible degree of immobility and disability, Mr L. was an avid reader (the pages had to be turned by someone else), the librarian at the hospital, and the producer of a stream of brilliant book reviews which appeared in the hospital magazine every month. It was obvious to me, from my first meeting with Mr L. – and this impression was reinforced by all my subsequent meetings with him – that this was a man of most unusual intelligence, cultivation, and sophistication; a man who seemed to have an almost total recall for whatever he had read, thought, or experienced . . . and, not least, a man with an introspective and investigative passion which exceeded that of almost any patient I had ever seen. This combination of the profoundest disease with the acutest investigative intelligence made Mr L. an 'ideal' patient, so to speak, and in the six and a half years I have known him he has taught me more about Parkinsonism, post-encephalitic illness, suffering, and human nature than all the rest of my patients combined. . .

The picture which Mr L. presented in 1966 had not changed since his admission to the hospital, and indeed he himself – like so many other 'mummified' post-encephalitic patients – seemed a good deal younger than his chronological age: in particular he had the unlined face of a man in his twenties. He showed extreme rigidity of his neck, trunk and limbs and marked dystrophic changes in his hands, which were no larger than those of a child; his face was profoundly masked, but when it broke into a smile the smile remained for minutes or hours – like the smile of the Cheshire Cat; he was totally voiceless except at times of unusual excitement when he could yell or bellow with considerable force. He suffered from frequent 'micro-crises' – upturnings of the eyeballs, associated with transient inability to move or respond; these lasted a few seconds only, and occurred dozens, and sometimes hundreds, of times a day. His eye movements, as he read, or glanced about his surroundings, were rapid and sure, and gave the only external clue to the alert and attentive intelligence imprisoned within his motionless body.

At the end of my first meeting with Leonard L. I said to him: 'What's it like being the way you are? What would you compare it to?' He spelt out the following answer: 'Caged. Deprived. Like Rilke's "Panther".'[1] And then he swept his eyes around the ward and spelt out: 'This is a human zoo.' Again and again, with his penetrating descriptions, his imaginative metaphors, or his great stock of poetic images, Mr L. would try to evoke the nature of his own being and experience. 'There's an awful presence,' he once tapped out, 'and an awful absence. The presence is a mixture of nagging and pushing and pressure, with being held back and constrained and stopped – I often call it "the goad and halter". The absence is a terrible isolation and coldness and shrinking – more than you can imagine, Dr Sacks, much more than anybody who isn't this way can possibly imagine – a bottomless darkness and unreality.' Mr L. was fond of tapping out, or voicelessly murmuring – in a sort of soliloquy – passages from Dante or T. S. Eliot, especially the lines:

Descend lower, descend only
Into the world of perpetual solitude,
World not world, but that which is not world,
Internal darkness, deprivation
And destitution of all property,
Desiccation of the world of sense,
Inoperancy of the world of spirit. . .

'At other times,' Mr L. would tap out, 'there's none of this sense of pushing or active taking-away, but a sort of total calmness, a nothingness, which is by no means unpleasant. It's a let-up from the torture. On the other hand, it's something like death. At these times I feel I've been castrated by my illness, and relieved from all the longings other people have.' . . .

It was only very gradually, over the following years, with Mr L.'s help and that of his devoted mother – who was continually with him – that I was able to form any adequate picture of his state of mind and being, and the way in which this had developed in the preceding years. Mr L. had shown precocity and withdrawal from his earliest years, and these had become much accentuated with the death of his father when he was six. By the

[1] His gaze from going through the bars has grown so weary that it can take in nothing more. For him it is as though there were a thousand bars, and behind the thousand bars no world.

age of ten he would often say: 'I want to spend my life reading and writing. I want to bury myself among books. One can't trust human beings in the least.' In his early adolescent years Leonard L. was indeed continually buried in books, and had few or no friends, and indulged in none of the sexual, social or other activities common to boys of his age. At the age of fifteen his right hand started to become stiff, weak, pale and shrunken: these symptoms – which were the first signs of his post-encephalitic disease – were interpreted by him as a punishment for masturbation and for blasphemous thoughts; he would often murmur to himself the words of the 137th psalm ('If I forget thee, O Jerusalem, let my right hand forget its cunning') and 'If thy right hand offend thee cut it off.' He was reinforced in these morbid phantasies by the attitude of his mother who also saw his illness as a punishment for sin.

. . . Despite the gradual spread and progression of his disability, Leonard L. was able to go to Harvard and to graduate with honours, and had almost finished a thesis for his Ph.D. – in his twenty-seventh year – when his disability became so severe as to bring his studies and activities to a total halt. After leaving Harvard, he spent three years at home; and at the age of thirty, almost totally petrified, he was admitted to Mount Carmel Hospital. On his admission he was at once given charge of the hospital library. He could do little but read, and he *did* nothing but read. He indeed became buried in books from this time on, and thus, in a sense, achieved a dreadful fulfilment of his childhood wish.

In the years before I gave him L-DOPA I had many conversations with Leonard L., conversations which were necessarily somewhat one-sided and cursory since he could only answer my questions by painfully tapping out answers on his spelling-board – and his answers tended to assume an abbreviated, telegraphic, and sometimes cryptic form. When I asked him how he felt he would usually tap out 'meek', but he would also intimate that he sometimes had a sense of intense violence and power which was 'locked up' inside him, and which he experienced only in dreams. 'I have no exit,' he would tap out. 'I am trapped in myself. This stupid body is a prison with windows but no doors.' Although for much of the time, and in many ways, Mr L. hated himself, his disease and the world, he also had a great and unusual capacity for love. This was especially apparent in his reading and his reviewing, which showed a vital, humorous, and at times Rabelaisian relish for the world. And it was sometimes evident in his reaction to himself when he would spell out: 'I am what I am. I am part of the world. My disease and deformity are part of the world. They are beautiful in a way like a dwarf or a toad. It's my destiny to be a sort of grotesque.'

There existed an intense and mutual dependence between Mr L. and his mother, who came to the hospital to look after him for ten hours a day – a looking-after which included attention to his most intimate physical needs. One could see, when his mother was changing his nappies or bib, a look of blissful baby-like contentment on Mr L.'s face, admixed with impotent resentment at his degraded, infantilized and dependent state. His mother, similarly, showed and expressed a mixture of pleasure with her life-giving, loving and mothering role, admixed with intense resentment at the way in which her life was being 'sacrificed' to her grown-up but helpless 'parasite' of a son. . . Both Mr L. and his mother expressed uncertainty and ambivalence about the use of L-DOPA; both of them had read about it, but neither had actually seen its effects. Mr L. was the first patient in Mount Carmel whom I put on L-DOPA.

Course on L-DOPA

L-DOPA was started in early March 1969 and raised by degrees to 5·0 gm. a day. Little effect was seen for two weeks, and then a sudden 'conversion' took place. The rigidity vanished from all his limbs, and he felt filled with an access of energy and power; he became able to write and type once again, to rise from his chair, to walk with some assistance and to speak in a loud and clear voice – none of which had been possible since his twenty-fifth year. In the latter part of March, Mr L. enjoyed a mobility, a health and a happiness which he had not known in thirty years. Everything about him filled him with delight: he was like a man who had awoken from a nightmare or a serious illness, or a man released from entombment or prison, who is suddenly intoxicated with the sense and beauty of everything round him. During these two weeks, Mr L. was drunk on reality – .on sensations and feelings and relations which had been cut off from him, or distorted, for many decades. He loved going out in the hospital garden: he would touch the flowers and leaves with astonished delight, and sometimes kiss them or press them to his lips. He suddenly desired to see the night-city of New York, which (although so close to) he had not seen, or wanted to see, in twenty years: and on his return from these night-drives he was almost breathless with delight, as if New York were a jewel or the New Jerusalem. He read the 'Paradiso' now – during the previous twenty years he had never got beyond 'Inferno' or 'Purgatorio' – with tears of joy on his face: 'I feel saved,' he would say, 'resurrected, re-born. I feel a sense of health amounting to Grace . . . I feel like a man in love. I have broken through the barriers which cut me off from love.' The predominant feelings at this time were feelings of freedom, openness and exchange with the world; of a lyrical appreciation of a real world, undistorted by phantasy, and suddenly revealed; of delight and satiety with self and the world – 'I have been hungry and yearning all my life,' said Mr L., 'and now I am full. Appeased. Satisfied. I want nothing more.' He experienced a vanishing of hostility, anxiety, tensions and meanness – and in their place felt a sense of ease, of harmony and safety, of friendship and kinship with everything and everyone which he had never in his life experienced before – 'not even before the Parkinsonism', as he was the first to admit. The diary which he started to keep at this time was full of expressions of amazement and gratitude. *'Exaltavit humiles!'* he wrote on each page: and other exclamations like 'For *this* it was worth it, my life of disease,' 'L-DOPA is a *blessed* drug, it has given me back the possibility of life. It has opened me out when I was clammed tight-shut before,' and 'If everyone felt as good as I do, nobody would think of quarrelling or wars. Nobody would think of domination or possession. They would simply enjoy themselves and each other. They would realize that Heaven was right here down on earth.'

In April, intimations of trouble appeared. Mr L.'s abundance of health and energy – of 'grace' as he called it – became *too* abundant and started to assume an extravagant, maniacal and grandiose form; at the same time a variety of odd movements and other phenomena made their initial appearance. His sense of harmony and ease and effortless control was replaced by a sense of *too-muchness*, of force and pressure, and a pulling-apart – a pathological driving and fragmentation which increased, obviously and visibly, with each passing day. Mr L. passed from his sense of delight with existing reality, to a peremptory sense of mission and fate: he started to feel himself a Messiah, or the Son of God; he now 'saw' that the world was 'polluted' with innumerable Devils, and that he – Leonard L. – had been 'called on' to do battle with them. He wrote in his diary: 'I have Risen. I am still Rising. From the Ashes of Defeat to the Glory of Greatness. *Now* I must Go Out and Speak to the World.' He started to address groups of patients in the corridors of the hospital; to write a flood of letters to newspapers, congressmen, and the White House itself; and he implored us to set up a sort of evangelical lecture-tour, so that he could exhibit himself all over the States, and proclaim the Gospel of Life according to L-DOPA.

Where, in April, he had had a marvellous sense of ease and satisfaction he now became uneasy and dissatisfied, and increasingly filled with painful, insatiable appetites and desires. His hungers became transmogrified into insatiable passions and greeds. He ascended to heights of longing and phantasy which no reality could have met – least of all the grim and confining reality of a Total Institution, an asylum for the dilapidated and dying, or – as he himself had described it three years earlier – a 'human zoo'. The most intense and the most thwarted of these yearnings were of a sexual nature, allied with desires for power and possession. No longer satisfied with the pastoral and innocent kissing of flowers, he wanted to touch and kiss all the nurses on the ward – and in his attempts to do so was rebuffed, at first with smiles and jokes and good humour, and then with increasing asperity and anger. Very rapidly, in May, relationships became strained, and Mr L. passed from a gentle amorousness to an enraged and thwarted erotomania. Early in May he asked me if I could arrange for various nurses and nursing aides to 'service' him at night, and suggested – as an alternative – that a brothel-service be set up to meet the needs and the hungers of DOPA-charged patients.

By mid-May, Mr L. had become thoroughly 'charged up', in his own words, 'charged and super-charged' with a great surplus, a great *pressure*, of libidinous and aggressive feelings, with an avidity and voracity which could take many forms. In his phantasies, in his notebooks, and in his dreams, his image of himself was no longer that of the meek and mild and melancholy one, but of a burly caveman equipped with an invincible club and an invincible phallus; a Dionysiac god packed with virility and power; a wild, wonderful, ravening man-beast who combined kingly, artistic and genital omnipotence. 'With L-DOPA in my blood,' he wrote at this time, 'there's nothing in the world I can't do if I want. L-DOPA is power and irresistible force. L-DOPA is wanton, egotistical power. L-DOPA has given me the power I craved. I have been waiting for L-DOPA for the past thirty years.' Driven at this time by libidinal force, he started to masturbate – fiercely, freely, and with little concealment – for hours each day. At times his voracity took other forms – hunger and thirst, and licking and lapping, biting and chewing, and sucking his tongue – all of which stimulated him and yielded something very similar to sexual pleasure. . .

Coinciding with this surge of general excitement, Mr L. showed innumerable 'awakenings' and specific excitements – particular forms of urge and push, repetition, compulsion, suggestion, and perseveration. He started to talk with great speed, and to repeat words and phrases again and again (palilalia). He continually seized and held different objects with his eyes, and would be unable to relinquish his gaze voluntarily. He showed urges to pant and to clap his hands, and once he had started to do either of these he was unable to stop, but proceeded with continually increasing violence and speed until a sort of clench or freezing set in: these frenzied crescendoes – a catatonic equivalent of Parkinsonian hurry and festination – yielded 'a surge of excitement, just like an orgasm'. In the latter half of May, reading became difficult because of uncontrollable hurry and perseveration: once he had started to read he would read faster and faster without regard for the sense or syntax, and unable to stop this festinant reading he would have to shut the book with a snap after each sentence or paragraph, so that he could digest its sense before rushing ahead. Tics appeared at this time, and grew more numerous daily: sudden impulsions and tics of the eyes, grimaces, cluckings, and lightning-quick scratchings. Finding himself distracted and decomposed by this increasing furor and fragmentation, Mr L. made his final effort at control, and decided – at the start of June – on an act of supreme coherence and catharsis – the writing of an autobiography: 'It'll bring me together,' he said; 'it'll cast out the devils. It'll bring everything into the full light of day.'

Using his shrunken, dystrophic index-fingers, Mr L. typed out an autobiography 50,000 words in length, in the first three weeks of June. He typed almost ceaselessly – twelve or fifteen hours a day, and *when* he typed he indeed 'came together', and found himself free from his tics and distractions, from the pressures which were driving and shivering his being; when he left the typewriter, the frantic, driven, ticcing palilalia would immediately assert its hegemony again. . .

In the last week of June, and throughout July, Mr L. returned to his violently frenzied and fragmented state, and now this passed beyond all bounds of control, and brought into action ultimate physiological safeguards which in themselves were highly distressing or disabling.

His sexual and hostile phantasies now assumed hallucinatory form, and he had frequent voluptuous and demoniac visions[2], and erotic dreams and nightmares each night. His tics, his palilalia, his frenzies increased. His speech became broken by sudden intrusions and cross-associations of thought, and by repeated punning and clanging and rhyming. He started to experience forms of motor and thought 'blocking' . . . at such times he would suddenly call out, 'Dr Sacks! Dr Sacks! I want . . .', but be unable to complete what he wished to say; the same block was also manifest in his letters to me, which were full of violent, exclamatory starts (usually my name, followed by two or three words – in one such letter, impotently repeated twenty-three times) followed by sudden haltings and blocks. And in his walking and movements such blocks were apparent, which suddenly arrested him in mid-motor stream: he seemed, at such times, to be in collision with an invisible wall. . .

The closing scene of this so-mixed summer was precipitated by institutional disapproval of Mr L.'s ravening libido, the threats and condemnations which this brought down on him, and his final, cruel removal to a 'punishment cell' – a tiny three-bedded room containing two dying and dilapidated terminal dements.[3] Deprived of his own room and all his

[2] At first, Mr L. ingeniously controlled these hallucinations by confining them to the blank screen of his television set or a picture which hung on the wall opposite his bed. The latter – an old picture of a Western shanty-town – would 'come to life' when Mr L. gazed at it; cowboys on horses would gallop through the streets, and voluptuous whores would emerge from the bars. The screen of the television set was 'reserved' for the production of grinning and leering demoniac faces. Later in July, this 'controlled' hallucinosis broke down, and his hallucinations 'escaped' from the picture and screen, and spread irresistibly in his whole mind and being.

[3] I thought at this time, and still think, that among the important non-pharmacological determinants of the reactions of these patients to L-DOPA – and especially the form and severity of their 'side-effects' after a period of enormous improvement – the repressive and censorious character of the institution they found themselves in played a considerable part. In particular, the hospital administration frowned upon any manifestations of sexuality among the inmates and often treated this with an irrational and cruel severity. Leonard L. . . and many other patients were, I think, driven at times into depressive or paranoid psychoses by the combination of a DOPA-induced libidinous arousal and its frustration or punishment by the conditions and policies of institutional life. If, as Mr L. suggested, some mode of sexual release had been provided or permitted, the effects of L-DOPA might – perhaps – have been less malignant. A further factor, which doubtless added to Mr L.'s sexual drives and their guilty moral recoil, was the too-close relation between him and his mother. His mother – who, in a sense, was herself in love with her son, as he was with her – became indignant and jealous of Mr L.'s new thoughts: 'It's ridiculous,' she spluttered. 'A grown man like him! He was so *nice minded* before – never spoke about sex, never looked at girls, never seemed to think about the matter at all . . . I have sacrificed my life for Len: I am the one he should constantly think of; but now all he thinks of is those *girls*!' On two occasions, Mr L.'s thwarted sexuality became incestuous in direction, which outraged (but also titillated) his ambivalent mother. Once she confided to me that 'Len was trying to *paw* me today; he made the most horrible suggestions. *He said the worst things in the world* – Bless him,' and she blushed and giggled as she said this to me.

belongings, deprived of his identity and status in our post-encephalitic community, degraded to the physical and moral depths of the hospital, Mr L. fell into suicidal depression and infernal psychosis.

During this dreadful period at the close of July, Mr L. became obsessed with notions of torture, death and castration. He felt the room was a network of 'snares'; that there were 'ropes' in his belly which were trying to strangle him; that a gibbet had been set up, outside his room, for his impending and deserved execution for 'sin'. He felt that he was going to burst open, and that the world was coming to an end. He twice injured his penis, and once tried to suffocate himself by burying his head in his pillow.

We stopped his L-DOPA towards the end of July. His psychoses and tics continued for another three days, of their own momentum, and then suddenly came to a stop. Mr L. reverted during August to his original motionless state.

During August he scarcely moved or spoke at all – he had been returned to his original room – but reflected deeply on the preceding few weeks. In September he 'opened up' again to me, tapping his thoughts on his original letter-board. 'The summer was great and extraordinary,' he said (paraphrasing, as he was prone to, a poem of Rilke's), 'but whatever happened then will not happen again. I thought I could make a life and a place for myself. I failed, and now I am content to be as I am; a *little* better perhaps, but no more of – all that.'

(Sacks, 1976, pp. 240–56)

Does this account enable you to add any more to your list of general characteristics of personal worlds?

Notes

1   Of all the windows we have glimpsed through, Leonard's world is perhaps farthest removed from our experience. But the extremity of his condition makes us aware of features of normal personal worlds which we might otherwise take for granted.

2   It emphasizes the *importance of body functioning.* The body is the instrument of expression and realization of our particular personal world, our means of relating to the world about us. Leonard's personal world is totally transformed by physical intervention in the form of the initial administration of the drug L-Dopa.

3   But again we also suspect the significance of *social context* and the opportunities and constraints it brings. Individuals such as his mother and the nursing-staff serve as a source of frustration as well as of vital support and potential gratification. And, as Sacks remarks in the final footnote, Leonard's eventually negative response to L-Dopa treatment may have had something to do with the repressive nature of the institution in which he spent his days.

4   What comes across vividly is the strength of Leonard's feelings. His dramatic changes of mood demonstrate the way in which personal worlds can be transformed by the presence of *emotions of very different qualities*: in Leonard's case, for example, despair, fear, strangeness, pressure, joy, lust, surges of excitement, and feelings, at different times, both of power and impotence. Such feelings have a 'dynamic' feel. They seem to be capable of radically altering behaviour and their impact is difficult, often impossible, to resist; at times, they can overwhelm him. They seem closely related not just to events, but also to biological changes and interventions: for example, the administration of L-Dopa.

5   Leonard's *self-image* is also subject to dramatic shifts, e.g. from being a caged panther to experiencing himself as a Dionysiac god. Some shift of self-image, albeit in less extreme form and depending on mood and situation, might be regarded as a feature of most personal worlds.

6   The enormous variation in Leonard's functioning and capacities brings home to us the *wealth of skills and abilities* which underpin normal personal worlds.

7   Leonard experiences himself as *accountable* for his actions: for example, when he interprets his symptoms as a punishment for masturbating.

8   Much of Leonard's personal world does not take the form of experiences which others share but is made up of *imagination, private fantasies* and even hallucinations.

9   This description of Leonard is set in the form of a *narrative.* Leonard's experience changes with the passage of time and events. Sacks reveals him to us by setting him in the context of the pattern of his earlier life. This emphasizes the significance in a personal world of an awareness of one's personal past. Can you imagine how you would experience yourself without a history?

10   In spite of its unusual character, Leonard and Dr Sacks seem able to communicate the nature of Leonard's personal world in a remarkably vivid way. They do this by their skill in using words to reconstruct what Sacks calls the 'thoughtscape' of his patient. Note also Leonard's frequent resort to metaphor and poetry as a means of effectively communicating the special quality of his experience. This raises questions as to *what is likely to be the most powerful method for eliciting and representing personal worlds.* But however effective an account of someone's personal experience may be, there usually seem to be some aspects and feelings which are impossible to describe effectively.

Window 4

These final excerpts taken from the autobiographical reflections of a French writer and intellectual Roland Barthes differ from the others in that they use photographs to supplement words. As Barthes points out, this is especially useful as a technique for recreating the personal world of childhood in which sensations and images have a particular importance. As the book proceeds, pictures become fewer: with the increasing dominance of ideas and abstract thought as he matures into an adult, words become more suitable as a means for expressing experience. The commentary given with the photos below is not always easy to read, but you may well find that it can stimulate (both by what it implies as well as what it directly expresses) your thinking about the nature of personal worlds.

Window 4   Roland

And, as it happens, only the images of my youth fascinate me. Not an unhappy youth, thanks to the affection which surrounded me, but an awkward one, because of its solitude and material constraint. So it is not a nostalgia for happy times which rivets me to these photographs but something more complicated . . .

It provokes in me a kind of obtuse dream, whose units are teeth, hair, a nose, skinniness, long legs in knee-length socks which don't belong to me, though to no one else . . .

The childhood photograph is both highly indiscreet (it is my body *from underneath* which is presented) and quite discreet (the photograph is not of 'me').

Bayonne, Bayonne, the perfect city: riverain, aerated with sonorous suburbs (Mouserolles, Marrac, Lachepaillet, Beyris), yet immured, fictive: Proust, Balzac, Plassans. Primordial image-hoard of childhood: the province-as-spectacle, History-as-odor, the bourgeoisie-as-discourse.

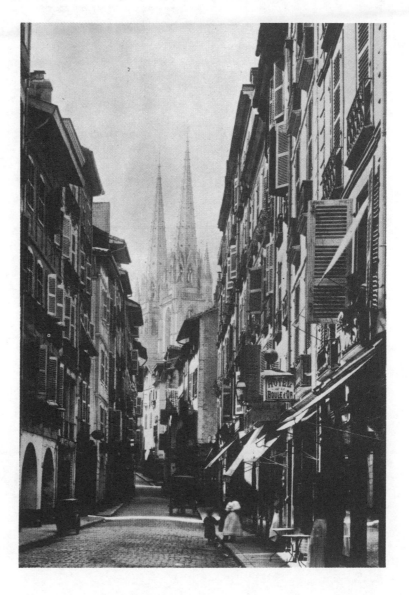

The three gardens

'That house was something of an ecological wonder: anything but large, set on one side of a considerable garden, it looked like a toy model (the faded gray of its shutters merely reinforced this impression). With the modesty of a chalet, yet there was one door after another, and French windows, and outside staircases, like a castle in a story. The garden, though continuous, was arranged in three symbolically different spaces (and to cross the boundary of each space was a significant action). You crossed the first garden to reach the house; this was the "worldly" garden, down which, taking tiny steps, pausing often, you accompanied the ladies of Bayonne to the gate. The second garden, in front of the house itself, consisted of narrow paths curving around twin lawns; in it grew roses, hydrangeas (that awkward flower of the southwest of France), carpet grass, rhubarb, kitchen herbs in old crates, a big magnolia whose white flowers bloomed on a level with the upstairs bedrooms; here in this garden, undaunted under their mosquito netting, the B. ladies, each summer, settled into canvas chairs with their elaborate knitting. At the far end, the third garden, except for a tiny orchard of peach trees and raspberry bushes, was undefined, sometimes fallow, sometimes planted with vegetables that needed no tending; you didn't go there much, and only down the center path.'

The worldly, the domestic, the wild is this not the very tripartition of social desire? . . .

(The house is gone now, swept away by the housing project of Bayonne.)

Coming home in the evening, a frequent detour along the Adour, the *Allées marines*: tall trees, abandoned boats, unspecified strollers, boredom's drift: here floated the sexuality of public gardens, of parks.

The father's sister: she was alone all her life.

The father, dead very early (in the war), was lodged in no memorial or sacrificial discourse. By maternal intermediary his memory – never an oppressive one – merely touched the surface of childhood with an almost silent bounty.

The family novel

Where do they come from? From a family of notaries in the Haute-Garonne. Thereby endowing me with a race, a class. As the (official) photograph proves. That young man with blue eyes and a pensive elbow will be my father's father. Final stasis of this lineage: my body. The line ends in a being *pour rien*.

The mirror stage: 'That's you'

Contemporaries?
I was beginning to walk, Proust was still alive, and finishing *À la Recherche du Temps perdu*.

As a child, I was often and intensely bored. This evidently began very early, it has continued my whole life, in gusts (increasingly rare, it is true, thanks to work and to friends), and it has always been noticeable to others. A panic boredom, to the point of distress: like the kind I feel in panel discussions, lectures, parties among strangers, group amusements: wherever boredom can *be seen*. Might boredom be my form of hysteria?

Distress: lecturing

Boredom: a panel discussion

'The pleasure of those mornings in U.: the sun, the house, roses, silence, music, coffee, work, sexual quiescence, holiday from aggressions . . .'

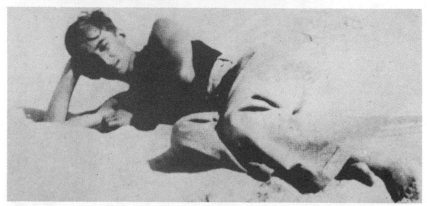

'Ourselves, always ourselves . . .'

. . . among friends

Where does this expression come from? Nature? Code?

1942

'But I never looked like that!' – How do you know? What is the 'you' you might or might not look like? Where do you find it – by which morphological or expressive calibration? Where is your authentic body? You are the only one who can never see yourself except as an image; you never see your eyes unless they are dulled by the gaze they rest upon the mirror or the lens (I am interested in seeing my eyes only when they look at you): even and especially for your own body, you are condemned to the repertoire of its images.

1970

Gaucher – Left-handed

To be left-handed – what does it mean? You eat contrary to the place assigned to the table setting; you find the grip of the telephone on the wrong side, when someone right-handed has used it before you;

the scissors are not made for your thumb. In school, years ago, you had to struggle to be like the others, you had to normalize your body, sacrifice your good hand to the little society of the *lycée* (I was constrained to draw with my right hand, but I put in the colours with my left: the revenge of impulse); a modest, inconsequential exclusion, socially tolerated, marked adolescent life with a tenuous and persistent crease: you got used to it, adapted to it, and went on . . .

La baladeuse – **The caboose**

There used to be a white streetcar that ran between Bayonne and Biarritz, in the summer, an open car was attached to it: the caboose. Everyone wanted to ride in that car: through a rather empty countryside, one enjoyed the view, the movement, the fresh air, all at the same time. Today neither the streetcar nor the caboose exists, and the trip from Biarritz is anything but a pleasure. This is not to apply a mythic embellishment to the past, or to express regrets for a lost youth by pretending to regret a streetcar. This is to say that the art of living has no history: it does not evolve: the pleasure which vanishes vanishes for good, there is no substitute for it. Other pleasures come, which replace nothing. *No progress in pleasures*, nothing but mutations. . . .

La côtelette – **The rib chop**

Here is what I did with my body one day:

At Leysin, in 1945, in order to perform an extrapleural pneumothorax operation, a piece of one of my ribs was removed, and subsequently given back to me, quite formally, wrapped up in a piece of medical gauze (the physicians, who were Swiss, as it happened, thereby professed that *my body belongs to me*, in whatever dismembered state they restored it to me: I am the owner of my bones, in life as in death). For a long time I kept this fragment of myself in a drawer, a kind of body penis analogous to the end of a rib chop, not knowing quite what to do with it, not daring to get rid of it lest I do some harm to my person, though it was utterly useless to me shut up in a desk among such 'precious' objects as old keys, a schoolboy report card, my grandmother B.'s mother-of-pearl dance program and pink taffeta card case. And then, one day, realizing that the function of any drawer is to ease, to acclimate the death of objects by causing them to pass through a sort of pious site, a dusty chapel where, in the guise of keeping them alive, we allow them a decent interval of dim agony, but not going so far as to dare cast this bit of myself into the common refuse bin of my building, I flung the rib chop and its gauze from my balcony, as if I were romantically scattering my own ashes, into the rue Servandoni, where some dog would come and sniff them out. . . .

J' aime, je n' aime pas – **I like, I don't like**

I like: salad, cinnamon, cheese, pimento, marzipan, the smell of new-cut hay (why doesn't someone with a 'nose' make such a perfume), roses, peonies, lavender, champagne, loosely held political convictions, Glenn Gould, too-cold beer, flat pillows, toast, Havana cigars, Handel, slow walks, pears, white peaches, cherries, colors, watches, all kinds of writing pens, desserts, unrefined salt, realistic novels, the piano, coffee, Pollock, Twombly, all romantic music, Sartre, Brecht, Verne, Fourier, Eisenstein, trains, Médoc wine, having change, *Bouvard and Pécuchet*, walking in sandals on the lanes of southwest France, the bend of the Adour seen from Doctor L.'s house, the Marx Brothers, the mountains at seven in the morning leaving Salamanca, etc.

I don't like: white Pomeranians, women in slacks, geraniums, strawberries, the harpsichord, Miró, tautologies, animated cartoons, Arthur Rubinstein, villas, the afternoon, Satie, Bartók, Vivaldi, telephoning, children's choruses, Chopin's concertos, Burgundian branles and Renaissance dances, the organ, Marc-Antoine Charpentier, his trumpets and kettledrums, the politico-sexual, scenes, initiatives, fidelity, spontaneity, evenings with people I don't know, etc.

I like, I don't like: this is of no importance to anyone; this, apparently,

32

> has no meaning. And yet all this means: *my body is not the same as yours*. Hence, in this anarchic foam of tastes and distastes, a kind of listless blur, gradually appears the figure of a bodily enigma, requiring complicity or irritation. Here begins the intimidation of the body, which obliges others to endure me *liberally*, to remain silent and polite confronted by pleasures or rejections which they do not share. . . .
>
> (Barthes, 1975, pp. 1–116)

Do these excerpts give you any further ideas about the nature of personal worlds?

Notes

1 Barthes' account brings home how much of our personal worlds, perhaps particularly when we are children, consists of *sensations*: e.g. the smells of gardens and streets, images of the park, the river, old ladies; and also *feelings*: e.g. loneliness and boredom. *Objects* too (like the 'precious' contents of the drawer described in the paragraph about the 'rib chop') may be invested with special emotional significance because of our contact with them or the associations which they have for us.

2 The use of photographs and the commentary point up nicely the double aspect of our *sense of self*. We both experience ourselves from within, as it were, and yet are capable of recognizing that we are an 'object' for others. A photo of Barthes is, he feels, both him and not him. For in spite of our recognition that others can see us, we can never directly experience our own selves in this way. Barthes' ambivalent attitude to his piece of rib also expresses how our bodies too are both the object and a direct manifestation of our experience of self. His comment on the photo of himself lying on the beach ('Ourselves, always ourselves . . .') raises another issue here, for it points to the inexorable way our selves are always with us; there is no escape from their containment and therefore our fundamental 'aloneness'.

3 The family photograph of his ancestors stimulates our awareness of how each of us is *rooted in a family past* – the end product of an extraordinary chain of meetings, relationships and events, any of which may well have not happened.

4 That the people in the photograph are now dead and gone emphasizes the *transience and vulnerability* of our personal worlds. Once they were conscious of existing as we are now. In the not too distant future we shall exist only as a faded photograph seen by someone not yet born. (This is brought home by the fact that Barthes himself is now no longer alive.)

5 We become aware that not only do we emerge from a family background (and adopt the class status, benefits or deprivation that this may bring with it) but that we are also interrelated with a *wider context of social events*. As Barthes plays as a child, Proust is taking up his pen, men are dying in battle.

6 People (family and friends, etc.) do not just form an intrinsic part of his personal world but often serve to actively shape or *construct* it, even Barthes' attitude to himself. So because it is unorthodox, left-handedness becomes an issue rather than just a simple difference between himself and others. His terse comment on his expression when sitting on the grass ('Nature? Code?') alerts us also to the possible role of biology as well as culture in influencing the way we are.

7 There is an effective sense of *life narrative*, beginning with the first incipient awareness of self in the mirror image. The bored child develops into the bored adult. Child and adult may be different beings with very different personal worlds and yet they are linked in a *continuity*.

8 The different situations depicted in the photographs illustrate the *multiplicity* of our personal worlds – a holiday, work, a morning spent relaxing,

time among friends – each is a distinct though related island of experience.

9 Barthes formulates general principles on the basis of his experiences. A memory of a streetcar ride as a child prompts him to a theory of pleasure. He seeks for *meaning* – for principles which make sense out of the complex and changing pattern of personal experience.

10 Barthes can reflect on his likes and dislikes. Experiences are clearly organized in terms of their *value* for him. He recognizes the personal nature of his preferences. (Also the restraint which social life demands in tolerating the different values which other people have.)

ACTIVITY 1

Look back now over any notes you have made on reading the four Windows and consider what these reveal about the nature of personal worlds. You might like to draw up a list of what you regard, in the light of your analysis and the comments I have given, as their more significant general characteristics.

1.2 Key features of personal worlds

I want now to draw together and expand on the notes above to produce a list of general characteristics which structure our personal worlds: I will call these key features (KFs). Before doing this though, it may be appropriate to comment on the nature of the analysis we are engaged in. While there may have been considerable overlap, it would be surprising if you picked exactly the same kind of features in your analyses of the windows as I did in the notes. What we have been doing is rather like analysing a series of complex landscapes. There are many features which can be detected and different kinds of general category which we could use to conceptualize these (e.g. contours of terrain, kind of soil, vegetation, the presence of trees, water, etc.). Any analysis – of physical landscape or personal world – is inevitably selective as to the features it focuses on and the categories it uses to classify these (see Metablock Paper 7). It will be influenced too by the particular set of examples chosen for analysis. We all of us have *direct* experience of one landscape – that of our own personal world, and *indirect* access to many others. The samples we looked at were designed to stimulate our thinking about our experience of personal worlds and to illustrate the categories suggested, not to establish them as an exhaustive list.

The features which will be proposed in this section represent what seem to me, on the basis of my own experience, significant general characteristics of personal worlds. Most of these have been illustrated in our samples. I am not offering them as the definitive set: there may be other categories which you would want to add or you might prefer to see those I have suggested refined into further sub-categories. Nor do I mean to imply that people are necessarily conscious of all these characteristics. If they are not, though, I would suggest that they *can* be made aware of them. A person may never have reflected before that they have the power of agency, for example. Once understood, however, then it becomes self-evident. It cannot be wished away. In Saint-Exupéry's phrase which began this unit, it is seen to be true, not because it can be demonstrated but because it cannot be escaped.

What we are trying to do is to differentiate systematically something of the nature of our experience as persons (a procedure perhaps not dissimilar to taxonomy in natural history). Such an analysis cannot be validated by formal experimental test. (As will be argued later,* this is generally an inappropriate procedure for studying the content of subjective experience.) But it can be tested against your own experience. Are the features discussed below consistent with your experience of your personal world?

* See, for example, Unit 14, Part 2 and also Metablock Papers 5 and 10.

1 Specific consciousness

KF (key feature) 1: Specific consciousness Any personal world is experienced from a specific point of view, the conscious awareness of the person concerned, and seems therefore to 'belong' to that person.

2 Time

KF2: Time Underlying conscious awareness there is a sense of the movement of time. All the accounts form some kind of narrative – a flow of experiences, actions and events. Situations and moods change – the most extreme example of the latter in the worlds we have sampled being Leonard. Pervading the present world of experience is an implicit awareness of events which have happened before and which will happen in the future. While it is by no means a clear progression, there is a sense too of personal, *biographical* flow. The current personal world represents a kind of distillation of this so far, coloured by anticipation of what life may hold in the future. Awareness of the stage of life one is at represents an important (if usually implicit) aspect of the personal worlds of most people.

3 Space

KF3: Space Most of the accounts are related to some point in *space*. Our immediate experience is located in a specific setting (e.g. an aeroplane, a hotel room, the grounds of a manor house, a hospital ward, or a beach or garden in southwest France). Most personal worlds involve a changing repertoire of specific settings. These have different qualities (for example, private versus public) and some, such as 'home' or 'my own room', take on special emotional significance.

However, personal worlds are capable to some extent of transcending temporal and spatial location. As we saw with Liv, conscious awareness can be focused on a time and place other than where we are. Also, we may express our experience of our personal world as a metaphor or abstraction. For example, at one point in his book *Notes to Myself* (1970), Prather describes his life as a 'constant irony of maturity and regression'. This represents his experience and yet is quite divorced from any specific time or place.

4 Emotional tone

KF4: Emotional tone The personal worlds represented here all have a particular emotional quality. A constant backdrop is provided by feelings and emotions of some kind, such as pity, security, surprise, lust or boredom. These may be consistent or, as with Leonard, subject to dramatic change. They may just form part of the background or become a central, even overwhelming, dynamic in the pattern of our lives. Over time, the prevailing emotional tone (e.g. contentedness, depression, anxiety) is likely to generate a distinctive feel to each person's experience of their personal world.

5 Rooted in a body

KF5: Rooted in a body Our personal worlds are inextricably coupled with a body. This can act as a constraint or as a means of realization and expression. We are subject to our body's needs and demands. If our biological functioning changes (for example, as a result of taking L-Dopa) so too may our subjective experience. One implicit consequence of this physical grounding is that personal worlds are *vulnerable and transient*. We are conscious that existence is limited. We are also implicitly aware that events and the actions of others or ourselves can radically change, even perhaps destroy, the world of our experience. And yet, paradoxically, there is a sense in which, once expressed, a personal world can live on, even after it may have ceased to exist. When we read the extracts by Barthes, an autobiographical account by a historical figure, or a suicide note, it may well be possible to reconstruct something of the author's personal world even though the person concerned is no longer alive.

6 Physical environment

KF6: Physical environment

As we exist bodily so we are part of a physical world. Sensory qualities attributed to the environment – temperature, comfort, colour – all form an intrinsic part of personal experience. Objects themselves are also important constituents of a personal world. Some smells, sounds and tastes, as well as particular things, may carry special significance because of associations they have for us (e.g. Liv's flowers and champagne, for Barthes his school report card and grandmother's dance programme).

7 Social context

KF7: Social context

Personal worlds form part of a larger social world. Other people play influential roles in the narrative – helping or serving, making demands, controlling events; and in emotional experience – instilling fear, eliciting desire, offering warmth and security. How far and in what ways people figure in any personal world varies. For those who are lonely, other people are significant because of their very absence. There is an uncertain predictability about our social context. Much of our development involves getting to know it – how it works and what to expect of it – the rules and conventions which govern its operations. But however well we succeed, it usually retains the potential to surprise us.

It is worth noting that others do not just form a part of our personal worlds. They help to create them. We saw how Christopher's early life essentially reflected the demands of his employers. Their concerns became his. For Liv, her lover and her daughter Linn form an intrinsic part of her personal world and can influence her feelings, it is implied, even when they are not physically present. As others define us by their actions, beliefs, values and our love or need for them, so we define them. Personal worlds are enmeshed together in a complex process of mutual definition and construction. (For further examples and discussion of this interdependence see the family system studies in Unit 2.)

legitimation

In the comments about Christopher's personal world, it was noted that some people exert greater power of definition over social reality than others. Their values and view of the world come to be accepted as the legitimate or valid ones. Alternative perspectives may be dismissed as irrelevant, suspect or even immoral. Even those who hold such perspectives may come to assimilate the dominant value system and come to regard their own experienced reality as in some way inferior. (You might compare this process with that of superego development. This also involves the 'introjection' or assimilation of someone else's values, although, in this case, at an early age and in the context of a close emotional relationship.)

8 Sense of self

KF8: Sense of self

Biographical flow, social context, bodily awareness and specific consciousness cohere together in a particular sense of self. We are aware that, although we share features in common, each of us is distinct from other people. For example, we are of one or other sex and a particular age, and each of us has a more or less unique combination of physical attributes and personality style. We have our own individual patterns of experience and life histories. Although we are aware of continuity from the younger selves we once were, there is also a sense in which we are continually renewed. Each of us is a different person today from the person he or she was as a small child, or even last year. As was highlighted by Barthes' comments on the photographs of himself, our sense of self, because of our capacity for reflexiveness (see KF 12), also has a double aspect: the self of our experience and the self as others see us (see Box 2). An important part of the self of our experience is the private, inner world of thoughts, feelings and fantasies which is only shared with others if we choose and are able to do so.

9 Agency

KF9: Agency

The protagonists in the windows seem capable of bringing about change. They

Box 2 Seeing the self through others' eyes

In the extract below, the Argentinian writer Jorge Luis Borges experiences his public image (himself as seen by others) as almost another self, a stranger to the Borges he feels himself to be:

> The other one, the one called Borges, is the one things happen to. I walk through the streets of Buenos Aires and stop for a moment, perhaps mechanically now, to look at the arch of an entrance hall and the grillwork on the gate; I know of Borges from the mail and see his name on a list of professors or in a biographical dictionary. I like hourglasses, maps, eighteenth-century typography, the taste of coffee and the prose of Stevenson; he shares these preferences, but in a vain way that turns them into the attributes of an actor. It would be an exaggeration to say that ours is a hostile relationship; I live, let myself go on living, so that Borges may contrive his literature, and this literature justifies me. It is no effort for me to confess that he has achieved some valid pages, but those pages cannot save me, perhaps because what is good belongs to no one, not even to him, but rather to the language and to tradition. Besides, I am destined to perish, definitively, and only some instant of myself can survive in him. Little by little, I am giving over everything to him, though I am quite aware of his perverse custom of falsifying and magnifying things. Spinoza knew that all things long to persist in their being; the stone eternally wants to be a stone and the tiger a tiger. I shall remain in Borges, not in myself (if it is true that I am someone), but I recognize myself less in his books than in many others or in the laborious strumming of a guitar. Years ago I tried to free myself from him and went from the mythologies of the suburbs to the games with time and infinity, but those games belong to Borges now and I shall have to imagine other things. Thus my life is a flight and I lose everything and everything belongs to oblivion, or to him.
>
> I do not know which of us has written this page.

(Borges, 1970, pp. 282–3)

can initiate actions and events and carry out personal projects. At the same time, as we have already observed, there are powerful constraints, both biological and social. A critical aspect here is the degree to which personal worlds are determined by 'outside' forces or are under a person's own control. There is a lot of variation in the accounts on this score. In some, the pervasive feeling is of being imposed on by other people or influences. The most striking is the extract which describes the world of Leonard who is imprisoned within his malfunctioning body and subjugated to its changing states and the intervention of agents like L-Dopa. For the gardener, Christopher, the controls are exerted by the social conventions in which he is locked, dominated by the dictatorial authority of autocratic employers. But none react as passive pawns. In all, there is some glimmer and occasionally a fire of *autonomy*, an awareness that they themselves have a part to play in exerting control over their destiny. In the case of Leonard, perhaps because the constraints on him are so overwhelming, we sense a fierce struggle to assert himself in the face of hostile reality. But agency may be exerted not just by action but also by taking a particular attitude. Humour can be used to cope with a difficult situation – reframing it, for example, by laughing at ourselves or at our antagonists. One consequence of our awareness of our power of agency is that we are likely to hold ourselves and each other *responsible* for our own actions. We accept that we may be called upon (if only by ourselves) to *account* for them – to give reasons for why we behaved as we did.

10 Values

KF10: Values

Coupled with this interplay of self- and other-directiveness (see KFs 7 and 9) is sometimes, though not always, a sense of underlying evaluation – of values or 'moral attitude': i.e. a notion that some things are good and others bad; that some things are right to do and others not. Such judgements may not necessarily be acted upon, nor even articulated, but they provide implicit guidance for our own actions and a means of judging those of others. Such principles may require us to justify or excuse to ourselves what we have done. They may even lead us to accept the appropriateness of retribution when we believe that we have transgressed (as Leonard does by linking the onset of his illness with his masturbation). Our values do not only concern the moral principles we believe in. Most of the experiences in our personal world can be scaled in terms of their value to us. Barthes is quite explicit about this, listing a selection of those things he likes and dislikes. But, while most of us, like him, have little difficulty in identifying what we value, our assessments are always, of course, open to revision and change.

11 Multiplicity

KF11: Multiplicity

Although each is identifiable as in some way part of a larger whole, there is a sense in which we inhabit multiple worlds. For Liv there is the rather unreal world of her Hollywood hotel and the more solid reality of her life in Norway. Barthes' photographs gives us a sample of the different worlds which he experiences – a holiday beach, for example, or lecturing, or relaxing with friends. For each of us, in the course of our daily lives, the 'frame' of our personal world is continuously changing. At one time it may become fused with, almost part of, the television play we are watching or the book we are reading: they become our reality. At others it may be immersed in the mechanics of the car as we struggle to renew the brake linings, or in the flow of the action as we play tennis. In all these cases, there may be moments when we 'come to' and become aware again of a different form of our personal world.

12 Reflexiveness

KF12: Reflexiveness

Not only does an individual's personal world exist in multiple forms, but he or she can adopt different *perspectives* towards it: for example, by being immersed in it or by standing back and reflecting on it.

Can you remember which of the accounts in the Windows came in first person form and which in third person? The curious feature is that these are so similar. When recounting our own experience it is almost as if we stand back and describe it as if we were observing another person. (Barthes, as you may have noticed, does this deliberately. See also the discussion earlier of KF8 (sense of self) and the account by Borges in Box 2.)

It should be remembered, however, that such reflections, like any other account of personal experience, are reconstructions – particular ways of making sense of what is going on – and as such will be limited by the cognitive capacity and constructs of the reflector. It is also possible for a person to reflect on his or her experience in more than one way.

A consequence of our capacity for reflexiveness is that, not only can we think of our own personal world as if it were that of someone else, we can also think of someone else's world as if it were our own. In other words, we have the capacity for empathy – for putting ourselves in other people's shoes. In such ways we become alert to the idea that other people's worlds may be different from our own.

13 Search for meaning

KF13: Search for meaning

One effect of the complexity of our personal experience is that we are likely to try to interrelate its various aspects in whatever way we can to give them meaning and coherence. Our capacity to reflect may, as we saw with Leonard, prompt us to apply the search for meaning to ourselves as well as life around us. We may search for some superordinate conception to give meaning, order and direction to the whole, to guide us in the choices we make. Many of us seem to need not only to be able to give some account of whom we are but also to ask questions about the point and purpose of our existence. Traditionally, this has been the province of religion. But this search for 'meaningfulness' is found in philosophy as well and among reflective people everywhere regardless of whether or not they subscribe to a particular brand of religious belief.

These thirteen key features should not be regarded as independent for they influence and interpenetrate each other. Because they have been generated by empirical analysis of personal experience and of the accounts given in the Windows rather than by theoretical discussion, the do not easily fall into distinctive sub-groups; but Figure 1 and its associated commentary represents an attempt to indicate ways in which they interrelate, and may help you to see the logic underlying the order of presentation. (While this may be useful, it is ultimately an unsatisfactory representation as the key features interconnect in a more integrative and complex way than it is possible to portray here.)

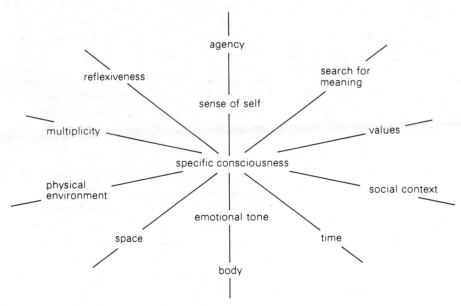

Figure 1   Key features of a personal world

Notes on Figure 1

1   At the core of a personal world is a specific sense of consciousness associated with a sense of self.

2   The flow of consciousness is characterized by the dimensions of time, space and emotional tone.

3   It is experienced as rooted in a body and as existing in a world of both physical objects and events (physical environment) and of people and their actions and products (social context).

4   In our experience of the world, our consciousness is engaged by, and moves from, one setting or frame of meaning to another (multiplicity).

5   The self is experienced as being capable of acting and bringing about change (agency).

6   Our consciousness is capable of monitoring and reflecting on our flow of experience (reflexiveness) and tries to integrate and make sense of what is going on (search for meaning).

7   Our values and beliefs are influenced and to some extent generated by these processes, and, in turn, serve to guide both them and our actions.

A related way in which we might group the key features is into four sub-groups:

1   *Aspects of self:* specific consciousness, sense of self, rooting in a body, agency.

2   *Aspects of world:* physical environment, social context.

3 *Dimensions of experience of self and world:* time, space, emotional tone.

4 *Ways in which we organize experience and actions:* values, multiplicity, reflexiveness, search for meaning.

1.3 Methodological issues

So far we have concentrated on the nature of personal worlds. But the accounts we have examined also suggest something of the methodological problems we confront as psychologists interested in studying personal worlds. We begin to realize the difficulties involved in gaining access to and describing them.

Our contact with the personal worlds presented here has been largely through *language*. That is not so artificial as it may seem at first, for it is our primary mode both of expressing to others our own personal world and of gaining some understanding of theirs. We can observe their actions, but to understand them requires attributing meanings and significance. We can infer these on the basis of what we know of similar situations for ourselves. But this is limited and depends to a very great extent on guesswork. For a more detailed understanding of someone else's world, we rely on what they communicate and our interpretation and reconstruction of this.

Because most salient meanings and significances can only be grasped through language of some kind, the question arises as to how far any personal world would be possible without language and what kind of personal world this would be? Certainly, as we saw in Unit 6, our awareness and sensitivity to different aspects of our experience are likely to be influenced by the particular form of language which we use. Language comes in different forms and can be used to express different aspects of personal worlds with differing degrees of power (see Box 3). So Leonard resorts to poetry to try to express more powerfully the character of his personal world. Christopher the gardener finds it useful to conceptualize his place in the scheme of things with a metaphor – being a part of a functioning machine. But whatever form of language is used, accounts of personal worlds, because they have to be expressed in *some* way, can only ever be partial. We can only catch glimpses of them. There is no way of conceptualizing the totality of another person's world.

Box 3   Sign language can express some things better than words

Mark Medoff's play *Children of a Lesser God* (1982) raises the point that sign language may be able to convey some meanings more effectively than the spoken words. Sarah, the central character, was born deaf and refuses to learn any other mode of communication except Ameslan, the sign language of the deaf, in which she is very proficient. She claims that it has the power to express what vocalization can never do. At one point in the play, she supports this by showing with subtle movements of her two hands the many variations possible in the way that two people can relate to each other, and she does this so vividly that even an audience untutored in Ameslan can understand!

Another reason for the inevitably partial and selective quality of any account of a personal world is that, by their very nature, *personal worlds only exist as constructions* (see Metablock Paper 7). To a large extent, we create our awareness of even our own personal world according to whichever aspects of our experience we focus on and the ways in which we choose to conceptualize and react to them. The accounts given in the Windows are of real persons. But could you have detected if any of them had been fictional? (Barthes actually prefaces his book

40

with the statement: 'It must all be considered as if spoken by a character in a novel'.) A curious feature is that, in skilful hands, fictional representations of personal worlds can be constructed which are impossible to distinguish from representations of 'real ones'. What does that tell us about the 'reality' and nature of personal worlds and/or the way they can be described? One thing it suggests is that any personal world is not a 'fixed reality'. Any apprehension of it is to a considerable extent created and can change according to the perspective and attitude of the person experiencing or describing it. Thus, as people grow older, they often view their past life in a new way: they construct a different account of their personal world in the light of their experience of the present.

PROGRESS BOX 1   Thirteen features of personal worlds

1	Specific consciousness	8	Sense of self
2	Time	9	Agency
3	Space	10	Values
4	Emotional tone	11	Multiplicity
5	Rooted in the body	12	Reflexiveness
6	Physical environment	13	Search for meaning
7	Social context		

Methodological problems in studying personal worlds

1 Access to the personal worlds of others is dependent on inferences based on what they do and tell us.

2 A personal world is inherently a *construction*, even for the person experiencing it, and can change depending on the perspective and attitude of whoever is construing it.

3 Thus any account of experience of a personal world is inevitably partial and selective.

ACTIVITY 2

1 Take each of the thirteen features of personal worlds indicated above and apply them in a consideration of your own personal world. Are there any features that you feel just do not hold for you: i.e. which have no possible place in your experience? Are there any other features *not* covered there which you feel are intrinsic to (i.e. that do form a fundamental and necessary dimension of) your personal world?

2 If you choose, or have chosen, to do the Interview Project, especially Option 1, you might like to see how far these features apply to accounts which you obtain there.

PART 2: PROBLEMS OF HUMAN EXISTENCE

You will remember that the Block Introduction promised that two primary perspectives adopted in this Block would be phenomenological and existential. So far the analysis has been broadly of a phenomenological kind. We have attempted to infer from other people's accounts, and to identify in our own awareness, the general characteristics of the experience of being a person. Now, in Part 2 of the Unit, I want to extend the discussion to 'existential concerns' – in other words **existential issues** issues which are rooted in the experience of being a self-aware and existing human individual. I want to discuss four of these:

1 *Time* A major problem here is coming to terms with our *finiteness* – the knowledge that our existence as a person has a limited span.

2 *Choice* Our capacity to reflect on our power of agency (i.e. our ability to initiate action) raises the problem of choice. What actions shall we take and why?

3 *Meaningfulness* People vary in the degree to which life is meaningful for them. Meaningfulness is based on a distinctive sense of values, of what is important in life, and the opportunity to experience this or express it in one's actions. Our power of reflexiveness makes it possible for us to question the meaningfulness of our life experience, to review the values which we ourselves hold, and to search for new and more satisfactory forms.

4 *Identity* As pointed out already, neither our parents nor the time and place of our birth are of our own choosing. As we grow older, we become capable of shaping to some extent what we are to become. The issue of identity (e.g. What shall I do? How shall I relate to others? Who shall I be?) is particularly a problem during adolescence, but for many people it remains a potent issue throughout their lives. The fact of being a particular person faces us too with inevitable isolation: because we are confined to being ourselves we are ultimately alone.

As can be seen from the brief descriptions above, such existential issues are linked to the general features of personal worlds which have already been discussed. The problem of *finiteness*, for example, arises from our experience of *time*. *Choice* becomes an existential issue because we are aware of being able to act and of consequences these actions may have. The importance of values coupled with the capacity for reflexive awareness and the need to search for meaning generate a concern for and perhaps pursuit of *meaningfulness* in our lives. The question of *identity* is premised on a sense of self and the capacity to reflect on this, as well as awareness of a particular body in which one's own experience seems to be rooted. It is influenced by social context and it becomes an issue because of the power of agency – the sense that what we become can be influenced by our own actions.

But while these existential concerns are related to the general features of our experience as persons, there is also a difference. For each represents an issue which we have to *confront*. In some way we have to come to terms with the questions it poses. We have to form some kind of response, even if this is only to ignore it. I am not suggesting that all persons are necessarily concerned by these issues or even think very much about them. As we shall see, there are substantial individual differences in how personally salient they are. But I would assert that to confront them is made possible only because of the self-awareness which humans are capable of, and that to do so is part of the distinctive experience of being an existing human being. Such issues have been a powerful force in the shaping of human culture and beliefs, in religions and mythologies. For a few people, the search for some resolution of the questions they entail becomes the driving force in their lives. But none of us remains untouched by them.

Existential psychotherapists work from the assumption that one of the primary sources of neurotic problems lies in the blocks and defences which we erect against the anxiety which our experience of existing may create. Thus one person may try to repress awareness of the fact of his eventual death: another may avoid all opportunity for making choices which could affect her life.

The four issues I have selected have been of particular interest both to existential psychotherapists (see, for example, May, 1958 and Yalom, 1980) and to existential philosophers and thinkers such as Nietzsche, Kierkegaard, Sartre and Camus.

In the sections which follow there will not be the space to give each topic the exhaustive treatment it deserves, but the discussions are intended to stimulate your own thinking about them as existential issues. For they are areas with potentially transforming power, in that reflecting on them can well have the effect of modifying the way you think about (and even live) your life.

Set reading

At some stage you might like to read pages 71–3 of Chapter 8 of the Set Book *Freud and Psychoanalysis*. This introduces the work of Erich Fromm. Note, in particular, the quotations which emphasize how the human capacities for self-awareness and reason create fundamental 'dichotomies' in the human experience of existence. Note also the sorts of resolution which Fromm advocates for the existential problems of isolation and the search for some meaning in life.

Existential issues

2 TIME

'... life can only be understood backwards. But ... it must be lived forwards' (Kierkegaard)

The centrality of time as a dimension of our personal worlds was clearly revealed in the accounts presented in section 1.1. Each one is set in a narrative of events, and involves memories of past experiences and anticipation of future ones.

time We are not here concerned with the concept of time in physics and philosophy. From an experiential point of view the word 'time' is an abstraction used to refer to the *flux* – the ongoing flow-like nature of our experience, coupled with our capacity to remember fragments of the past and to envision possibilities in the future. This flow seems to be not so much a continuity but a succession of phases or cycles, each with its distinctive qualities and marked out by our involvement in the ecological and social contexts in which we live. So winter days follow the autumn; Monday morning has a decidedly different feel from Saturday night. (Such differences may well be reflected in the values assigned when we come to sell our time. In the UK, for example, work on a Sunday night is typically paid at 240 per cent of the standard rate (Wedderburn, 1981).)

Another feature of the flow of time is its sense of being 'the continuous creation of unforeseeable novelty' (Bergson, 1965). We may know what to expect, but when it happens it is never *precisely* as we predict. Although we are located in an ever-changing present, this contains within it both our awareness of the past and anticipations of the future. As St. Augustine pointed out in his *Confessions* there are 'three times: a present of past things, a present of present things, and a present of future things' (1961, p. 269). Awareness of the past is sustained not just by present memory but by objects in our present experience which are associated with earlier times. Photographs often provide particularly powerful links (see Box 4). Nevertheless, experientially, it may be a misconception to regard the past as immutable. For although it cannot be regained, it can be reconceptualized in the present and seen as something other than it appeared to be at the time.

For most people in contemporary western society, the future plays a potent role. Knowing that an exam or a visit to the dentist is in the offing or that if we graduate in four years time we will be able to practice medicine, can drastically modify our actions and experience in the present. Anticipations of the future may also influence our awareness of the past. As Rollo May has expressed it, 'What an individual seeks to *become* determines what he remembers of his *has been*' (May, 1958, p. 69).

The experience of time is set in a series of widening perspectives: our personal biography, awareness of how this meshes with the lives of significant others, broader historical perspectives and, for some people, superordinate frameworks of unimaginable scale – the evolution of our species, of life and the planet. There is clearly substantial individual variation in the clarity and extent of the time perspectives we use. Some people claim that, while in moments of rapture or involvement ('peak experiences') or under the influence of drugs, they have experienced 'being out of time' altogether. Timelessness may be sensed too in the world of myths or in the ending of a fairy story when 'they live happily ever after'.

Time becomes an existential issue because we are aware that, once experienced, it cannot be turned back; and that the allotment to each of us, although variable, is finite. In other words, each of us has to confront in some way the fact that at some stage we shall cease to be. This prospect of non-being can profoundly influence our experience and understanding of being (as Heidegger (1962) has made much of). Although in this section we will briefly consider some of the features influencing our general experience of time, it is this topic of finiteness which is our primary concern.

Box 4   Photographs as present encapsulations of the past

In their book *The Meaning of Things* (1981) Csikszentmihalyi and Rochberg-Halton discuss how objects can form a link with a past which we may not even have experienced ourselves. The following account was given by a woman who was born and raised in Chicago:

> Photographs. . . That is the link with the past, the pictures of people that I never knew, and whom my children will certainly never know. I'm the kind of person who looks up relatives. It's a link with the past, the knowledge that these people are a part of our lives. I consider the loss of an irreplaceable photo a terrible, terrible loss. When I took a photo I liked, I always had a zillion copies made – but often forgot to give them to people – but I wanted to make sure somewhere there was another copy, in case anything happened to the original. But the ones my mother has from Europe are just irreplaceable. The people are all dead. All of their belongings were confiscated. There's nothing left.
>
> It's a very emotional issue for Jews who lost family during the Holocaust, and I don't know any Jewish people who didn't lose someone, some members of his family, whether it was someone he knew or didn't know. . . All of my mother's five brothers and sisters, their husbands and wives, their children, her cousins, all of her childhood friends, everybody was slaughtered. Some died in the concentration camps, starvation and torture. Some were killed, pulled right out of their homes, and murdered, not just by the Nazis. One niece remained, the one whose paintings I have, she lives in Paris. And her contact with her sister – the only other [one] left of the whole family, dozens and dozens of people – she learned from her sister what happened to the family. They all lived in neighboring towns. . . Some were sent to concentration camps. Others were just killed on the spot. Butchered by the local townspeople, who were given free rein by the Nazis to kill the Jews.
>
> My mother came to America when she was fifteen, her brother and sister were here. On her it was even worse, because she knew these people, I didn't. But I have the pictures and I see them.

(Csikszentmihalyi and Rochberg-Halton, 1981, p. 223)

2.1   Factors underlying variations in the experience of time

The flow of experience seems highly variable: sometimes it flies by, on other occasions it drags. This seems intrinsically bound up with the kind and amount of *activities and events we are engaged in,* how pleasurable and how involving these are. Our awareness of how much time has elapsed seems dependent on perspective too. Have you found, as I have, that while you are involved in many activities, time seems to pass rapidly, but in retrospect it always seems as though a long time has elapsed? On the other hand, when life is more humdrum, time seems to flow more slowly, but in retrospect it seems difficult to believe a week, say, has gone by.

Our experience of time depends very much on the *context* we are in. It is particularly when a person is cut-off from the normal flow of everyday life that the differences possible in the experience of time are brought home forcibly. For example, Victor Serge has written powerfully about the experience of time in prison:

> So as not to lose track of the date, you have to count the days attentively, mark each one with a cross. One morning you discover that there are forty-

seven days – or one hundred and twenty, or three hundred and forty-seven! – and that it is a straight path leading backwards without the slightest break: colourless, insipid, senseless. Not a single landmark is visible. Months have passed like so many days; entire days pass like minutes. Future time is terrifying. The present is heavy with torpor.

Each minute may be marvellously – or horribly – profound. That depends to a certain extent on yourself. There are swift hours and very long seconds. Past time is void. There is no chronology of events to mark it; external duration no longer exists.

(Serge, 1970, pp. 56–7)

For most Open University students and staff at least, time dominates much of our life. We plan ahead, marking dates of events, meetings and deadlines in calendars and diaries, and struggle to get our work in on time. Time becomes a commodity which we carefully allot according to the priority of the experience or activity in question or the pressure put upon us. Time can too easily become an enemy to fight against, which seems to be harrying and hurrying us into the future. Our attention can become focused not on the here and now but absorbed by the present of things future. However, there are periods in our lives when all this changes. For most of us, there are spaces of 'free time', such as when we are relaxed or on holiday, when we allow life to take its course – marking and shaping it only by a few rather flexible parameters generated by our needs to eat and sleep, the schedules of planes or trains, or habits which we find difficult to lose completely.

ACTIVITY 3

Payne (1974) has suggested the following exercises as a way to help break the feeling of being imposed on by the flow of events, to help bring us back to experiencing the present. You might like to try them sometime:

1   Stop reading for a minute or two and try to be here-now. Quiet your breathing and increase the pauses before and after exhalation. Take in as much of what is going on as you can – the sounds, the motions of things, the flow of feelings within you, the positions and tensions of your body, your thoughts. Especially attend to any other persons, and your own sense of yourself as being present, right here, right now. As you do this, *stop time*. Be aware that everything happening or existing is just as it should be, was to be, will be, is. There is no time, there is only now, this moment.

2   Gather together a few friends who are familiar with the notion of being here-now and have practised a bit. Pick a relaxed and pleasant spot away from distractions of noise or other persons and sit closely together so that you can easily see and touch each other. Take a few minutes to attend to what is present – the sensory environment, your own internal states and the presence of those around you. Then concentrate your attention primarily on being with each other. Talk or not as you wish. But help one another not to stray into reveries or away from the group. Try to be fully here-now with each other. Maintain eye contact by looking into the eyes of the others and as you look, feel, and sense what is going on, *reflect on the timelessness of it. Make the effort to stop time*. Be aware, understand that *there is no time within you*, that here the past and the future flow together into the now and now is forever. This moment is eternal.

(Payne, 1974, pp. 123–4)

Time structures, however, should not necessarily be regarded in a wholly negative light. There is evidence, for example, that one of the major negative consequences of becoming unemployed is the loss of the time structuring which goes with work (Jahoda, 1982). And when Fryer and Payne (1984) studied a sample of

46

people identified as coping with their unemployment in a creative and positive way, they found that one of their distinguishing characteristics was the ability to generate their own personal structuring of time.

Our experience of time is not just bound up with the situation but also with *mood states*, for example of excitement and depression (which in turn relate to physiological functioning). If you look back at the account of Leonard L. in section 1.1 and compare the various phases of his experience of taking L-Dopa, there is a different feeling about the flow of his experiential time – periods of mad rush and impulsion, others of quiet emptiness. He is clearly aware of such differences, and later reported having experienced more during his time on L-Dopa than in all the previous years of his life combined.

Perhaps you have noticed that the years seem to be getting shorter as you grow older. Perhaps one reason for this is that the length of any particular unit of time taken as a proportion of the span of life we have lived does become progressively smaller. There is some evidence that the way we experience time is related to the *stage of life* we have reached (Cottle and Klineberg, 1974). For children, for example, time seems to have a more expansive feel, in the sense that what for us are short periods are long ones for them: and the younger the child the less ability he/she seems to have to conceive of the future. The change in cognitive capacity which comes with the attainment of formal operational thinking (see Piaget's theory, discussed in Unit 4) opens up time perspective for adolescents. But while there may be preoccupation with thoughts and plans for the future, adolescence is also often characterized by a sense of interminable waiting for it all to begin:

> So much of adolescence is an ill-defined dying,
> An intolerable waiting,
> A longing for another place and time,
> Another condition.
>
> (Roethke, 1968, p. 162)

2.2 The significance of social context

If our experience of time is dominated by the situations and activities we engage in, this in turn points to the role of social context in constructing the way we experience events. The constant time checks we use today – the radio signals and the bleep of digital watches in workplace and at home – are, of course, of relatively recent origin. Fromm (1960) links the increasing importance of clock time to the growth of capitalism. He points out that towards the end of the Middle Ages:

> Minutes became valuable; a symptom of this new sense of time is the fact that in Nurnberg the clocks have been striking the quarter hours since the sixteenth century. Too many holidays began to appear as a misfortune. Time was so valuable that one felt one should never spend it for any purpose which was not useful.
>
> (Fromm, 1960, p. 49)

With the development of a technological society time becomes a commodity, equivalent to money; a scarce resource to be budgeted carefully and not to be wasted, for there is never enough. As measured by the rate of social and technological change, the pace of events accelerates and, with the elaboration of theories of evolution and the origins of the universe, the contextual time-scale in which we set ourselves vastly expands.

The ways in which contemporary technological society can influence the nature of subjective experience is a topic which will be looked at in the next unit. Two aspects discussed there are particularly relevant to why time has become dominant in a technological society. One feature of contemporary life is the multiplicity of different settings which we experience: for example, the worlds of work, home and different leisure activities. Time has to be budgeted and activities synchronized to make possible such multiple involvements. Another aspect of living in modern society is the sense it fosters (although this may be something of an illusion) that there are numerous opportunities and possibilities open to us. As this encourages us to plan our future with the aim of maximizing these, any free time is likely to be quickly absorbed.

The concern with the future that characterizes our society does not necessarily seem to be found in others. John Mbiti has argued, for example, that in traditional African consciousness the concept of a future, apart from events which inevitably will occur as natural cycles, is virtually absent. There is an almost exclusive focus on 'what is present and what is past' (Mbiti, 1969).

It seems reasonable to suppose that the experience of time is not just strongly influenced by the wider nature of society but also interrelates with the subculture in which a person lives and the kind of life he or she leads. A nice example of this is given in Box 5.

Box 5   Time and cool people

John Horton examined the experience of time for the 'street people' of Venice, Los Angeles. His analysis was based on observations and interviews with twenty-five young (18–25-year-old) blacks over a period of two years. Horton's account illustrates how 'Time is diverse; it is always social and subjective. A man's sense of time derives from his place in the social structure and his lived experience' (Horton, 1967, p. 9).

The structure of street time

Keeping cool and out of trouble, hustling bread, and looking for something interesting and exciting to do created the structure of time on the street. The rhythm of time is expressed in the high and low points in the day and week of an unemployed dude. I stress the pattern of the unemployed and full-time hustler because he is on the street all day and night and is the prototype in my interviews. The sometimes employed will also know the pattern, and he will be able to hit the street whenever released from the bondage of jail, work, and the clock. Here I describe a typical time schedule gleaned through interviews, and field observation.

Characteristically the street person gets up late, hits the street in the late morning or early afternoon, and works his way to the set. This is a place for relaxed social activity. Hanging on the set with the boys is the major way of passing time and waiting until some necessary or desirable action occurs. Nevertheless, things do happen on the set. The dudes 'rap' and 'jive' (talk), gamble, and drink their 'pluck' (usually a cheap, sweet wine). They find out what happened yesterday, what is happening today, and what will hopefully happen on the weekend – the perpetual search for the 'gig,' the party. . . .

On the set, yesterday merges into today, and tomorrow is an emptiness to be filled in through the pursuit of bread and excitement. Bread makes possible the excitement – the high (getting loaded with wine, pills, or pot), the sharp clothes, the 'broad,' the fight, and all those good things that show that one knows what's happening and has 'something going' for himself. The rhythm of time – of the day and of the week – is patterned by the flow of money and people.

Time is 'dead' when money is tight, when people are occupied elsewhere – working or in school. Time is dead when one is in jail.

One is 'doing dead time' when nothing is happening, and he has got nothing going for himself.

Time is alive when and where there is action. It picks up in the evening when everyone moves on the street. During the regular school year it may pick up for an hour in the afternoon when the 'broads' leave school and meet with the set at a corner taco joint. Time may pick up when a familiar car cruises by and a few dudes drive down to Johnny's for a 'process' (hair straightening and styling). Time is low on Monday (as described in the popular song, 'Stormy Monday'), Tuesday, Wednesday, when money is tight. Time is high on Friday nights when the 'eagle flies' and the 'gig' begins. On the street, time has a personal meaning only when something is happening, and something is most likely to happen at night – especially on Friday and Saturday nights. Then people are together, and there may be bread – bread to take and bread to use. . . .

Clock time vs personal time

Negro street time is built around the irrelevance of clock time, white man's time, and the relevance of street values and activities. Like anyone else, a street dude is on time by the standard clock whenever he wants to be, not on time when he does not want to be and does not have to be.

When the women in school hit the street at the lunch hour and he wants to throw them a rap, he will be there then and not one hour after they have left. But he may be kicked out of high school for truancy or lose his job for being late and unreliable. He learned at an early age that school and job were neither interesting nor salient to his way of life. . . .

. . . whatever 'respectable' society says will help him, he knows oppresses him, and he retreats to the streets for security and a larger degree of personal freedom. Here his control reaches a maximum, and he has the kind of autonomy that many middle-class males might envy.

In the street, watches have a special and specific meaning. Watches are for pawning and not for telling time. When they are worn, they are decorations and ornaments of status. The street clock is informal, personal, and relaxed. It is not standardized nor easily synchronized to other clocks. In fact, a street dude may have almost infinite toleration for individual time schedules. To be on time is often meaningless, to be late an unconsciously accepted way of life. 'I'll catch you later,' or simply 'later,' are the street phrases that mean business will be taken care of, but not necessarily now.

Large areas of street life run on late time. For example, parties are not cut off by some built-in alarm clock of appointments and schedules. At least for the unemployed, standard time neither precedes nor follows the gig. Consequently, the action can take its course. It can last as long as interest is sustained and die by exhaustion or by the intrusion of some more interesting event. A gig may endure all night and well into another day. . . .

Personal time as expressed in parties and other street activities is not simply deficient knowledge and use of standard time. It is positive adaptation to generations of living whenever and wherever possible outside of the sound and control of the white man's clock. The personal clock is an adaptation to the chance and accidental character of events on the street and to the very positive value placed on emotion and feeling.

(Horton, 1967, pp. 7–11)

ACTIVITY 4

To explore your dependence on structuring time, you might like to try going for half or even a whole day without wearing a watch and deliberately avoiding any form of time check (including listening to the radio). Later, reflect on your experience. What did it feel like? How important did it become for you to know what the time was? Why?

I have argued that the experience of time is interrelated with social life and social context and have illustrated this. However, it would I think be inaccurate to assume that an underlying sense of fleeting time is constructed through the experience of life in a particular segment of modern society. It is a theme that recurs in the literature of many cultures. The Persian poet Omar Khayyám wrote in *The Rubáiyát* many centuries ago:

> The Moving Finger writes; and, having writ,
> Moves on; Nor all thy Piety nor Wit
> Shall lure it back to cancel half a Line,
> Nor all thy Tears wash out a Word of it.

The irrevocable nature of the flow of experience is something which is experienced as a fundamental dimension of human existence. Deeds done cannot be undone; possibilities unrealized never will be. It is this irrevocability which makes time an existential issue. For it confronts us with our own role in creating the future and with *finiteness* – the limited time span of any experience, even existence itself:

> Time present and time past
> Are both perhaps present in time future,
> And time future contained in time past.
> If all time is eternally present
> All time is unredeemable.
> What might have been is an abstraction
> Remaining a perpetual possibility
> Only in a world of speculation.
> What might have been and what has been
> Point to one end, which is always present.
> Footfalls echo in the memory
> Down the passage which we did not take
> Towards the door we never opened
> Into the rose-garden. My words echo
> Thus, in your mind.
>   But to what purpose
> Disturbing the dust on a bowl of rose-leaves
> I do not know.

(Eliot, 1974, p. 189)

2.3 Finiteness

finiteness   Time or the flow of experience is inevitably bound up with change – the sense that things future will become things present, that that which is now will never be again. For many of us, for much of our lives, this may be experienced as a sense of *progression* – of moving towards brighter, richer, more developed horizons. But as we grow older, perhaps, the future may become more circumscribed, more definitive. Under some circumstances, such as unemployment, the flow may be experienced as *deterioration*. Taylor notes this also in his study (with Cohen) of long-term prisoners:

> The problem that these men had to face was how to get through each day of their very long sentences. They were in prison for up to thirty years (in some

cases the judge's recommendation was for 'natural life') and they therefore realized, unlike shorter-term prisoners, that they had literally been given 'life'. The prison was now where they lived; it was not a temporary interlude after which normal life might be resumed. It was reality. It was their new world, although it was hardly of their making.

Their greatest concern was deterioration. The physical aspect of this was not too serious; it might be countered by the resources available within the wing. (Weightlifting, for example, was almost an obsession – one prisoner spoke ironically about an inmate who would 'rather add an inch to his biceps than lose a year off his sentence'.) But psychological deterioration was another matter. In the outside world this hardly concerns us. We go from day to day without too much worry about our sanity or our grip on life. We might just consider that we are becoming less intelligent, perhaps even that our memory is failing, or our capacity for abstract thinking declining. But we can usually shrug off such concerns; those around us are unlikely to point to any developing deficiencies and it is easy to ignore any changes. However, for these long-term prisoners there was a continuous anxiety about psychic degeneration. They had no events which might carry them unthinkingly through the day; monitoring their own psychic state therefore assumed a special importance. And as a further stimulus to such self-monitoring and the concomitant anxiety it induced, there were all around them in the wing, frightening examples of men who appeared to have lost all contact with reality. These were the men who had already been inside for years and exhibited the type of obsessive neurotic concern with particulars, the type of unselfconscious involvement in the most absurd prison routines, that they become known as 'zombies', 'vegetables' and 'catatonics'.

(The Open University, 1976, pp. 13–14)

The most profound conflict which underlies human existence, and which we all have to confront in our own ways, is the gradual movement through our lives towards non-being. As Yalom asserts: 'The fear of death plays a major role in our internal experience; it haunts as does nothing else; it rumbles continuously under the surface; it is a dark, unsettling presence at the rim of consciousness' (Yalom, 1980, p. 27). Uncertainty about the actual time when we will die may help to make it more tolerable to bear but does not subtract from the certainty that it will come someday. We may react with anger at our impotence in the face of it. As Dylan Thomas exhorted his father:

> Do not go gentle into that good night,
> Old Age should burn and rave at close of day:
> Rage, rage against the dying of the light.

(Thomas, 1952, p. 159)

We are more likely though to erect defences against full awareness of its inevitability – an implicit feeling perhaps that somehow we are 'special' and that 'it cannot happen to us'. For most of us, such defences are fragile at best. They are easily disturbed, particularly as we grow older, by reminders of ageing or mortality – the death of a friend, retirement, a bout of illness, or even annual rituals such as birthdays or New Year's Eve which mark the passing of the years. Entering a new phase in our lives, through divorce, for example, or even by commitment to a new relationship, may also remind us that we are one stage nearer to the end. And, of course, existence is full of 'little deaths' where friendships fade, children grow up and houses are lived in no more.

defences against awareness of death Society tends to support (indeed may actively encourage) our attempts to shield ourselves from the prospect of non-being. A widespread reaction, particularly by many religions, has been in effect to *deny* it. This is done by asserting that, while our physical bodies may die, the important essence of ourselves or soul continues to exist in some form of 'afterlife'. A rather different approach which is common in present-day secular societies is to *ignore* it – staving off the awareness of eventual death by involvement in a continuous round of projects and activities. As each one is completed so a new one is taken up in its place.

Perhaps the most realistic way to cope, in that it does not seek to ignore or deny the reality of death, is to attempt to *transcend* it. This may be done by seeking some form of 'immortality' in this world: for example, by having children, by creating products which will live on after you have gone, by influencing other people's lives in some way, or by being remembered for some achievement (see Box 6). Many of the most strenuous activities we engage in are fuelled by this underlying need. Joyce Smith, the first woman to finish in the 1982 London Marathon seemed to indicate this when asked why she had entered: 'It would be nice to be remembered as an outstanding marathon runner. A lot of athletes achieve a lot, but in the end they're forgotten. Deep down I just want to be remembered' (*Daily Mail*, 11 May). Another way of transcending it comes with the exuberant emotional release on festivals and occasions when we break free of normal restraints of time and responsibility to celebrate existence here and now with song, dance, drink and laughter.

It has been suggested (e.g. by the psychoanalyst Rank) that underlying a concern with death may be a fear of separation and disintegration. Another way of coping is therefore to reframe it, much as Buddhism does; to see it not as separation but as a fusion with universal and continuing life. Related to this perhaps is the

---

Box 6 The search for immortality through creation

This means of seeking immortality is nicely expressed by Jerzy Kosinski in his description of a character in his book *Pinball*:

> Domostroy dreaded death – not illness or pain or the humiliation of disability associated with dying, but death itself: the sudden cessation of the self, the end of being, the final, arbitrary dissolution, as it were, of the entire concrete history of Patrick Domostroy.

> The thought of it came to him often, both in the daytime – during a spell of joy or pleasure – and at night, when nightmares about dying would wake him up to conscious fear of it as he lay alone in the dark.

> All men were subject to death at any time and, he knew for most men their past – their lived life – was the only reality death could not take from them. Still, whereas death could terminate the existence of Patrick Domostroy as a physical being, it could not terminate the existence of his music, which, being an abstract entity, would extend into the future. His music was a shadow cast before him, and as long as he was composing, Domostroy regarded himself as existing without a history, as creating the means to outlive himself.

> In his composing days Domostroy thought of his music as a key that could open the door to the future. Since many of his admirers were young, they would outlive him and thus become his standard-bearers and messengers in the years ahead. When his music was widely known and he himself famous, he kept the lock and hinges of that door well oiled. He would answer piles of letters from young men and women enthusiastic in their praise of his talent – all of them sincere, a few actually perceptive. Occasionally, for the sake of vanity, but even more for the sake of securing his future, he even encouraged them and went so far as to make an appointment and talk to one or another of these eager fans.

(Kosinski, 1963)

attitude of *acceptance* of eventual non-being suggested by T. S. Eliot's lines from 'East Coker':

> Houses live and die: there is a time for building
> And a time for living and for generation
> And a time for the wind to break the loosened pane . . .

(Eliot, 1974, p. 196)

It also seems to be echoed in Erikson's idea that out of the final phase of life, and emerging from the dominant polarity then between 'ego integrity' (acceptance of one's life for what it has been) and despair, comes the virtue of *wisdom* – 'the detached yet active concern with life itself in the face of death itself' (see discussion of the life-cycle in Unit 14).

Whatever resolution of this existential issue is attempted, the awareness that we will eventually die and that the end could come unexpectedly through accident or illness or even as a consequence of our own or another's action generates an underlying sense of *vulnerability* in our personal world which was noted earlier in the analysis of the Windows. There are times in the experience of many people when this insecurity of existence surfaces. In *The Varieties of Religious Experience* (based on the Gifford Lectures delivered at Edinburgh University, 1901–2) William James provides an example which, although in the book he attributes to an anonymous 'French correspondent', he later admitted to be autobiographical (see James, 1920, p. 145):

> I went one evening into a dressing-room in the twilight to procure some article that was there; when suddenly there fell upon me without any warning, just as if it came out of the darkness, a horrible fear of my own existence . . . it was like a revelation; and although the immediate feelings passed away, the experience has made me sympathetic with morbid feelings of others ever since . . . I dreaded to be left alone. I remember wondering how other people could live, how I myself had ever lived, so unconscious of that pit of insecurity beneath the surface of life. My mother in particular, a very cheerful person, seemed to me a perfect paradox in how unconscious she was of danger, which you may well believe I was very careful not to disturb by revelations of my own state of mind.

(James, 1960, pp. 166–67)

There have been those, from the Greek Stoics and the Romans Cicero and Seneca, who have argued that awareness of our vulnerability and the prospect of death can enrich rather than impoverish our zest for life. When Gulliver in Jonathan Swift's book visits the Island of Luggnag, the most miserable beings he meets there are the Struldbuggs who have a spot on their foreheads which signifies that they will be alive forever, though their bodies continue to age and their minds to deteriorate. Several existential philosophers and humanistic psychologists in particular have emphasized that, paradoxically, far from casting a pall of gloom, awareness of the inevitability of one's own eventual death can intensify the vitality of our experience of living. Martin Heidegger (1962), for **authenticity** example, has asserted that, for 'authentic' existence, we need to live with **mindfulness of being** *mindfulness of being* rather than with the forgetfulness which is so characteristic of our ordinary everyday experience. It is the need to confront unavoidable 'urgent experiences' like the fact of death that can jolt one into mindfulness. This effect has been clearly documented in several studies where people who have confronted near-death experiences have been asked about its subsequent effect on their lives (e.g. Rosen, 1975; Schmitt, 1976; Noyes, 1981). A common occurrence is that it changes their experience of life. One patient had come close to death through kidney failure. After a length of time on renal dialysis she had received a successful kidney transplant:

> Actually the only way I can describe myself is that I think of myself as having lived two lives. I even call them the first and the second Kathy. The

first Kathy died during dialysis. She could not make it long in the face of death. A second Kathy had to be born. This is the Kathy that was born in the midst of death. . . . The first Kathy was a frivolous kid. She lived only one minute at a time. She quibbled about cold food in the cafeteria, about the boredom of surgical nursing lectures, about the unfairness of her parents. Her goal in life was to have fun on the weekends. . . . The future was far away and of little concern. She lived for trivia only.

But the second Kathy – that's me now. I am infatuated with life. Look at the beauty in the sky! It's gorgeously blue! I go into a flower garden, and every flower takes on such fabulous colours that I am dazzled by their beauty. . . . One thing I do know, had I remained my first Kathy, I would have played away my whole life, and I would never have known what the real joy of living was all about. I had to face death eyeball to eyeball before I could live. I had to die in order to live.

(Schmitt, 1976, p. 54)

Becoming more fully aware of our finiteness can intensify the delight we have in the time that is left to us. It can serve to turn our attention from trivialities and encourage us to live in a richer and more authentic way.

ACTIVITY 5

1 *Life-line:* Draw a line. At one end represent the moment of your birth: at the other the likely point of your death. Estimate and mark in where you are now in your life on the scale of this line. Meditate on this for a few moments.

Other entirely optional activities which you might like to try at some time

2 *Life time:* Working on the basis of likely correlates, such as the average age of death of people closely related to you, whether you smoke or are overweight, your state of health, etc., estimate roughly the year when you think you might die. Then work out (i) how many years and (ii) how many weeks there are between then and now.

3 *Time budgeting:* Section 2 of this Unit has been concerned with the way we experience time. But awareness of the finiteness of existence may make it important to us to think about how we *use* time as well.

You might like to keep a diary of how you spend your time, breaking up the days into twenty-four one-hour periods and noting what you do during each. At the end of each week, analyse the pattern, breaking it down into appropriate subcategories and noting how much time you spend overall on each kind of activity. Reflect on whether this is how you *want* to use your time and, if necessary, on ways in which you can modify your schedule to bring the pattern more into line with what you would like.

(There have been a number of studies of how people spend their time (how long they sleep, work, spend on leisure activities of different kinds, etc.). If you are interested in the topic, see J. P. Robinson (1977) *How Americans Use Time: A Social-Psychological Analysis of Everyday Behaviour*, especially the summary and conclusions on pp. 180–95.)

```
PROGRESS BOX 2   Time

1   Our concern is with the way time is experienced.

2   Factors influencing our experience of time:
– nature of activities engaged in
– context
– states of excitement or despair (physiological functioning)
– stage of life.

3   Significance of social context:
– clock time and capitalism
– technological society makes time a commodity
– need to synchronize life worlds
– influence of subculture.

4   But the sense of time flow is fundamental.

5   Time and personal change: flow of time may be experienced as
progression or deterioration.

6   Attitudes towards the prospect of eventual non-being:
– defy, deny or ignore
– try to transcend through search for immortality of some kind; through
  emotional release; by reframing/acceptance.

7   Awareness of death as a means of creating an authentic awareness of
life.
```

3   CHOICE

Time as an existential problem is not just a question of coming to terms with the prospect of change and eventual non-being. It is compounded by our power of *agency* – the capacity to initiate change through our own action. To a considerable extent we can create our own futures. How we choose or choose not to do this may well have irrevocable consequences.

3.1   Autonomy and determinism

choice

Our concern in this Block is with the way we experience ourselves and our personal worlds. We certainly *experience* some capacity for self-direction, for choosing what we do – these are attributes which (to borrow a phrase) no self-respecting person would be caught without. It is therefore unnecessary to embark on a philosophical debate as to whether we actually are free to choose or whether this is an illusion masking a situation where our actions are determined by factors quite outside our control. However, the course so far (and later this Block too) discusses many factors on which our action and experience clearly do depend: for example, physiological processes (themselves the culmination of millions of years of evolution), socialization, and the nature of the society in which we happen to live. So some comment on the ontological status of our sense of freedom might seem appropriate. Though we experience being free to choose, what sort of freedom can this be?

One problem with discussion of this issue is that too often determinism is posited as an irreconcilable alternative to something called 'free-will'. Another difficulty is the failure to make clear what this 'free-will' is actually supposed to mean. Once you have accounted for the influence of factors of the kind we have noted above, what else is there which could be said to generate experience and behaviour?

One way of breaking through this impasse is to think of our actions as analogous to language.* It is clear that we are totally dependent on both biological inheritance and social context. Had you inherited the genes of a frog you would not be anything like the person you are now. But had you grown up as a member of a Chinese family, this also would have been a radically different life experience from that you have had. These kind of statements are true also for the language you speak. That too is totally dependent on vocal apparatus and brain centres of a specific kind, and also on the opportunity to assimilate from society a particular set of language conventions.

ACTIVITY 6

Stop reading and speak or write down a sentence which you are pretty sure no-one has ever uttered before.

You have thereby created something completely original by means of an ability which itself might be regarded as totally dependent on factors outside your control. Although the form of the language we speak may be determined for us, some at least of the content would appear not to be. The critical factor here, as you will remember from Block 2, is that it is a *rule generated* system. The capacity to use the rules and the particular conventions which govern them may be laid down by biology and society, but the way you use them is a product of you. It could be argued that the ways in which we frame our experience, interact with each other and plan and execute our actions are also generated by implicit rules. So this analogy would seem an appropriate one to enable us to conceptualize how, even given the biological and social construction of our personal worlds, we are still able to generate novel and personal structures in what we think and do. A better term than 'free-will' for this ability is perhaps 'autonomy'.

The point of drawing on this analogy with language is not to suggest that this is sufficient to account for what autonomy is, but rather to demonstrate that autonomy and the genetic and social shaping of behaviour need not be regarded as incompatible. In fact, it can be argued that the two are inherently linked. As Rollo May has put it, 'a person moves *toward* freedom and responsibility in his living as he becomes more conscious of the *deterministic* experiences in his life. . . . *Freedom* is thus not the opposite to determinism' (1967, p. 175). The analogy does however imply that individual human actions are best understood (and predicted) when they are seen as generated by a person who is capable of reflection and autonomous choice, and that they cannot be explained away solely in terms of the influence of and interactions between genetic and social factors.

Another point which suggests the operation of autonomy *with* determinism is that through our attitudes and actions we can often modify the influence of the environment (and sometimes biology) which is acting upon us – what Bandura (1978) has called 'reciprocal determinism'.

reciprocal determinism

autonomy

Much of the traditional confusion here and difficulty in reconciling the notions of autonomy (or 'freedom') and determinism (or 'nature') has arisen, I would suggest, because they are different paradigms generated by different contexts: in the former case our subjective experience of living, in the latter our observation of the natural world.

* See also Metablock Paper 9, 'Autonomy and determinism'.

56

3.2 The experience of autonomy

The exercise of autonomy is a personal act of creation. Experientially, it would seem to have two facets. It involves *reflection* (KF12) on what alternatives we feel are open to us; and also the *commitment* to one or other of them in thought, word or action (KF9). (The emphasis on reflection is not to deny that spontaneous, undeliberated action may also be experienced as autonomous, but for it to be considered so we do need at some level to be aware of what we are doing and to accept that this is what we choose to do.)

responsibility

accountability

intentionality

Exercising autonomy involves taking *responsibility* for or 'owning' one's own actions. As noted in the commentaries on Christopher (Window 2) and Leonard (Window 3) and in the subsequent discussion of agency (KF9), in everyday life people do hold both themselves and others responsible for what they do, provided, as is usually the case, that this is assumed to have been freely chosen. Being responsible means being *accountable*, i.e. we may be called upon to account for (if only to ourselves) *why* we chose to do what we did. Some existentialists, like Sartre, have taken the extreme position of regarding people as responsible for *all* that they experience and do including actions which they choose *not* to carry out. (There is not the space here to go into the detail of existentialist philosophy but it might be worth noting in passing that one basis for this position is the idea of *intentionality*: that our perception and awareness are 'directed at' objects and the world and that the world as we experience it is therefore constituted by our own consciousness as well as by the nature of the objects themselves. A useful example offered by Rollo May (1969, p. 224) to illustrate intentionality is to imagine a house as seen by an estate agent, an artist, a person looking for a house to rent, or someone coming to visit friends. In each case it is the same house but, because of their different needs, it is likely to be constituted very differently in the consciousness of each of the people mentioned. In this sense, we 'own' and are responsible for the *way* we experience the world as well as for the actions we take.)

3.3 Fear of freedom

Although it seems difficult to envisage human existence without some implicit sense of personal autonomy, some writers have questioned how far this is dependent on historical and cultural context. Erich Fromm (1960) has suggested that personal autonomy assumed significance only fairly recently in human history, coming into prominence with the advent of capitalism and the rise of secularism. For with the weakening of cultural and religious belief systems which traditionally provided firm guidance for action, autonomy becomes a problem. People are aware of their power to choose. But they do not always know *what* to choose – at least not when they try to act with a reflective eye for the nature and potential consequences of what they do.

A basic problem here, as existentialists see it, is that autonomy is yours and yours alone. There are no real guidelines and there is no-one else to tell you what to do,

groundlessness

for that would be to relinquish your autonomy. Such *groundlessness* is a fundamental source of existential anxiety, deeper, some believe, than the fear of death (as Kierkegaard put it (1957, p. 139) 'dread is the possibility of freedom'). By taking responsibility for our actions and attitudes we acknowledge that they are what we are. Choosing is thus an act of self-creation. To choose also means, of course, to exclude the rejected alternatives – to know that this event will not happen, that this is an experience we may never know.

defences against autonomy

Confronted with such onerous responsibility, people often seek to escape. Irvin Yalom (1980) has described some of the defences against autonomy which he typically finds among his clients. They may attempt to *displace responsibility* for their lives on to other people – the therapist, for example, or their spouse, or a friend, or astrology. They may avoid it by *refusing to take decisions*, by *behaving impulsively* without thought, by *compulsive behaviour*, or even by *going 'crazy'*, acting in a way which can be assumed to be beyond their control.

Fromm also asserts that people find it difficult to accept their freedom to choose. They shirk the responsibility it demands and fear the isolation it may bring. The mechanisms of escape which he describes focus on the ways in which individuals relate to society. One way, for example, is by submission to the orthodoxy of a political ideology or a religious belief system. One reason why authoritarian regimes (and perhaps some contemporary cults) may appeal to some people is that they offer the means to escape from their freedom. Another escape route common, according to Fromm, in contemporary 'marketing' societies is to allow our choices to be dictated by fashion. The changing tastes and reactions of other people become a key arbiter in determining what we do and how we are to be.

But, the existentialist would argue, there is no escape. Human beings, according to Sartre, are 'doomed' to freedom. To try to avoid this existential reality is equally to choose. To live authentically, it is necessary, they assert, to accept our responsibility, to 'own' what we do (and what we do not do) and to acknowledge **existential guilt** this as *our* personal choice. For an existentialist, guilt arises not because of transgressions against the moral code of someone else but as the result of transgressing against ourselves by failing to live in an authentic way.

3.4 Cultivating autonomy

There is, of course, much variation in the scope which people have to behave in the ways that they would like. Being in prison, for example, closes quite a few doors. And if it helps to provide sustenance and shelter for your family, then you may accept the need to comply with the demands of others even if these are resented. But even where we are subject to physical constraints, we can still exert autonomy in our thoughts and attitudes, as Leonard (in Window 4) demonstrated so well. The Austrian therapist Victor Frankl was himself incarcerated in a German concentration camp and observed that, even there, some prisoners were able to 'preserve a vestige of spiritual freedom, of independence of mind, even in such terrible conditions of psychic and physical stress' (Frankl, 1959, p. 103).

It was the capacity to initiate thoughts, in fact, which finally convinced William James that 'free-will' was no illusion. In his notebook of 1870, he wrote:

> I think that yesterday was a crisis in my life. I finished the first part of Renouvier's second 'Essais' and see no reason why his definition of Free Will – 'the sustaining of thought *because I choose to* when I might have other thoughts' – need be the definition of an illusion. At any rate, I will assume for the present – until next year – that it is no illusion. My first act of free-will shall be to believe in free-will. . . I will go a step further with my will, not only act with it, but believe as well; believe in my individual reality and creative power.

(James, 1920, pp. 147–8)

James's words here remind us of the significance of what we *believe* we are for the way in which we live. In this respect, there is a self-fulfilling quality about human experience. The first step towards developing one's capacity for autonomy is to believe that one has it. (Incidentally, this raises the interesting point that, because psychology is concerned with statements about why we behave in the way that we do, it cannot remain morally neutral. One of the criticisms which has been made of experimental psychology (see, for example, Heather, 1976) is that it tends to constrain our freedom by presenting us with a determinist account of human behaviour – see Unit 14, Part 2 and Metablock Paper 10 for further discussion of this issue.)

ACTIVITY 7

Recall the account of *reframing* in Unit 2. Can you see how this technique is related to the discussion above? By reframing yourself as having the capacity for self-direction, so you come to increase the autonomy you exercise.

As suggested in the quotation from Rollo May in section 3.1, degree of personal autonomy would seem to rest also on awareness of factors influencing our behaviour and experience. Once we become alerted to these, we have greater scope to counteract their effects and to initiate different patterns if desired. Thus 'liberation' movements like gay and women's groups often place emphasis on **consciousness raising** 'consciousness-raising'. Psychology would seem well-placed to play a potentially important role here by throwing light on possible ways in which we are constructed and influenced by biological, developmental and social forces (see the reference to 'critical psychology' in the box in Metablock Paper 10). It can also help us increase the scope of our autonomy by sensitizing us to the potentials and possibilities in ways of experiencing, and of relating to others.

The analysis of the experience of autonomy made earlier suggested that to act autonomously involves not just reflection on alternatives but commitment to or action on the one selected. In some cultures, particular attention has been paid to this aspect. In Japan, for example, one function of the martial arts and their accompanying exercises is to increase the capacity for self-control of body and mind. *Hara-kiri* and ritual violence are thus framed very differently from the way they are in western society – potentially as ultimate expressions of autonomy.

In a rather different way, a concern with cultivating autonomy can be found in North American culture. It is presumed in the conventional notion that anyone is capable of bringing about what they desire, and encouraged in a spate of popular books with titles like *Pulling Your Own Strings* (Dyer, 1978).

Western psychology, in contrast, has been extremely wary about the notion of will. Both experimental psychology and psychoanalysis almost totally disregard it. The reason for this, of course, is that the concept makes no sense within the determinist paradigm within which both operate. Two notable exceptions to this trend have been Roberto Assagioli and the psychoanalyst Otto Rank. Rank **will** (1936) has made a useful analysis of the nature of *will*, distinguishing, for example, between negative or *counterwill* (opposing the demands made on one), *positive will* (bringing about what one has accepted from others as appropriate), and *creative will* (bringing about what one autonomously wants): he considers that these unfold in turn in the course of development. Assagioli was originally a psychoanalyst but later founded psychosynthesis – a therapeutic approach aimed at developing the intellectual, emotional, physical and spiritual potential of a person into a harmonious whole. One of Assagioli's books, *The Act of Will* (1974) explores the different facets of our experience of willing and making choices. A contribution he makes is to broaden the concept of will well beyond the Victorian notion of 'strong will'. Rather he sees it as the active, creative process at the heart of the experience of self. Though not required reading, it is worth looking at this book if you want to pursue this topic for your own interest.

But however we conceive of autonomy and its cultivation, a fundamental problem remains: that of *groundlessness*. If we are responsible for the choices we make and if there are no guidelines other than our own deliberations, on what kind of basis can we choose? Unless autonomous action is to be merely random (which on the basis of the analysis presented here it is not) then it requires some sense of direction premised on values and beliefs. This brings us to our third existential issue – the need for *meaningfulness*.

ACTIVITY 8   Creating actions

1   Think of something you would like to do but would not ordinarily do (e.g. going to a museum, taking a taxi instead of a bus, holding a party, giving a present to someone).

2   Imagine yourself doing this.

3 Do it. Be aware that you have chosen to do it and have created an action which otherwise would not have happened.

4 You might like to repeat the exercise with other things you would like to do. (Or, alternatively, try *not* doing something you would usually do and modify the rest of the exercise accordingly.) Try incorporating a more conscious sense of creative autonomy into your everyday life.

PROGRESS BOX 3   Choice

1 The notion of *agency* is intrinsic to the experience of ourselves as persons.

2 Autonomy is not necessarily incompatible with determinism:

– analogy of language: a rule-generated system which can produce creative and novel utterances (openness)

– 'reciprocal determinism'

– autonomy and determinism stem from different paradigms.

3 The experience of autonomy = reflection on alternatives plus commitment. It also implies responsibility and accountability.

4 Fear of freedom:

– autonomy is a particular issue in contemporary society (Fromm)

– the problem of *groundlessness*

– choice as an *irrevocable* creation

– *defences* against autonomy (displacing responsibility or avoiding it by refusing to decide, by impulsive or compulsive behaviours, or by 'going crazy'.

– the existential argument: need to accept freedom and responsibility for our actions for *authentic* living; existential guilt.

5 Cultivating autonomy:

– autonomy in thought as well as actions

– self-fulfilling nature of human experience

– importance of consciousness-raising

– social encouragement of self-control (Japan) and autonomy (USA)

– disregard of 'will' in psychology and psychoanalysis

– two exceptions: Rank and Assagioli

– the problem of groundlessness remains.

---

4   MEANINGFULNESS

ACTIVITY 9

Spend at least ten minutes thinking about the meaning of your life. What would you say you live for? What principles guide your actions? What do you regard as the point and purpose of your existence?

Reflect too on the nature of such questions. What kinds of answers are possible?

---

meaningfulness In the sense in which I want to use the word, 'meaningfulness' has two aspects. It refers to a way of *making sense of reality* as we experience it: in particular, having a sense of its relevance – what it is for, what it is 'about'. It also implies an emotional aspect: a feeling of *engagement* or involvement with living, welcoming certain experiences and events (perhaps, though not necessarily, with delight), finding them, for whatever reason, desirable. In terms of the analysis of personal worlds presented earlier in this unit, *meaningfulness* essentially involves a combination of two key features – *search for meaning* (KF 13) and *values* (KF 10).

A life which is deficient in meaningfulness is one which is experienced as lacking point, purpose and vitality; living is merely 'going through the motions'. Such *meaninglessness* is expressed in classical mythology by the fate of Sisyphus, who was condemned forever to repeatedly roll a rock up a hill only to watch it come tumbling down again.

Lack of meaning in our lives is not something which may be immediately obvious. It may manifest itself only in a generalized apathy and lack of involvement in what we experience or do. But at moments when, for whatever reason, we reflect on the pattern of our lives, it may suddenly seem empty. In his book *Existential Psychotherapy* (strongly recommended to students interested in this general area), Yalom (1980) includes a suicide note which vividly illustrates such an awareness:

> Imagine a happy group of morons who are engaged in work. They are carrying bricks in an open field. As soon as they have stacked all the bricks at one end of the field, they proceed to transport them to the opposite end. This continues without stop and everyday of every year they are busy doing the same thing. One day one of the morons stops long enough to ask himself what he is doing. He wonders what purpose there is in carrying the bricks. And from that instant on he is not quite as content with his occupation as he had been before.
>
> I am the moron who wonders why he is carrying the bricks.
>
> (Yalom, 1980, p. 419)

So the significance of meaning in life is that it generates a sense of vitality and of meaningful engagement as opposed to passivity, withdrawal and alienation.

4.1   Sources of meaning

What then are the origins of such a sense of meaningfulness? One source is biology. When you are starving, or in peril for your life, the need to find a meaning in existence is not an issue. Meaning is a given, provided presumably by biological process. It is sufficient to survive.

In this sense then our existence as biological beings has some relevance. But this is not all that we are. We are also symbolic beings, capable of communicating and attributing meanings to our experiences over and above their biological significance. Meaningfulness is culturally as well as biologically constructed. It can be as important to eat the right foods prepared in the right way as it is to eat at all. Cultural values serve to give meaning and direction which often have no relation to individual physical survival and may indeed be in opposition to it – as demonstrated by those many times when people have chosen or have been persuaded to die for their beliefs. Cultural conventions as sources of meaning and direction can retain all the potency of biological needs. (For example, in a plane crash in the Andes, a number of the survivors refused to eat the flesh of their dead companions even though not to do so meant certain death from starvation (Read, 1974).) In traditional and coherent societies, cultural values and conventions are likely to retain their potency as a source of meaningfulness. The framework they provide is accepted by others in the same community and, like biological imperatives, it takes on a quality of 'givenness', of having an existence as it were outside the individual as the unquestioned 'way things are'.

4.2 The problem of meaning in contemporary society

The advent of more complex forms of social organization (in particular, technological society) undermines the sense of meaning and direction provided by these biological and cultural sources. On one level, it reduces the pressure of biological need. Life in western industrial societies rarely if ever needs to become a matter of finding enough food to survive. It serves also to break up the coherence of a shared, culturally constructed frame of reference. In part, this comes about through the means it provides for vastly increased communication through broadcasting, literature of all kinds and travel. We are flooded with a plethora of alternative belief and value systems. Coherence is also undermined (as we shall see in Unit 13 when we look at Berger's analysis of modern consciousness) by the multiple worlds which are part of life experience in modern society. Not only does each of us inhabit a number of settings (e.g. work, home, etc.) where beliefs and purposes may differ, but the fact that we can escape from one into another reduces the potency of the influence of any one. A further factor in modern society which contributes to undermining an all-embracing framework of meaning in life is the development of scientific thought. The essence of the scientific approach is scepticism – questioning and enquiring into established views. One effect of this in everyday life has been to raise doubts about many of the assertions made by the religions and ideologies on which traditional beliefs and values depend. Science's own attempts to exclude values from its operations has also had the effect of reducing the salience of values in secular world views built upon its foundations. Science explains but provides no guidance or direction in the choices we confront in daily existence.

So how does a person in the modern world find ways of giving direction and meaning to his or her life? For a happy few, religious experience continues to provide a source of faith and inspiration – a way of making sense of life and deciding on priorities in action and experience. The major function of religions is to offer principles of moral guidance together with ways of making sense of reality which serve both to justify and give coherence to the moralities they espouse.

Where such certainty is no longer possible, what then? One common pattern would seem to be that values become centred on aspects of people's daily lives, such as family, leisure, work and material comforts. This is certainly what Cottrell (1979) found in an intensive interview study of a sample of middle-class people in the UK. Apart from a general concern with contentment among the older subjects and some signs of a romantic vision of a 'back-to-the-land good life', there seemed to be little concern with overarching values and ways of making sense of reality of the kind offered by religion. Nor was there much evidence of anguish over this. Most of the non-religious respondents seemed quite content to get on with whatever immediate projects they were engaged in without worrying too much about the need to make sense of it all. Although in a few cases political ideology had to some extent come to serve as a functional equivalent to religion, her conclusion was that, for the general run of her subjects, 'no new religions were being born', nor were they felt to be necessary.

Cottrell's study was limited both in the number (34) and type (professional) of her subjects. How far her findings can be generalized remains open to question (and the current interest among quite a few people in cults of various kinds makes it seem desirable at least to test them further). In any case, an existentialist might well consider that the subjects in this study were merely manifesting 'forgetfulness' and failing to live authentically with real awareness of their existential situation. Be that as it may, it would seem possible that the need for meaningfulness often asserts itself insistently only at particular stages in a person's life (this is a point which we will consider when discussing the life-cycle in Unit 14). It may be prompted by increasing age (e.g. the so-called 'mid-life crisis') or the changes which come about through time (e.g. children leaving home), or it may arise in the wake of crises such as unemployment or divorce. People who have lived much of their lives content with *ad hoc* projects may suddenly awaken to a powerful desire to find a more all-embracing meaning to their lives. In his *Confession*, Leo Tolstoy vividly describes such an awakening in his own life:

> ... five years ago something very strange began to happen to me. At first I began having moments of bewilderment, when my life would come to a halt, as if I did not know how to live or what to do; I would lose my presence of mind and fall into a state of depression. But this passed, and I continued to live as before. Then the moments of bewilderment recurred more frequently, and they always took the same form. Whenever my life came to a halt, the questions would arise: Why? And what next?

> At first I thought these were pointless and irrelevant questions. I thought that the answers to them were well known and that if I should ever want to resolve them, it would not be too hard for me; it was just that I could not be bothered with it now, but if I should take it upon myself, then I would find the answers. But the questions began to come up more and more frequently, and their demands to be answered became more and more urgent. And like points concentrated into one spot, these questions without answers came together to form a single black stain.

> ... The questions seemed to be such foolish simple, childish questions. But as soon as I laid my hands on them and tried to resolve them, I was immediately convinced, first of all, that they were not childish and foolish questions but the most vital and profound questions in life, and, secondly, that no matter how much I pondered them there was no way I could resolve them. Before I could be occupied with my Samara estate, with the education of my son, or with the writing of books, I had to know why I was doing these things. As long as I do not know the reason why, I cannot do anything. In the middle of my concern with the household, which at the time kept me quite busy, a question would suddenly come into my head: 'Very well, you will have 6,000 desyatins [1 desyatin equals 2.7 acres] in the Samara province, as well as 300 horses; what then?' And I was completely taken aback and did not know what else to think. As soon as I started to think about the education of my children, I would ask myself, 'Why?' Or I would reflect on how the people might attain prosperity, and I would suddenly ask myself, 'What concern is it of mine?' Or in the middle of thinking about the fame that my works were bringing me I would say to myself, 'Very well, you will be more famous than Gogol, Pushkin, Shakespeare, Molière, more famous than all the writers in the world – so what?'

> And I could find absolutely no reply. . . .

> Expressed differently, the question may be: Why should I live? Why should I wish for anything or do anything? Or to put it still differently: Is there any meaning in my life that will not be destroyed by my inevitably approaching death?

> (Tolstoy, 1983, pp. 26–7, 35)

4.3   The search for meaning

Such questions pose a curious paradox. On one hand, they seem to demand an answer of a definitive kind – some firm sense of meaning which can provide a necessary basis for a fully authentic, engaged and vital existence. On the other, once you get beyond the need for survival, there is no one definitive meaning to life. Or at least, as we shall see in our examination of the nature of subjective experience in the next unit, such answers cannot be provided by rational means. For meanings are metaphors, constructions not absolutes, created by the particular constellation of circumstance and experience which happens to mark our existence. From the standpoint of existential psychological analysis, there exists no meaning other than that created by ourselves as biological, social and experiencing beings. It is worth noting all three of these adjectives, for all three aspects would seem to be involved in whatever meaning life comes to possess.

ways to seek meaning Yalom (1980) has made some attempt to classify the kinds of secular meaningfulness which people have sought in the face of such a paradox. There are those concerned essentially with self-gratification or development: *hedonism* is one example, where meaning is found in pleasure, the view that 'life is a gift, take it, unwrap it, appreciate it, use it, and enjoy it'. Another is *self-actualization* – the attempt to 'fulfil one's potential' by freeing oneself and trusting in 'one's organismic wisdom' to develop towards a sense of 'fuller being'. Meaning can also be found in *creativity*, not necessarily expressed only in some form of art but also in a general delight in bringing things into being and in relating to life in an imaginative and spontaneous way. There are also those solutions which transcend the self, *altruism* – finding meaning in serving others and trying to leave the world a better place (the road incidentally which Tolstoy was to take), and *dedication to a cause*. Yalom points out that these various forms of personal meaning are not mutually exclusive. In particular, different ones may be embraced at different stages in one's life (see Unit 14). The psychologist who has perhaps been most concerned with the problem of meaning, Victor Frankl (1969), has suggested a somewhat different classification. Meaningfulness may be sought, he asserts, not just through *creativity* and the *experience of beauty* but also through *fortitude* – the capacity to face up to adversity and to find meaning in doing so.

To conclude this cursory survey of ways of searching for meaning, it might be worth mentioning an approach to life found among many Zen Buddhists. For this could perhaps be regarded as confronting the paradox which lies at the heart of any search for meaning. It is to regard all attempts to seek meaning in life as ultimately futile, whether this be through pleasure, creativity, altruism or dedication to a cause. But, by seeking to be fully conscious of immediate ongoing experience and what is happening for one at the moment, awareness in itself provides all the meaning required. This attitude is reflected in many Japanese haiku poems which capture the essence of an experience at a moment in time:

> Spring rain:
> Soaking on the roof
> A child's rag ball.
>
> (Buson, 1964)

There are no simple solutions to the paradox of how we find and create meaning – arguably one of the most formidable problems of our time. But as Kurtz has pointed out, at its root lies 'not the epistemological demand for proof of life's value – but the quest for psychological stimulus and motivational appeal. What is at issue here is whether we can find within life experience its own reward' (Kurtz, 1974, p. 92). The issue then becomes one of inspiration as well as understanding. If psychology is to facilitate human potentials rather than merely preserve the status quo, it is an issue with which it must surely be concerned. (This topic will be taken up and discussed further in Part 2 of Unit 14.)

PROGRESS BOX 4 Meaningfulness

1 Meaningfulness = a way of making sense of reality plus a feeling of engagement.

2 Basic *sources* of meaning:
– biological being
– culture (symbolic world).

3   In modern life the power of such sources of meaning has been undermined by:

– reduced pressure of biological need

– fragmentation of shared frames of reference

– development of scientific thought.

4   For some people, religion still provides a source of meaningfulness. For others, meaning may be fragmented in pursuit of *ad hoc* projects (e.g. family, material comforts, etc.)

5   Need for meaning perhaps has differential salience at different stages of life (e.g. Tolstoy)?

6   Paradox of meaningfulness – no rational basis for constructing a sense of meaning.

7   Meaning sought in:

– hedonism, self-actualization, creativity, altruism, or dedication to a cause (Yalom)

– in creativity or fortitude (Frankl)

   (Such solutions not mutually exclusive)

– Zen Buddhist paradoxical approach: no ultimate meaning but full awareness of 'here and now'.

8   The need for inspiration (can psychology play a role here?).

5   IDENTITY

identity   I am using the term 'identity' here to refer specifically to *self-awareness* – the human capacity to be aware of oneself as being a particular person distinct from all others and to reflect on the experience of being that person and on who that person is.

In terms of the key features of our personal world discussed earlier, *sense of self* (KF8) is clearly central to identity. But others are relevant too. Our identity is experienced as developing through *time* (KF2) for it is set in the context of a particular personal history – what has been done and experienced in the past and what expectations there are of the future. It is impossible also to separate out a person's identity from the *body* in which it is rooted (KF5). This not only locates identity in *space* (KF3) by linking us, for example, to where we live or come from, but what our body is like (e.g. male/female, fat/thin) may also form an important dimension of the person we think we are. In particular, self-awareness depends on capacity for *reflexiveness* (KF12) – on being able to reflect on who we are and who we might become.

Identity is an existential issue because it confronts us with the need to come to terms both with our awareness of ourselves and the knowledge that we may ourselves participate in creating who we are. It is appropriate to conclude the consideration of existential issues with identity for, in some respects, it could be regarded as the meeting point for the issues considered so far: it is our identity which is threatened by finiteness, which is defined by the choices we make and which is intimately bound up with the kinds of meaning we seek and find in our lives. Identity also effectively illustrates two significant and somewhat paradoxical features of existential issues: (1) our relationships and culture influence them and give shape to the ways in which we work them through, but (2) in the end each of us can only confront and try to resolve them alone.

5.1 Analyses of identity

Unlike the three issues we have discussed so far, identity has received considerable attention from psychologists, though it is usually treated more as an aspect of personality to be analysed than as an existential issue.

William James acknowledged that our sense of who we are is intimately bound up with our awareness of our body and our thoughts and feelings. He also considered it to be related to our material possessions (the house we live in, the car we drive, our clothes, etc.) and to our social roles and relationships. More recently Erik Erikson (1968) has produced a detailed elaboration of the concept of identity. He describes it as 'a subjective sense of an invigorating sameness or continuity' and sees it essentially as a *synthesis* of all the aspects which relate to the self (like those which James suggests) and of our consciousness of who we are in the various personal worlds in which we participate. He points out how we can experience 'ourselves' very differently depending on the time or situation:

> There are constant and often shocklike transitions between these selves: consider the nude body self in the dark or suddenly exposed in the light; consider the clothed self among friends or in the company of higher-ups or lower-downs; consider the just awakened drowsy self or the one stepping refreshed out of the surf or the one overcome by retching and fainting; the body self in sexual excitement or in a rage; the competent self and the impotent one; the one on horseback, the one in the dentist's chair, and the one chained and tortured – by men who also say 'I'. It takes, indeed, a healthy personality for the 'I' to be able to speak out of all of these conditions in such a way that at any given moment it can testify to a reasonably coherent Self.
>
> (Erikson, 1968, p. 217)

Erikson stresses that identity does not just emerge fully-fledged. It evolves over time as a function of our experiences and growth, and, in particular, the close emotional relationships of childhood. As a consequence of identifications which arise from these, the child begins to develop particular values and attitudes which form the basis of his or her identity. These are refined and shaped as we grow **identity formation** older by the more self-aware process of *identity formation* whereby we explore and try out different experiences and models of the kind of person we might wish to become. One important part of the identity formation process is *negative* **negative identification** *identification*. Erikson means by this that our identity is defined in part in terms of what we are *not* and by reference to those kinds of people we do not want to be like.

Self-awareness and identity problems take on greater significance at particular times in our life. For Erikson, the critical time is adolescence. It is then that we begin to explore in earnest what kind of person we can become. But identity development by no means stops with adolescence. Personal crises such as desertion or the death of a partner, or merely the process of ageing, may prompt us into a serious examination of who we are and what we might be. (The question of changing patterns of concern with identity as we mature through the life-cycle will be taken up in Unit 14.)

The rather different uses which Erikson makes of the 'I' and the 'Self' in the last three lines of the quotation above, is very like a distinction which has been made by George Mead (see Unit 4) between the self as processor (the active ego which makes sense of and acts on the world) and the self as object (the kind of person we perceive ourselves to be). It is also reminiscent of the double aspect of the sense of self which Barthes draws attention to in his comments on the photographs of himself (see Window 4 in section 1.1). Awareness of ourselves as objects depends not just on personal experience but on our capacity to see ourselves as we think others see us. One effect of this is that (as illustrated by the account of the private and public selves of Jorge Luis Borges in Box 2 in section 1.2) we are likely to be able to make sense of our identity in varied ways.

5.2 The social construction of identity

Erikson has emphasized that, with identity, 'we deal with a process "located" in *the core of the individual* and yet also *in the core of his communal culture*' (1968, p. 22). If we think back to the Windows in Part 1 of this unit, several examples there suggest how identity is sustained and shaped by social context. One way is by the manner in which other people relate to us. Thus, part of Liv's identity which is 'film star' is confirmed by the attention, the flowers and champagne she finds on her arrival. Christopher's social identity is sustained by the reactions of his employers towards him and the attitudes of his fellow workers. Another social source of our identities derives from the groups of which we are (or aspire to be) **group-related identity** members, be they to do with class, sex, nationality or religion. Such group-related identities may be deliberately fostered by particular styles of dress or customs which distinguish members of that group from other people. Such groups do not have to exist as established entities but may be only notional. Thus Barthes was likely to adopt a style of life and behaviour appropriate to an 'intellectual' or 'academic'.

Personal identity is therefore rooted in social comparisons between one person and another and in the identity images available in our culture. So the impact on a person's identity of becoming, say, unemployed will depend in part, as Kelvin (1980) has observed, on the image of the 'unemployed' in the community in which that person lives.

There is considerable individual and cultural variation in the degree to which personal identity is dependent on the social context. Feelings of self-esteem are particularly vulnerable to social definition. But although for some self-worth is highly dependent on how people in general seem to view them, for others it rests much more on self-assessment or on the regard only of 'kindred spirits'.

A final point worth noting in considering the social construction of identity is Berger *et al.*'s (1974) notion (which will be elaborated in the next unit) that the very sense of having an individual identity may be largely a product of a particular kind of society. In modern western society, for example, we live our lives in many contexts (work, family, etc.) and are never totally immersed in just one area of life. There is thus always a part of our identity which is separate from the situation we are in. It is this, they argue, which encourages a sense of individual, personal identity. Coping with the diverse selves we experience in different settings, it might be added, requires us as individuals to try to create some kind of integration and wholeness. It passes responsibility to us for choosing which selves we will emphasize and for constructing who we shall be. Thus, identity becomes an existential issue.

5.3 The psychosocial nature of identity

Personal identity is both a product of the social context in which we live and also **identity as psychosocial** an individual enterprise. Erikson uses the term 'psychosocial' to emphasize that identity emerges from the complex interplay between the two.

A good illustration of this interaction process is gender. A child sees him or herself as 'boy' or 'girl' and may act accordingly, but much, if not most, of what constitutes emergent maleness or femaleness is constructed by the way other people react to the child. Biological and hormonal factors may play a part in differentiating behaviour between the sexes, but a major influence also comes from people's expectations about how a boy or girl, a man or woman, should be treated and what they should be like. In a study which has become a classic, Harold Garfinkel (1967) has given a vivid account of Agnes who, in spite of the possession of a penis and scrotum and having been raised as a boy, saw herself as essentially female. What is interesting about this study from our standpoint is the detailed account which Garfinkel provides of the complex skills which Agnes had to learn to get other people to react to her as a woman. She needed them to respond appropriately in order for her to properly assume a female identity.

The term 'psychosocial' therefore draws our attention to the idea that identity emerges from a complex, continuous negotiation between an individual's characteristics and actions and the stereotypes and conceptions which govern the responses of other people in his or her community. An area in which considerable effort has been made to delineate more clearly the processes involved has been

deviance

the study of deviance (i.e. behaviours which run counter to the established norms of society and which are usually, though not necessarily, regarded by those in authority as anti-social). The most influential perspective here (labelling theory)

labelling theory

asserts that people are categorized according to physical characteristics, their behaviour or background (for example, having been in prison or mental hospital). Once a person has been labelled as 'sick' or 'criminal' or an 'addict', he or she has been allocated an identity based on social stereotypes, although this identity is not confined to the behaviours, etc., which provided the basis for the categoriza-

essentializing labels

tion. Such labels are 'essentializing' in that they impute that the labelled person is someone who is fundamentally different from normal people. The effect of this may be self-fulfilling: by having such identities thrust upon them, the persons concerned may come to think of themselves in this way and to behave accordingly. (For further discussion of labelling theory see the section on 'The interpersonal basis of personal reality' in Metablock Paper 7.)

In his detailed account of the complex sequence involved in the construction of a deviant identity, Matza (1969) has brought out very clearly how it emerges from the interaction between individual behaviours and self-conception and the responses to these by other people, particularly those in authority. The sequence begins with what Matza terms the 'invitational edge' of deviance. This is when a person imagines what it might be like to try the behaviour in question – perhaps taking drugs, or taking someone's car for a joyride without their permission, or offering sex in return for money or a favour. At this stage, he or she may never get round to doing it. To do so requires an act of impulse or will. Once done, there may be reflection on what it was like – how it made the person feel. That one act may be sufficient and the sequence need go no further. But if the person decides to continue the experiment, this is likely to involve learning techniques (e.g. starting a car without an ignition key, rolling a joint, or distracting a shopkeeper's attention). With this awareness of a new pattern of behaviour and skills comes a changing conception of self.

We see how Matza's description ascribes the exercise of choice and will to the apprentice delinquent and regards the process as one of exploring possible actions and other people's reactions to these. It is seen as an open affair where the individual can choose whether to proceed or not. But it also intrinsically depends on social context, for this determines the kinds of opportunities available in the first place and imposes meaning on the actions concerned. In some communities, for example, the action in question may be a source of status, in others of contempt.

The role of social processes becomes more dominant as the sequence shifts from this stage (which Matza calls primary deviance) to a secondary phase. This takes over when the behaviour in question is no longer an arbitrary, occasional event but is seen by the person as part of himself. A key factor in this development is

signification

signification. The deviant behaviours are signified as illegal and are subject to *ban*. This may require the person to cover up the true nature of one side of his life. If he or she is arrested and brought to court then the behaviour is clearly labelled as delinquent. Private awareness is synchronized with public image and a delinquent identity is confirmed by the reactions and definitions of others, particularly those in a social position to 'legitimate' the label they ascribe.

Delinquency is used here merely as an example. The same kind of pattern can be found in the construction of legitimate forms of identity such as becoming a doctor or a psychologist. The sequence is likely to begin with thinking about the possibility of becoming such a person, followed by experimenting and learning appropriate skills. The individual then becomes caught up in the relevant social processes until, finally, the identity is confirmed by the action of accredited others through the award of a degree or a professional post.

It is interesting also to consider the rise (and fall) of political figures in this psychosocial light. In some respects, political success is a function of an individual's skills, attitudes and behaviours. But it is also a complex sequence governed both by available opportunities and the reactions of influential people to the characteristics of the person concerned, which determine the eventual status (and thus the identity) which is attained. (See also the discussion of leadership in Block 6.)

ACTIVITY 10   Disidentification exercise

This analysis has suggested that identity is bound up with our thoughts, feelings and actions, as well as the social roles and stereotypes thrust upon us by others. One goal of Zen Buddhism is to encourage us to become more detached from all these aspects of identity. If we can do so, it is claimed, we may come to a more fundamental experience of self. If you are interested in this notion, you might like to try the following activity (adapted from Payne, 1974).

1   Find a time when you can be silent and alone for at least fifteen minutes.

2   Make yourself comfortable but preferably sitting straight in a chair.

3   Try, as far as possible to still other thoughts which may be rising in your mind and meditate (i.e. focus on and be as fully aware as possible) upon the following 'seed' thoughts:

(i)   'I am not my physical body but that which uses it.'

(ii)   'I am not my emotions but that which controls them.'

(iii)   'I am not my thoughts but that which creates them.'

(iv)   'I am.'

5.4   Existential isolation

To reflect on our identity is to become aware that, for all its embedding in a social context, we are fundamentally alone. Erich Fromm has asserted that the process of individual development, because of the human powers of reason and self-awareness, represents the gradual emergence of a sense of being a person distinct and separated from nature and from other people (see *Freud and Psychoanalysis*, pp. 71–3). To grow up is to assume a separate identity, to become a separate being.

existential isolation

As noted earlier in this unit, we seem to own our personal worlds. Our experience feels part of us and we are confined within it. This is what I mean by 'existential isolation': not the loneliness which comes from the need to be with people, but awareness of, as Yalom has expressed it, the 'unbridgeable gulf between oneself and any other being' (Yalom, 1980, p. 355) and indeed the world. Yalom quotes Thomas Wolfe: 'caught in that insoluble prison of being, we escape it never, no matter what arms may clasp us, what mouth may kiss us, what heart may warm us. Never, never, never, never, never' (Wolfe, 1929, p. 31).

productive love

Such separateness, Fromm asserts, generates profound anxiety which, not surprisingly, we seek to escape. The ways in which people do this have formed a theme running through his work. In *The Art of Loving* (1957), for example, Fromm suggests that one common mode is through conformity: 'If I am like everybody else, if I have no feelings or thoughts which make me different . . . I am saved . . . from the frightening experience of aloneness' (Fromm, 1957, p. 17). Another way in which we might try to alleviate our isolation is by fusion with another person in a personal and/or sexual relationship. Fromm argues, however, that such bonding is only of value if it does not seek to deny the existential reality of our aloneness and, therefore, the ultimate individuality of the partners involved. For him, the solution lies in 'productive love' where 'the paradox occurs that two beings become one and yet remain two' (Fromm, 1957, p. 21), though he does not elaborate in detail on what this idea implies.

For the existentialist, there is no authentic alternative save to accept that, as no-one can die or make our choices for us, so no-one else can take responsibility for who we are; that ultimately each of us can only stand alone. But this is not necessarily to despair: for such acceptance can bring with it heightened awareness and excitement in the creative process which existence, when we confront existential realities, can become.

PROGRESS BOX 5   Identity

1   *Identity is awareness of who we are.* It is focused on the sense of self but related to other key features of personal worlds such as time, space, rooting in a body and reflexiveness.

2   Why identity is an existential issue: it is the 'meeting point' for finiteness, choice and meaning; we experience some scope to create ourselves; it brings home to us our ultimate isolation.

3   *Analyses of identity*:
– William James
– Erikson: synthesis of experiences of self, the development of identity and our awareness of it as an issue
– the double aspect of identity: self as process and as object.

4   The *social construction* of identity:
– social sources of personal identity: the way people relate to us, group memberships, social images and comparisons. But there are individual variations in the power of such influences: e.g. differences in the basis for self-esteem
– the many *'life worlds'* of contemporary society intensify a sense of individual identity (Berger) and generate a need to integrate and construct it on a personal basis.

5   Identity as *psychosocial*:
– the development of identity as an interactive process between individual and social context
– gender as an example of this
– the psychosocial construction of an identity (both deviant and legitimate).

6   *Existential isolation*:
– confinement in our personal world of being
– escape attempts: conformity, dependent relationships with other people, sexuality
– Fromm's solution: productive love
– existential authenticity: accepting aloneness.

Epilogue

This unit has discussed and provided illustrations of what seem to be general characteristics of our experience of being a person. It has also explored some of the problems we have to confront because of the nature of our experience of existing. In doing so, it has raised a number of general questions. One is about the kind of understanding which is possible in areas of this kind: this will be taken up in Unit 14 in the conclusion to the Block. Another is how far the analysis presented in this unit is limited to our culture. For a theme which has been evident throughout is that personal worlds are eminently social: people not only form an important part of our experience but they help to constitute it by their reactions to us and by the conceptions and attitudes which we assimilate from them. Are then the key features identified and the existential issues discussed characteristic only of people in our culture: or can we assume that they apply to all human kind?

There is no easy answer to this question. Clearly cultural context profoundly shapes personal worlds, affecting, for example, the experience of time, personal identity, attitudes to the prospect of eventual death, and the kinds of values and meanings looked for in life. None the less, it is reasonable to suppose that the key features and existential issues explored in the unit occur in some form in every human being. There are certainly features of human experience which are universal across cultures. Everyone is born and will die; all have some capacity to initiate actions and some sense of what they value. Although the actual way in which time is experienced may vary, it would be difficult to imagine someone (unless brain-damaged) with *no* experience of time. And could anyone be regarded as a 'person' without a modicum of self-awareness? Cultures may suppress or modify our experience of existential issues, but in all of us some vestige of them is surely there. The theories we shall look at in the next unit take rather different positions on the question. Some view many of the features we have discussed as fundamental aspects of human experience which have emerged in the course of evolution. Others view them largely in historical and/or cultural terms.

This unit has been primarily descriptive and exploratory. It lays the groundwork for the theories and ideas which will be elaborated in the other two units in the Block. In the next one, Unit 13, we will dig a little more deeply into the nature of personal worlds by looking at some of the ways in which psychologists have conceptualized subjective experience.

References

ASSAGIOLI, R. (1974) *The Act of Will*, London, Wildwood.

BANDURA, A. (1978) 'The self-system in reciprocal determinism', *American Psychologist*, Vol. 33, No. 4, pp. 344–58.

BARTHES, R. (1977) *Roland Barthes* (trans. by R. Howard), London, Macmillan.

BERGER, P. L., BERGER, B. and KELLNER, H. (1974) *The Homeless Mind*, Harmondsworth, Penguin Books.

BERGSON, H. (1965) 'The possible and the real', in Browning, D. (ed) *Philosophers of Process*, New York, Random House.

BLYTHE, R. (1969) *Akenfield*, London, Allen Lane.

BORGES, J. L. (1970) *Labyrinths*, Harmondsworth, Penguin Books.

BUSON, Y. (1964) 'Spring rain', in *The Penguin Book of Japanese Verse* (trans. by G. Bownas and A. Thwaite), Harmondsworth, Penguin Books.

COTTLE, T. J. and KLINEBERG, S. L. (1974) *The Present of Things Future*, London, Collier Macmillan.

COTTRELL, M. (1979) 'Invisible religion and the middle class', unpublished paper, Linacre College, Oxford.

CSIKSZENTMIHALYI, M. and ROCHBERG-HALTON, E. (1981) *The Meaning of Things*, Cambridge, Cambridge University Press.

DYER, W. (1978) *Pulling Your Own Strings*, New York, Funk and Wagnalls.

ELIOT, T. S. (1974) *Collected Poems, 1909–1962*, London, Faber.

ERIKSON, E. H. (1968) *Identity: Youth and Crisis*, London, Faber.

FRANKL, V. E. (1959) *Man's Search for Meaning: An Introduction to Logotherapy*, Boston, Beacon Press.

FRANKL, V. E. (1969) *The Will to Meaning*, New York, New American Library.

FROMM, E. (1957) *The Art of Loving*, London, Unwin.

FROMM, E. (1960) *Fear of Freedom*, London, Routledge and Kegan Paul.

FRYER, D. M. and PAYNE, R. L. (1984) 'Proactive behaviour in the unemployed: findings and implications', *Leisure Studies*, Vol. 3, pp. 273–95.

GARFINKEL, H. (1967) *Studies in Ethnomethodology*, Englewood Cliffs, New Jersey, Prentice-Hall.

HEATHER, N. (1976) *Radical Perspectives in Psychology*, London, Methuen.

HEIDEGGER, M. (1962) *Being and Time*, New York, Harper and Row.

HORTON, J. (1967) 'Time and cool people', *Transaction*, No. 4, April, pp. 5–12.

JAHODA, M. (1982) *Employment and Unemployment*, Cambridge, Cambridge University Press.

JAMES, W. (1920) *The Letters of William James* (ed. by H. James), London, Longmans Green and Co.

JAMES, W. (1960) *The Varieties of Religious Experience*, London, Collins.

KHAYYAM, OMAR (1974) *The Rubáiyát* (trans. by E. Fitzgerald) London, Royal College of Art.

KELVIN, P. (1980) 'Social psychology 2001: the social psychological bases and implications of structural unemployment', in Gilmour, R. and Duck, S. (eds) *The Development of Social Psychology*, London, Academic Press.

KIERKEGAARD, S. (1957) *The concept of dread* (trans. by W. Lowrie) Princeton, Princeton University Press.

KOSINSKI, J. (1983) *Pinball*, London, Arrow Books.

KURTZ, P. (1974) *The Fullness of Life*, New York, Horizon Press.

MATZA, D. (1969) *Becoming Deviant*, Englewood Cliffs, New Jersey, Prentice-Hall.

MAY, R. (1958) 'Contributions of existential psychotherapy', in May, R., Angel, E. and Ellenberger, H. F. (eds), *Existence*, New York, Basic Books.

MAY, R. (1967) *Psychology and the Human Dilemma*, Princeton, D. van Nostrand.

MAY, R. (1969) *Love and Will*, London, Souvenir Press.

MBITI, J. (1969) *African Religions and Philosophy*, London, Heinemann.

MEDOFF, M. (1982) *Children of a Lesser God*, Ambergate, Amber Lane Press.

NOYES, R. (1981) 'Attitude change following near-death experiences', *Psychiatry*, Vol. 43, No. 3, pp. 234–41.

PAYNE, B. (1974) *Getting There Without Drugs*, London, Wildwood House.

PRATHER, H. (1970) *Notes to Myself*, Moab, Utah, Real People Press.

RANK, O. (1936) *Truth and Reality*, New York, Knopf.

READ, P. P. (1974) *Alive*, London, Alison Press (with Secker Warburg).

ROBINSON, J. P. (1977) *How Americans Use Time: A Social-Psychological Analysis of Everyday Behaviour*, New York, Praeger.

ROETHKE, T. (1968) *Collected Poems*, London, Faber.

ROSEN, D. (1975) 'Suicide survivors', *Western Journal of Medicine*, Vol. 122, pp. 289–94.

SACKS, O. (1976) *Awakenings*, New York, Vintage Books.

SAINT AUGUSTINE (1961) *Confessions* (trans. by R. S. Pine-Coffin), Harmondsworth, Penguin Books.

SAINT-EXUPÉRY, A. de (1975) *Wind, Sand and Stars*, London, Pan Books.

SCHMITT, A. (1976) *Dialogue with Death*, Lincoln, Virginia, Chosen Books.

SERGE, D. (1970) *Men in Prison*, London, Gollancz.

STEVENS, R. (1983) *Freud and Psychoanalysis*, Milton Keynes, The Open University Press (Set Book).

THE OPEN UNIVERSITY (1976) D305 *Social Psychology*, Block 9, *Man's Experience of the World*, Milton Keynes, The Open University Press.

THOMAS, D. (1952) *Selected Poems 1934–1952*, London, Dent.

TOLSTOY, L. (1983) *Confession* (trans. by D. Patterson), New York, Norton.

ULLMAN, L. (1976) *Changing*, New York, Bantam Books.

WEDDERBURN, A. A. (1981) 'Is there a pattern in the value of time off work?', in Reinberg, A. *et al.* (eds) *Night and Shift Work: Biological and Social Aspects*, Oxford, Pergamon Press.

WOLFE, T. (1929) *Look Homeward, Angel*, New York, Scribner.

YALOM, I. D. (1980) *Existential Psychotherapy*, New York, Basic Books.

Acknowledgements

Grateful acknowledgement is made to the following sources for material used in this Unit:

Text

R. Blythe, *Akenfield*, Penguin Books, 1969, reprinted by permission of David Higham Associates; O. Sacks, *Awakenings*, Gerald Duckworth and Co. Ltd, 1973; R. Barthes, *Roland Barthes*, trans. R. Howard, Macmillan, London and Basingstoke, 1975.

Illustrations

pp. 25–31 from R. Barthes, *Roland Barthes*, trans. R. Howard, Macmillan, London and Basingstoke, 1975, reprinted by permission of Editions du Seuil; *p. 43* from M. Calman, *Calman Revisited*, Methuen, London.

Index of concepts

UNIT 13 MAKING SENSE OF SUBJECTIVE EXPERIENCE

Prepared for the course team by Richard Stevens

CONTENTS

'What an absurd amount of energy I have been wasting all my life trying to figure out how things "really are", when all the time they weren't.'

(Prather, 1970)

Study guide

At the core of any personal world is the flow of subjective experience or consciousness. The purpose of this unit is to look at some of the ways in which psychologists have tried to make sense of or conceptualize this. We will examine and contrast six approaches:

1 One of the themes which emerged in the last unit was the social nature of individual experience. The first theory we look at works from this premise. Goffman in his *frame analysis* tries to show how subjective experience reflects the basic frameworks provided in society for making sense of events.

2 In contrast, the second approach is firmly focused on the individual. How can we account for the richness and variety of subjective experience and its intangible, evanescent feel? Jaynes and Romanyshyn, two psychologists working largely from a phenomenological approach (the analysis of individual subjective experience – remember?), propose that a useful way to try to do this is to think of consciousness in terms of.*metaphor*.

3 The next perspective concerns the part played by *fantasy and imagination* in personal worlds. Here, we also consider the significance of unconscious meaning and, with the help of the Set Book (Stevens, 1983), the implications of psychoanalysis for understanding subjective experience.

The final three approaches are grouped together because they are all concerned in their different ways with trying to make sense of subjective experience by considering the conditions which have made it possible.

4 The fourth approach thus discusses how taking into account the *evolutionary development* of our species might cast light on the origins of consciousness.

5 We then go on to look briefly at a controversial theory which has proposed that the nature of subjective experience has changed during *historical* time.

6 Finally, we turn again to the idea that individual experience is *socially constructed*. Do different social contexts foster the emergence of particular forms of consciousness? We shall look particularly at the ideas of Berger and his colleagues about the nature of modern consciousness and the links which they assert that it has with the structures of contemporary society.

While most of the themes are presented here for the first time in the course, they do reflect general perspectives and 'tensions' within social psychology which you have encountered before. Some approaches emphasize, for example, the role of the individual in constructing his or her own experience (as personal construct theory has in Unit 8); others (like symbolic interactionism discussed in Unit 4) see consciousness as essentially a product of society. Some place stress on the need to look at evolutionary development; others on historical and social change. Each theory highlights different facets of subjective experience. Taken together, they provide a well-differentiated account of it, as well as deepening our understanding of the features of personal worlds discussed in the preceding unit. The range of perspectives presented also helps us to appreciate how it is possible to conceptualize subjective experience in very different ways. The difficulties involved in making sense of such an elusive subject-matter are taken up in the final section of the unit.

Objectives

After having studied this unit, you should be able to:

The nature of consciousness

1 Reflect on the nature of your *own conscious experience* and the problems of introspection.

2 Briefly describe the basic ideas in William James's analysis of consciousness.

Frame analysis

3 Give an account of and evaluate the usefulness of frame analysis, including concepts such as natural and social frameworks, keying, frame disjunction and frame maintenance.

Subjective experience as metaphor

4 Outline and evaluate the proposition that consciousness is metaphorical in nature.

5 Show how understanding of the physical world, of subjective realities, and in science depends on the use of metaphor.

6 Know what is meant by a 'subjective reality of reflection', 'figuring experience', and 'understanding by imaginal reconstruction'.

7 Discuss the implications for psychology of the idea that both understanding and consciousness are metaphorical in nature.

8 Discuss personal construct theory in relation to (i) the notion of subjective experience as metaphor and (ii) the key features of personal worlds presented in Unit 12.

The significance of imagination

9 Discuss the role of *fantasy* and *unconscious meanings* in subjective experience.

Conditions shaping subjective experience

10 Assess the possible relevance of *evolutionary development* to our understanding of subjective experience.

11 Offer a critique of Jaynes's view of possible *historical changes* in the nature of consciousness and discuss what its implications might be for understanding the consciousness of people today.

12 Demonstrate what is meant by the *social construction of reality* and the possible impact of modern society on consciousness.

Ways of studying subjective experience and the problems involved

13 Compare and contrast the different perspectives on subjective experience presented in the unit.

14 Appreciate the intrinsic problems involved in making sense of subjective experience.

1   TRYING TO GRASP AWARENESS

What do I mean by subjective experience?

ACTIVITY 1

1   For about three minutes try to be consciously aware of what you are conscious of.

2   Then, reflect for a few minutes on what goes on in your consciousness. How would you describe it?

These are not easy activities! Here is how one psychologist, Julian Jaynes, has written about the experience of consciousness:

> O, what a world of unseen visions and heard silences, this insubstantial country of the mind! What ineffable essences, these touchless remember-ings and unshowable reveries! And the privacy of it all! A secret theater of speechless monologue and prevenient counsel, an invisible mansion of all moods, musings, and mysteries, an infinite resort of disappointments and discoveries. A whole kingdom where each of us reigns reclusively alone, questioning what we will, commanding what we can. A hidden hermitage where we may study out the troubled book of what we have done and yet may do. An introcosm that is more myself than anything I can find in a mirror. This consciousness that is myself of selves, that is everything, and yet nothing at all – what is it?
>
> And where did it come from?
>
> And why? . . .
>
> It is the difference that will not go away, the difference between what others see of us and our sense of our inner selves and the deep feelings that sustain it. The difference between the you-and-me of the shared behavioral world and the unlocatable location of things thought about. Our reflections and dreams, and the imaginary conversations we have with others, in which never-to-be-known-by-anyone we excuse, defend, proclaim our hopes and regrets, our futures and our pasts, all this thick fabric of fancy is so absolutely different from handable, standable, kickable reality with its trees, grass, tables, oceans, hands, stars – even brains! How is this possible? How do these ephemeral existences of our lonely experience fit into the ordered array of nature that somehow surrounds and engulfs this core of knowing?
>
> (Jaynes, 1979, p. 1)

Should you find the declamatory and literary style of this quotation somewhat off-putting, you might like to recall the methodological point made in Unit 12 (section 1.3) that the capacity to get at personal worlds may depend on facility with language. Stylistic use of language and metaphor may also be helpful in capturing something of the essential features of consciousness itself. Try reread-ing each phrase a little more closely. You may well find that, if you can pick up the full flavour of the images and connotations which Jaynes uses, they get you thinking more deeply about what consciousness is and the kind of questions which might be asked about it.

In the early days of psychology, when in Wundt's laboratory in the latter part of the nineteenth century the 'methods of physiology began to be applied to the problems of philosophy', the study of consciousness was recognized as a central concern. A common approach then was to train observers to analyse their introspections, rather like a painter breaks down a scene he or she is about to paint, in terms of its component 'sensations' of light, contour and colour. William James was among those objectors to this method who pointed out that sensations are an abstraction we impose on our experience, they are not an intrinsic part of that experience itself. *His* starting point was only that 'thought goes on'.

James was one of the first psychologists to try to deal with the kind of questions posed in the quotation above. In his *Principles of Psychology* (first published in 1890), he emphasized how subjective experience is characterized by continual change:

> Our state of mind is never precisely the same. Every thought we have of a given fact is strictly speaking, unique, and only bears a resemblance of kind with our other thoughts of the same fact... experience is remoulding us every moment, and our mental reaction on every given thing is really a resultant of our experience of the whole world up to that date.
>
> (James, 1950, pp. 233–4)

stream of consciousness He also stressed its *continuity* and flow – the *stream-like* nature of consciousness:

> It *feels* unbroken; a waking day of it is sensibly a unit as long as that day lasts, in the sense in which the hours themselves are units, as having all their parts next to each other, with no intrusive alien substance between.
>
> (James, 1950, p. 238)

James recognized, nevertheless, that subjective experience does not come in a homogeneous web. He distinguished sub-worlds of experience like that of the senses, science, that of a madman, philosophical and abstract beliefs, the supernatural and myths, etc., each with 'its own special and separate style of existence'.

He worked towards a definition of consciousness:

> ... the mind is at every stage a theatre of simultaneous possibilities. Consciousness consists in the comparison of these with each other, the selection of some, and the suppression of the rest by the reinforcing and inhibiting agency of attention. The highest and most elaborated mental products are filtered from the data chosen by the faculty next beneath, out of the mass offered by the faculty below that, which mass in turn was sifted from a still larger amount of yet simpler material, and so on. The mind, in short, works on the data it receives very much as a sculptor works on his block of stone. In a sense the statue stood there from eternity. But there were a thousand different ones beside it, and the sculptor alone is to thank for having extricated this one from the rest.
>
> (James, 1950, p. 288)

Even in these brief extracts from James's account of consciousness, we can see traces of the features of personal worlds identified in the preceding unit. The flow of *time (KF2)* is implicit in his notions of change and continuity, and his concepts of sub-worlds of experience and of the mind as a 'theatre of simultaneous possibilities' (with awareness at any one point being a particular selection and construction from these possibilities) relate to our notions both of the *multiplicity* of personal worlds *(KF11)* and the *reflexiveness* which enables us to adopt different perspectives *(KF12)*.

Introspective accounts like those of James ran into difficulties. Arguments arose which there was no way to resolve. Could there be thought without any kind of implicit images involved in it, for example? What one psychologist would assert, another could equally deny. The behaviourist movement sprang up to cut the

Gordian knot by sweeping away altogether the notion that consciousness has relevance to psychology. In time, moderate behaviourists came to assert a more methodological position: i.e., it is not that consciousness does not matter, only that it is not possible to study it scientifically. For it is a private and exclusive affair. It cannot be laid bare to the public eye as a set of observable events. (One might question this though. We all have access to our own conscious awareness and, as with the 'Windows' in Unit 12, are able to some extent to share the world of other people's experience.)

In spite of James's conviction of the importance of studying consciousness, until recent years, mainstream academic psychology has been largely content to ignore his initiative. But one of the exciting though confusing features of psychology is the variety of ways in which its subject-matter is studied. There have been schools of thought traditionally associated with sociology (like symbolic interactionism which, you will remember, you encountered in Unit 4) which, because of their interest in how people make sense of the world, have provided useful insights into subjective experience. Alfred Schutz (1962), for example, has **multiple realities** put forward a notion of 'multiple realities' or provinces of meaning, which is not dissimilar to James's sub-worlds (and also of course *KF11 – multiplicity*). So the child enters the play world of his toys; we settle down to watch a television play or penetrate the world of a good book; the religious person withdraws into communion with God, perhaps a mystic world; we drift into fantasy or dreams. One of the most interesting analyses of the different forms of experience which make up our personal worlds is to be found in a book by Erving Goffman called *Frame Analysis* (1975) and it is to this we now turn.

PROGRESS BOX 1

1   William James describes consciousness as:

(i)   ever-changing;

(ii)   a continuous flow;

(iii) comprising sub-worlds of experience;

(iv)   involving selection/creation from simultaneous possibilities.

2   Problems of introspection. Irresolvable arguments about claims made about the nature of consciousness based on 'private' experience.

---

2   FRAME ANALYSIS

Goffman was a Canadian sociologist working broadly within the symbolic interactionist perspective (see Unit 4, section 5). His interests were centred on the strategies involved in social interaction, how these are generated by 'social scripts', and the complex rituals and processes of negotiation and interpretation they involve. His approach is sometimes called 'dramaturgical' because he broadly conceived of interaction as being rather like improvisation in the theatre. (Some aspects of his work in this area have already been introduced in section 3 of Unit 10/11.)

In *Frame Analysis* though, his primary concern is how subjective experience is organized for us. His aim is to 'try to isolate some of the basic frameworks of understanding available in our society for making sense out of events' (1975, p. 10). He is interested in what different provinces of meaning there are. What con-

frame

ventions and rules underlie them, set their limits and cue us in so that we recognize what is going on? Goffman borrows from Bateson (1972) the term 'frame' to denote the way we define a particular situation. As the term suggests, when we 'frame' an experience, we put it in context and this provides an implicit set (i.e. expectations) which allows us to anticipate and make sense of what is happening (cf. the idea of 'reframing' discussed in Unit 2, section 6.4).

2.1 Primary frameworks

natural framework

social framework

Goffman first distinguishes two broad frameworks of primary experience – the natural world and the social. The physical world of the *natural* framework is conceived of as undirected and unguided, as due to 'natural causes'. Examples might be the state of the weather or the operation of an engine. We explain the natural world by reference to *causes*. When it comes to the *social* world, however, we are more likely to explain with *reasons*. For its distinguishing feature is that it is constituted by deeds rather than mere events. Motive and intention are assumed to be involved:

> Social frameworks, . . . provide background understanding for events that incorporate the will, aim, and controlling effort of an intelligence, a live agency, the chief one being the human being. Such an agency is anything but implacable; it can be coaxed, flattered, affronted, and threatened. What it does can be described as 'guided doings'. These doings subject the doer to 'standards', to social appraisal of his action based on its honesty, efficiency, economy, safety, elegance, tactfulness, good taste, and so forth.

(Goffman, 1975, p. 22)

As individuals we straddle both worlds. Our bodies form part of the natural order of events. There are some circumstances too under which our actions can be regarded as outside our intentional control (when we are drunk, for example, asleep, or hypnotized). Excuses often involve reframing our behaviour by placing it in a natural rather than social perspective and hence outside our responsibility – 'I did not know what I was doing', 'The traffic made me late', 'I couldn't do it because I was ill'.

The line between natural and social frameworks varies with culture and historical period. Whereas *we* may ascribe no malevolence to the fact that it rains on our feast-day, others may think of it as due to the actions of the gods. Goffman points out our fascination with the boundary areas between the two. Stunts, where a person manages to maintain voluntary control under what may be seen as impossible conditions, enthrall us at the circus. 'Muffings' (occasions when something that started as a guided action, like driving a car, for some reason gets out of control) make the newspapers, as do reports of strange events which stretch our normal conceptions of the natural – like ESP and visitations from outer space. But while we tolerate and are intrigued by the unexplained, we tend, according to Goffman, to dislike the inexplicable, and we are anxious to assimilate it within one or other of our primary frameworks.

Goffman goes on to discuss the tension which can be created where the usual framework is supplanted by another, as when a doctor presumes to adopt a 'natural' rather than a 'social' perspective to the naked body of his patient. The social rules of such situations are carefully defined and, if there is a departure from them, means are provided (like undressing in private) to 'bracket' it off and make the shift of perspective quite clear.

(You might like to relate the distinction which Goffman makes between natural and social frameworks to the suggestion made in Metablock Paper 2 (section 3) and Paper 5 that one key difference between psychological theories is whether they frame the subject matter of psychology as being part of the *natural* world (and therefore to be explained in terms of causes) or as part of the *social and personal* world (and thus to be explained in terms of reasons).)

2.2 Keys and keying

keyed experience Drawing on a musical analogy, Goffman introduces the notion of keys and keying to refer to the way that primary experience can be transformed or transcribed into a different register and thus take on new form. Playing, pretending to do something, or a television play are obvious examples, but there are many kinds of keys. Thus 'we can *stage* a fight in accordance with a script, or *fantasize* one, or describe one *retrospectively* or *analyse* one and so forth' (p. 45). As examples of keys, Goffman includes rehearsals, simulations, role-play, experiments, daydreaming, ceremonies and demonstrations. Keyed experiences may be quite as engrossing as primary ones, or we may be a stage removed from them, as it were, and fully aware that they are not 'for real'. More likely we will operate in more than one key at once or at least shift rapidly between them. At a good play we are likely to be involved in the action on stage and yet quite capable of appreciating the performances of the actors. Laughter will be in key when we respond to the jokes of the characters but reverts to primary experience when we giggle as the set falls down. There are established social conventions to cue in different keys. The curtain-call cues us to applaud the performance of the actors not the virtue of the characters they are playing and, in a conversation, a wink establishes that what is said is to be taken with a pinch of salt.

There are also social (and thus variable) conventions to mark the limits of what is *permissible* in different keys. Whereas simulated violence may be acceptable on stage, simulated sex will probably not be. In psychology experiments, there are limits as to what subjects are expected to do and to undergo, though they may only become apparent when they are reached. (See, for example, the discussion in Block 6 of the experiments by Milgram (1974) on obedience to authority. His subjects were required to give what they believed to be electric shocks to someone in the next room whom they thought suffered from heart trouble. Even so, many subjects were willing to do this, and some were prepared, when instructed, to continue even after the 'victim' had stopped giving signals in response.) Sometimes the limits of what is permissible are subtle and involve the crossing of keys. It was thought all right for the actress Marilyn Chambers to appear in Ivory Snow soap-powder advertisements when she was unknown but not after she had appeared in hard-core pornographic films. Certainly any actor who aspires to play Christ should be careful about the roles he accepts as well as his private life!

As with the distinction between natural and social frameworks, there are occasions when the borderlines between keyed and primary experience become unclear. Thus a ceremonial like a wedding or a funeral may be scripted and performed, but is quite likely to constitute primary experience for those taking part. In some situations keys can be so engrossing that people come to treat them as primary, as when many listeners went into mourning on the death of the radio character Grace Archer. In more everyday situations too, a keyed experience may be retransformed into reality, as when the practical demonstration of a new carpet cleaner in your home has the happy result of also getting your carpets cleaned. The form which a keyed presentation may take is also governed by conventions and these may vary even within subcultures. To take an example from psychology, a report of research in which relevant personal experience was included in frame is likely to be disqualified by an experimental journal. By a humanistic one it would be welcomed. Keying conventions also, of course, change with time. Twenty years ago a 'mix' (i.e. a slow fusing through from one scene to another) was needed in a film to key the passage of time. Now a straight 'cut' does just as well.

lamination Keying can take place in multiple or laminated form, as illustrated by the play within a play in *Hamlet*. A book may be written of a film which, in turn, is based on a novel, or a simulated exercise (such as an army war-game) may itself be rehearsed. A nice example of lamination was occasioned by Sean Connery's performance as James Bond when he often managed with a lift of the eyebrow or the turn of a phrase to 'send up' the character he played.

2.3 Frame disjunction and maintenance

frame disjunction In most of our interactions, participants will agree on the frame that they are in. But various kinds of disjunction can occur. In such a case both or all the participants may be aware that they are framing it differently ('For God's sake will you take this seriously!'), or one person may not realize the key the others are in, taking seriously, for example, what is intended as a joke or as sarcasm. Some disjunctions are created through deliberate deception. While these may be 'cons' aimed at exploiting a victim for gain, they can also be generally benign with (as in the case of practical jokes and leg-pulls) no more evil intent than a laugh at someone else's expense. In this very mixed category of benign come attempts to protect others (as when the captain of a plane hesitates to tell his passengers that an engine has failed in order to avoid panic), the misleading information given in certain social psychology experiments, and loyalty tests like the following:

> *Dear Abby:* Roy and I have been going around together for three years. We're not kids – we're both in our fifties.
>
> Roy has mentioned marriage several times, but nothing definite was said about 'when.'
>
> I always suspected that Roy could still be interested in other women, although he kept telling me I was wrong. Well, I decided to put him to the test, so I wrote him a note saying I had seen him somewhere and I asked him to meet me at a certain place at a certain time. Then I signed another woman's name. I went to the 'meeting place' at the appointed time and hid, and sure enough, there was Roy all spruced up and waiting!
>
> Isn't this a sign that he would go to meet another woman if he had the chance?
>
> (quoted in Goffman, 1975, pp. 98–9)

frame maintenance Goffman's analysis brings home to us the skill and subtlety which goes into both social behaviour and the framing of experience. We are quite capable of ignoring much of what is going on in order to *maintain* the frame, as when *saving face* in conventional social life demands that we 'disattend' when someone fails to contain their flatulence or do up their flies. And in Alan Ayckbourn's play *How the Other Half Loves*, two sets are intertwined and characters not in the action sometimes remain on stage, yet the audience has little difficulty in attending to where the action is. Our *capacity to reframe* a situation can powerfully transform our experience of it. Mountain climbers can frame as an exhilarating adventure what might in other circumstances be experienced as intense discomfort and fear. London commuters frame as a normal acceptable part of everyday life travelling conditions which would be condemned as inhumane if imposed on cattle.

2.4 Evaluation

As Goffman himself admits, his analysis is somewhat 'bookish' in that it leans heavily on anecdote and story rather than on direct observations of behaviour and experience. It does, nevertheless, provide a very useful system for differentiating some of the ways in which we organize subjective experience, and it extends our understanding of some of the features of personal worlds discussed in the previous unit. Goffman distinguishes and illustrates, for example, the various kinds of experience which contribute to the *multiplicity (KF11)* of personal worlds. The notion of frames also suggests one way in which the dominant values of a culture can be *legitimated* and imposed on its members (see *KF7 – social context*). Behaviours consistent with this are framed as 'normal', perhaps even 'praiseworthy', and those which conflict are framed as a 'joke' or 'perversion'.

Frame analysis helps us in particular to make a little more sense of some of the paradoxical qualities of subjective experience. For example, the world as we experience it has a decidedly permanent and solid feel in spite of the continually changing flow of consciousness. After long consideration, William James was inclined to attribute this solidity to the rooting of subjective experience in a physical body (you may remember that this was our *KF5* in the features of personal worlds listed in Unit 12). James in fact gave special weight to the world of the senses. This seems reasonable. What we can feel, smell, and touch does seem to have an unquestionable existence. The sensory processes of different people are much the same and are likely to remain relatively stable throughout life. So the physical world we perceive is confirmed in its reality both by its consistency over time and by the fact that other people seem to respond to it in much the same way as we do.

But there is a compelling quality not only about sensory experience but also about many features of our social world. Being in an embarrassing or hurtful situation, for example, may not have quite the same kind of tangibility as the table in front of you but it feels real enough. Such an event appears to have a similar quality of independent existence which is not likely to evaporate even if we try to dismiss it by, say, laughing it off. The reason for this is that such situations involve constructs which, because they are shared and are part of our culture, have a reality outside of us. The ways we frame our experience in general have a similar quality of shared and social reality.

Frame analysis, then, accounts for the stability of subjective experience. But it also makes sense of some of its confusion and intangibility. For framing boundaries are often unclear and they are subject to change and open to challenge. Social experience often has a quality of uncertainty: we are aware that we can misframe it, and of the possibility of pretence.

Another paradoxical quality of subjective experience, as we saw in the last unit, is that it is both a social and an individual construction. Goffman's analysis is consistent with this. On one hand, it demonstrates how other people have the power to define the nature of the situation we are in and to set its conventions and boundaries by the way they frame it. It shows how vulnerable we are to the **frame traps** manipulative framing which they may impose – as in teasing and frame 'traps' where we are encouraged into thinking the situation is other than it is. On the other hand, Goffman makes it clear that we have considerable autonomy. We can impose *our* framing too. And if we choose, we can often break those which others try to get us to go along with. This is illustrated by a story, not from Goffman but from the *San Francisco Examiner*:

> Stockton – the worst possible fate befell two young masked robbers here last night. They tried to hold up a party of thirty-six prominent, middle-aged women, but couldn't get anybody to believe they were for real.
>
> One of the women actually grabbed the gun held by one of the youths.
>
> 'Why,' she said, 'that's not wood or plastic. It must be metal'
>
> 'Lady,' pleaded the man, 'I've been trying to tell you, it is real. This is a holdup.'
>
> 'Ah, you're putting me on,' she replied cheerfully.
>
> The robbers' moment of frustration came about 9 p.m. at the home of Mrs Florence Tout, wife of a prominent Stockton tax attorney, as she was entertaining at what is called a 'hi-jinks' party.
>
> Jokes and pranks filled the evening. Thus not one of the ladies turned a hair when the two men, clad in black, walked in.
>
> 'All right now, ladies, put your rings on the table,' ordered the gunman.
>
> 'What for?' one of the guests demanded.

'This is a stickup. I'm SERIOUS!' he cried.

All the ladies laughed.

One of them playfully shoved one of the men. He shoved her back.

As the ringing laughter continued, the men looked at each other, shrugged, and left empty-handed.

(quoted in Emerson, 1970, pp. 216–17)

reframing We have an extraordinary power to reframe social acts if we so choose. Goffman illustrates our ability to reinterpret other people's actions with an extract from Tomkins (1963) which describes the varied and skilful ways in which people with a low opinion of themselves can translate even the most fulsome praise so that it is consistent with self-image:

> Let us suppose the individual to be richly praised. What transformations can convert such positive evidence into the opposite? First, the sincerity of the judge may be questioned. He cannot really believe what he is saying and indeed he is using exaggerated praise to mock me. Second, he praised only this work because he knows that everything else which I have done is trash, and he is praising this work because there is nothing else to praise. Third, he may be sincere, but he is probably a fool to be taken in like this – and he is thereby exposing me all the more to the ridicule of those who can evaluate properly. Fourth, this is a temporary lapse of judgment. When he comes to his senses and sees through me, he will have all the more contempt for me. Fifth, the judges have incomplete information. They do not really have all the evidence which they would need to see the worthlessness of the work of the self. Sixth, this is a fluke. It is truly praiseworthy, and the judges are not mistaken but it was a lucky, unrepresentative accident, which will probably never occur again. Seventh, others are trying to control me, holding out a carrot of praise. If I eat this I am hooked, and I will thenceforth have to work for their praise and to avoid their censure. Eighth, they are exposing how hungry I am for praise and thereby exposing my inferiority and my feelings of humiliation, even though they do not intend to do this. Ninth, they are seducing me into striving for something more which I cannot possibly achieve. Ultimately this praise will prove my complete undoing by seducing me into striving for the impossible and thereby destroying myself. Tenth, he is acting as though he alone is the only judge of my work, as though I am incapable of correctly judging its worth and so I must forever be dependent upon his or their judgment.
>
> So may genuine respect be transformed in the monopolistic humiliation equation.

(Tomkins, 1963, pp. 442–3)

The first theory which we have considered in detail demonstrates then the *social psychological nature* of subjective experience; how it is a social as well as an individual construction. But frame analysis is limited in scope. It deals with whether we frame an event as social or natural, whether it is taken for real, as a joke or pretence. It reveals the shifts and negotiations of meaning on which social life and personal worlds depend. But all this hardly accounts for the richness and subtlety which characterize personal awareness. We turn in the next section to an approach to subjective experience which is firmly individualist. Its concern is not so much with shared ways of organizing experience but with a way of thinking about subjective awareness which can take account of its complex and insubstantial feel.

3   SUBJECTIVE EXPERIENCE AS METAPHOR

3.1   Understanding through the use of metaphor

metaphor

One of the most important means we have of extending our understanding is the use of metaphor. What metaphor does is to give us new insights into one concept by means of comparing it with another. In so doing we can often create from their fusion an emergent third experience which is more than just the sum of the other two. For example, the metaphorical idea that 'time is money' generates a whole set of related ideas (borrowing, investing and wasting time, etc.). It changes our way of thinking about time.

That language fundamentally depends on metaphor to extend its capacity to describe things is obvious. Our speech is stuffed with metaphors both dead and alive. We talk of pop stars and record sleeves, of being stumped and undermined, of going downhill or climbing the ladder of success. It is not easy to write a standard sentence without a metaphor lurking somewhere in the background, and any creative user of language is likely to coin his or her own. But the use of metaphor is more than a literary device. It is fundamental to our capacity to give meaning to and deal with the world about us. Metaphor serves to deepen one experience by imbuing it with all the connotations of the concept it is compared with. So (to use an example from Jaynes) to talk of the snow being a blanket is not just to view it as a cover but is also to infuse it with associated feelings of warmth, softness and cosiness. Let me give another example taken from Tennessee Williams's play *Orpheus Descending*. Val Xavier, the young wanderer who is the central character in the play, at one point talks of himself as a tiny, transparent bird that flies so high that it cannot be seen, and sleeps on the wind so that it never returns to earth. None of this literally describes Val, of course, but it radically influences our image of the kind of person he is.

The usefulness of metaphor for deepening our understanding is particularly apparent when we try to make sense of psychological life (see Box 1).

Box 1 The use of metaphor to make sense of love

Love is a physical force (electromagnetic, gravitational, etc.)

I could feel the *electricity* between us. There were *sparks*. I was *magnetically drawn* to her. They are uncontrollably *attracted* to each other. They *gravitated* to each other immediately. His whole life *revolves* around her. The *atmosphere* around them is always *charged*. There is incredible *energy* in their relationship. They lost their *momentum*.

Love is a patient

This is a *sick* relationship. They have a *strong, healthy* marriage. The marriage is *dead* – it can't be *revived*. Their marriage is *on the mend*. We're getting *back on our feet*. Their relationship is *in really good shape*. They've got a *listless* marriage. Their marriage is *on its last legs*. It's a *tired* affair.

Love is madness

I'm *crazy* about her. She *drives me out of my mind*. He constantly *raves* about her. He's gone *mad* over her. I'm just *wild* about Harry. I'm *insane* about her.

Love is magic

She *cast her spell* over me. The *magic* is gone. I was *spellbound*. She had me *hypnotized*. He has me *in a trance*. I was *entranced* by him. I'm *charmed* by her. She is *bewitching*.

Love is war

He is known for his many rapid *conquests*. She *fought for* him, but his mistress *won out*. He *fled from* her *advances*. She *pursued* him relentlessly. He is slowly *gaining ground* with her. He *won* her hand in marriage. He *overpowered* her. She is *besieged* by suitors. He has to *fend them off*. He *enlisted the aid* of her friends. He *made an ally* of her mother. Theirs is a *misalliance* if I've ever seen one.

(Lakoff and Johnson, 1980, p. 49)

ACTIVITY 2

You might like to look back at Julian Jaynes's description of subjective experience at the beginning of section 1 and consider the following questions:

1   What use of metaphor can you detect there?

2   Would it be possible to describe subjective experience without using metaphors?

It is not just our ordinary ways of describing and making sense of the world and psychological affairs which rest on metaphor but scientific theorizing too. Like any other theorizing, this is based on metaphors drawn from our experience and thus rooted in the historical and social context in which the theorist lives. If we take theorizing about mind and brain, for example, the conceptions of the seventeenth-century philosophers, and later the early psychologists (the mind as associations of elements of sensations, etc.), drew on the molecular theorizing of physics and chemistry after the invention of the microscope. With the advance of technology, we see continual updating of the concepts which are applied. As the phenomena of electricity and magnetism came to the fore in physics, so these were applied to 'make sense' of hypnotism and animal magnestism. Later as the concept of 'force' fields made their appearance in physics, so they were taken up by *Gestalt* psychologists. (Interestingly, the concepts borrowed from other disciplines are very often themselves metaphors. Thus understanding is extended by the propagation of metaphors themselves.)

Today, it is fashionable in much of psychology to draw on images taken from cybernetics and computer science. Most recent has been the importation of notions from laser and holographic technology. David Bohm, for example, has suggested that we are constrained in conceptualizing the *ideas* of relativity and quantum theory, even though their mathematics has been worked out, because of the dominance of the eye – a lens system – in constructing our conceptual realities. The hologram does not, like a lens, project the world as a set of defined images or objects. It represents it in the form of a register both of the microwaves an object emits (rather like the ripples from dropping a stone in a pond) and the interference patterns from other emissions (like the interlocking sets of ripples from two stones). Karl Pribram (1981) has made use of the holograph as a metaphor for modelling the organization of the brain and nervous system.

Jaynes (1979) has pointed out that, if to understand something is to deepen our capacity to conceptualize it by means of a metaphor based on another concept or experience, understanding consciousness will always pose problems – indeed we may even question how effective this could ever be. For the problem of making sense of subjective experience is the problem of finding a metaphor which is appropriate. It is not difficult to find other experiences which deepen through metaphor our understanding of events and objects in the physical world. We can even apply metaphors from the physical world to help to conceptualize and communicate feelings and mental states (as we saw in Box 1). But for subjective experience itself we have few, if any, comparisons which provide an effective source of metaphors to increase our awareness of its nature and properties. For, as Jaynes has put it, 'it should be immediately apparent that there is not and cannot be anything in our immediate experience that is like immediate experience itself. There is therefore a sense in which we shall never be able to understand consciousness in the same way that we can understand things we are conscious of' (1979, p. 53).

Jaynes points out that the metaphors we do tend to use are inadequate to the task. Subjective experience is, for example, by no means a 'copy' or 'picture' of the world. Nor does it have the tangible properties which are associated with any object to which it might be compared. The most common metaphors used for consciousness are taken from our experience of vision and three-dimensional space:

> The most prominent group of words used to describe mental events are visual. We 'see' solutions to problems, the best of which may be 'brilliant', and the person 'brighter' and 'clear-headed' as opposed to 'dull', 'fuzzy-minded', or 'obscure' solutions. These words are all metaphors and the mind-space to which they apply is a metaphor of actual space. In it we can 'approach' a problem, perhaps from some 'viewpoint', and 'grapple' with its difficulties, or seize together or 'com-prehend' parts of a problem, and so on, using metaphors of behaviour to invent things to do in this metaphored mind-space.

And the adjectives to describe physical behaviour in real space are analogically taken over to describe mental behaviour in mind-space when we speak of our minds as being 'quick', 'slow', 'agitated' (as when we cogitate or co-agitate), 'nimble-witted', 'strong-' or 'weak-minded.' The mind-space in which these metaphorical activities go on has its own group of adjectives; we can be 'broad-minded', 'deep', 'open', or 'narrow-minded'; we can be 'occupied'; we can 'get something off our minds', 'put something out of mind', or we can 'get it', let something 'penetrate', or 'bear', 'have', 'keep', or 'hold' it in mind.

As with a real space, something can be at the 'back' of our mind, in its 'inner recesses', or 'beyond' our mind, or 'out' of our mind. In argument we try to 'get things through' to someone, to 'reach' their 'understanding' or find a 'common ground', or 'point out', etc., all actions in real space taken over analogically into the space of the mind.

(Jaynes, 1979, pp. 55–6)

But Jaynes asserts that even 'mind-space', for all its uses, is still of only limited value as a metaphor for consciousness because it is drawn from our experience of the physical world.

3.2 Jaynes's ideas about consciousness

Two key points then emerge from the preceding discussion. One is the assertion that the way to make sense of any aspect of our experience is to find an appropriate metaphor. Another is the difficulty of finding any metaphors appropriate to subjective experience.

Jaynes's solution to this dilemma is to suggest that the most effective metaphor to use for making sense of subjective experience is *metaphor itself*. He argues that subjective consciousness is itself grounded in and generated by processes of comparison and conjunction similar to those of metaphor. The nub of his conception is expressed in the following paragraph:

> Subjective conscious mind is an analogue of what is called the real world. It is built up with a vocabulary or lexical field whose terms are all metaphors or analogues of behaviour in the physical world. Its reality is of the same order as mathematics. It allows us to shortcut behavioural processes and arrive at more adequate decisions. Like mathematics, it is an operator rather than a thing or repository. And it is intimately bound up with volition and decision.

(Jaynes, 1979, p. 55)

Let me try to unpack this rather difficult statement and clarify the main ideas which underlie it.

analogue 1 By the term *analogue*, Jaynes is suggesting that consciousness, rather like a map, is a *metaphorical representation*, not a direct copy, of the world as experienced. It is a metaphorical representation of the world which is itself built up with metaphors.

operator 2 Jaynes describes consciousness as an *operator* 'intimately bound up with volition and decision'. The point here is that consciousness is not just a representation of our experience of the world but it can act on that experience and transform it. For although a metaphor may be generated by the conjunction of two experiences (and by thus attaching the connotations of one to the other), once created, it has itself the power to transform our awareness of the experiences on which it is based. This, as we have already noted, is one way in which scientific theorizing proceeds. To take a further example from everyday life, to conceptualize our relationships with other people we might well draw on metaphors based on the skin and physical contact. So we think of a person as 'thick-skinned' or as someone who has to be 'handled' carefully in case we 'rub him up the wrong way', etc. Once such a way of looking at people has been generated (either by the metaphors provided by the conventions of our language and culture or by our personal capacity to generate our own) then this acts upon our experience and makes it more likely that we will abstract from and make sense of relationships in this kind of way.

The point is then that conceiving of consciousness as being both like a metaphor and constituted by metaphors is appropriate for (and draws attention to) both the capacity of consciousness to *represent* (in a metaphor-based way) the world we experience and also its power to act upon and *transform* the experience we have. Moreover, as it is possible to create entirely novel metaphors from further conjunctions of existing ones, Jaynes's conception of consciousness as metaphor allows both for the *openness* of consciousness (i.e. its power to generate itself in the form of new ways of framing experience) and its capacity to create abstract conceptions which are not directly related to perceptions or feelings.

Although Jaynes's scheme is, like consciousness itself, somewhat elusive and intangible, its end product is to provide us with a way of thinking about or conceptualizing consciousness (different, for example, from physically-based notions like 'mind-space') which deepens our understanding of it. It accounts, for example, for the stability of consciousness, and its predictability and effectiveness in dealing with the world while, at the same time, allowing for its power to transform and actively construct it. For the metaphors which make up consciousness are both, at the same time, *analogues* of the world of experience and *operators* upon it. Jaynes's scheme also throws further light on questions raised in Block 2 and in Unit 12 about the way personal consciousness emerges from the interactions and negotiations between an individual and the people and symbolic meanings (i.e. language and culture) which form his or her social world. For the metaphors which constitute our consciousness are generated not just by comparisons we make ourselves but by the metaphors provided by the language we use, other people's utterances and the social contexts in which we grow up and live. By assimilating their metaphors, we may come to see the world as others do.

Emphasizing the metaphorical essence of consciousness in this way perhaps makes it clearer why one way to express or become aware of the subtle nuances of consciousness or a new experience is to resort to poetry – the most intense way we have of generating and using new and powerful metaphors. (Note in Window 3 of Unit 12, Part 1, how Leonard does this.)

PROGRESS BOX 3   The relevance of metaphor to consciousness

1   The use of *metaphor* for making sense of the world we experience, especially psychological states:

(i)   Metaphor is not just a literary device but is a way of extending understanding.

(ii)   The use of metaphor in science and in theorizing about the mind and brain.

(iii)   The problem of finding *adequate* metaphors for conceptualizing subjective experience.

2   Jaynes proposes 'metaphor' itself as the best metaphor for consciousness. This suggests that:

(i)   Consciousness is an *analogue* of the world built up through metaphors.

(ii)   Metaphors (and therefore consciousness) work also as an *operator*.

Thus the notion of metaphor can account for the capacity of consciousness to transform as well as represent our experience of the world.

---

3   The conception of consciousness as metaphor is consistent with:

(i)   the *openness* of subjective experience (i.e. its capacity to generate itself);

(ii)   the *stability* of subjective experience;

(iii)   its openness to *change*; and

(iv)   the way it can be *socially constructed*.

3.3   Romanyshyn's conception of subjective experience

psychological life metaphor

In a difficult, rambling but in many ways important book *Psychological Life: From Science to Metaphor* (1982), a phenomenological psychologist, Robert Romanyshyn, apparently quite independently of Jaynes, has also elaborated the notion of psychological life as metaphor. (Note that Romanyshyn uses the term 'psychological life' in a way which is virtually indistinguishable from 'consciousness' and 'subjective experience'.) He sees metaphor as a subjective reality based on 'reflection', in that through it we deepen our grasp of one situation through its reflection in another. The result of the interplay is an emergent experience which cannot be reduced to the component experiences which are brought together in the metaphor. There is a paradoxical relation between the two conceptions involved in the comparison in that the metaphor relies on the existence of some similarity between them and yet depends for its effect on a difference. In an earlier paper (1981), Romanyshyn illustrated this by reference to the discovery by the seventeenth-century physician William Harvey of the circulation of the blood and his innovatory notion of the heart as a pump. With this idea, the people of the time were given, as it were, a 'new' heart, in that they experienced it as a new reality and could deepen their understanding of it through the metaphor. But the metaphor only worked because it postulated a similarity between a pump and a heart which, up till then, had been seen as entirely different entities, so enabling people to view the heart in (what was then) a novel way:

> Reality in its original metaphorical presentation *is what it is not* and/or *is not what it is*. Either of these phrases is meant to describe that elusive character of reality according to which in showing itself to be what it is, it alludes to being something more, something else, a difference.

(Romanyshyn, 1981, p. 9)

We can clarify this dense and difficult (but important) statement by reference to the previous example. In order to appreciate the nature of the heart, it is useful to allude to it as something which it is not, i.e. a pump. We get at its reality with the help of a comparison with something which is essentially different from it.

ACTIVITY 3

If you have a mirror nearby, spend a few seconds looking at yourself in it. What do you see?

For Romanyshyn, psychological life has a similar metaphorical character. By its very nature it is elusive and indirect. He illustrates this thesis by reference to a reflection in a mirror. What you *experience* in looking into a mirror is not a piece of flat reflecting glass but a dimensional figure. The subjective reality of the reflection is neither constituted by the glass nor by your usual experience of yourself. A new reality emerges through the reflection. By means of the reflection we deepen our understanding of ourselves in that we experience ourselves in a way which would not have been possible without it. And, Romanyshyn asserts, what we see in the reflection is not 'a visual double of the empirical me standing here on this side of the mirror. . .':

> On the contrary, when I look in the mirror I never see merely the double of myself on this side of the mirror but rather *a figure in a story*, . . . It is a character that I see when I look 'in' the mirror, a figure who may be a saint or a sinner. At times the figure may be the youth who has slipped away from my life; at times it may be the old man who too quickly approaches with the declining years. But whoever the figure may be, the reflection is never of the empirical person who stands on this side of the mirror. The lined face, sagging chest, and balding head tell a story, and in this sense the reflection gathers together these features, which would otherwise merely be statistical facts about the person reflected, and weaves around them a tale. In the wrinkled face and baggy eyes the middle-aged man may see the absence of an admiring glance, just as in the soft mouth and seductive eyes the young woman may read the furtive intentions of another's desire.

(Romanyshyn, 1982, p. 10)

Did your experience of looking at yourself in the mirror tally with the kind of thing Romanyshyn is saying?

3.3.1   Subjective experience as metaphorical reflection

With the mirror then, the reality of our experience exists neither in the mirror nor in us but in the reflection of one through the other. Romanyshyn extends this analogy to our personal worlds. Along with Jaynes (and other phenomenologists) he argues that consciousness is not experienced 'inside our heads'; rather it is

metaphorical reflection   constituted by reflections of thoughts and feelings *through* the things and people who make up our worlds. (N.B., reflection *through* rather than *in* serves to indicate that it is not a question of a straightforward *reflection* but a metaphor-like *transformation* into a new subjective reality by means of the conjunction of the perceiver's thoughts and feelings with the object perceived.) *Subjective experience consists then neither of concepts nor things but the reflections between them.* As with the mirror, this reflection is capable of deepening and transforming awareness. Let us try to make this clearer with an example from Romanyshyn:

> Last year I unexpectedly lost a friend through death. He was a young man, and we had been friends for a long time. Before he died, he had given to me a copy of a book which he had recently finished, and he had written within it

an inscription of our friendship. Today that book is the only piece of material remembrance I have of him, and I have placed it in a corner of my study. It rests solitary and alone on a table. Nothing else surrounds it. It is a simple memorial to a friend.

There have been times in the course of these days since he died when I have recalled my friend. Sadly, however, these moments have become rarer and are always brief. But on occasion when I enter my study I am called by that book which rests upon the table, and in those moments I remember him deeply and vividly. In those moments he is there in the room with me. His book is my memory. That book is my departed friend. Through the book my remembrance of him is a world. Through the book my memory of him has a place. That book is the reflection of my experiences of memory and of sadness. That book mirrors the story of our life.

Surely, however, one wants to object that this description pertains to my feelings, and that these feelings are private and belong to me. And surely one wants to add to this objection that the book is after all only a book, only an empirical material reality, which remains unchanged in spite of the addition of my feelings to it. Psychology certainly would agree with these objections. Psychology knows about feelings and their projection.

But I cannot take these objections seriously, any more than anyone can who preserves memories through the things of the world. The book *matters*, and the loss of it would matter now almost as much as the original loss of my friend. I do not deny that my feelings are revealed in this account, and that my feelings as feelings are private and belong to me. But I do insist that these feelings are not the experience. I do insist that *the feeling of an experience* is not the same thing, either logically or phenomenologically, as the *experience of a feeling*. And so insisting I would add that while my feelings are private and invisible, my experience is public and visible for others to see. Through that book which sits on that table, others are able to experience something of the sadness of a departed friend. Through that book others can and do participate in this psychological story of friendship and early death, even if not in detail or with the same depth. This psychological experience is, therefore, visible as a world, and the world through which it appears, this material book, does matter in another way. It is not exclusively an empirical object which receives my projections. It is on the contrary another kind of object, a psychological object, which reflects an experience of my life. That book, I said, *is* my departed friend. I am speaking psychologically. It is a metaphor. That book appears psychologically as a metaphorical reality.

(Romanyshyn, 1982, pp. 36–7)

This example certainly makes sense in terms of my experience. The objects of my world change with me, they become as it were part of me. Psychological realities are not external factual ones. I think of the trappings of other people's worlds in this way too. I remember visiting Lenin's apartments, seeing the pen he used, the bed he slept in, his clothes. They were not just any objects. In my experience it was as if they were imbued with him, as if by experiencing them I could grasp at least something of his personal world. You may be able to recall experiences of a similar kind when, by seeing where a person had lived, you experienced not just a house or a room or a garden but the personal world of the person who had lived there.

ACTIVITY 4

Find an old photograph of people, a place or events of significance in your life. Spend a few minutes looking at it. Afterwards, reflect on whether your experience matched this notion of subjective experience as consisting of reflections of feelings and memories through the people and objects concerned.

As this important conception is not an easy one to assimilate, one more example may be of help. I look out of the window at this moment and see sun sparkling on the water of the little pool below, trees and fields beyond and the bright sky. The scene is warm and inviting, imbued with a sense of joy and delight. That conscious experience is a subjective reality consisting of the reflection of my awareness through the landscape outside the window. It is not in the landscape. Nor is it merely a projection of my feelings. They are not just 'in me'. They could not exist in the form they do without the fields and the sun. My conscious experience is deepened and given reality *through* the scene it beholds.

The point is then that subjective experience is not constituted by thought and feelings in themselves. Like metaphor is a deepening of one experience through another, so psychological reality (i.e. what we experience as 'real') is a deepening of thoughts and feelings through the world of people, events and things in which we are immersed. They are, in Merleau-Ponty's phrase, 'the materialization of our subjectivity'.

3.3.2 Experiencing people

What applies to the experience of the reality of things applies equally to our relationships with people. In terms of Romanyshyn's analysis, the notion of the behaviour of people as objective, neutral categories makes no sense. For they can exist only as *experienced* and what is experienced will be a reflection dependent on the perspective of the observer as much as what is observed.

ACTIVITY 5

Think of someone whom you know well. Jot down five or six lines of notes which could help someone else to understand what kind of person he or she is.

Romanyshyn argues that the way we understand others is by an act of imagination whereby we set them in some kind of story. He cites in illustration his recollection of two old people he did not know whom, as a child, he saw regularly on a Sunday walking and sitting in the park. He remembers thinking:

> ... how much sadness they seemed to carry and yet also how much peace they seemed to have. The world seemed so special to them, so important, as if nothing else really mattered on Sunday morning. As I watched them I would imagine who they were and where they had come from. They had been emigrants, I supposed, and had come to America to struggle in a lifetime of work. She would have been a domestic or maybe a store clerk, and he would have been a laborer. I was sure they had children, a schoolteacher, a lawyer, and maybe a policeman. But they were all gone now, married, and living far away from these two old people. Maybe they telephoned on Sundays. I thought she would like that. Maybe that was why they would leave the park.

> One Sunday, however, the old man and woman were not there, and for several Sundays thereafter I did not see them. But finally on another Sunday I saw him. He came into the park, more slowly than usual, and alone. And I remember that as I watched him make his way slowly toward the bench and pass it I knew that his wife had died. I never went that way again, and I never saw the old man after that final Sunday morning.

> Today after so many years I recognize that I *understood* those two old people through a *story*. I understood them through a story of old age, of the course of life, and of dying. On those Sunday mornings a tale was spun between me and those two old people, and around that tale, among others, a little boy began to change. Was my understanding *in fact* correct? Had she *in fact* died? Were they *in fact* immigrants? To this day I do not know the answers to these questions, and while I suppose I could have talked to them,

the most important feature of those Sunday mornings would not have changed. Our conversation would have *continued* the story and perhaps it would have corrected and even changed it into another story. *But it would not have changed the story into a fact.* It could not without changing what mattered most about those Sunday mornings. *The story mattered.* It moved an eight-year-old boy toward a vision of life as biography. No empirical facts, however many he might have collected about those people, could have been more psychologically real.

(Romanyshyn, 1982, pp. 85–6)

Romanyshyn's point here is not that all stories are equally correct. Some may be more accurate than others in that they make more consistent sense of the events observed. His point is that all are *stories*. In our personal worlds, we make sense of people (and ourselves) by setting them in some kind of constructed narrative, albeit an implicit one. (You may remember that this was very much a feature of the accounts of personal worlds presented in Unit 12.) Such a narrative will be a construction – a function of both the storyteller and the people it concerns. It is not an 'objective fact'.

Though Romanyshyn does not make this point, this notion adds to our capacity to understand how our conceptions of people may be influenced by social context. Our culture, including fairy stories, TV soap operas, etc., and our education, both moral and scholastic, offer us ready-made narratives which we can implicitly utilize or adapt to make sense of the people and social situations we encounter. If we accept a psychoanalytic view of the unconscious, we might consider *transference* in this way also. Relationships once expressed but now forgotten or repressed provide us with a rich source of narratives which we unconsciously bring to bear in our reactions to and style of relating with others (see the discussion of transference in Chapter 7 of *Freud and Psychoanalysis* which was optional reading for Unit 4).

How far do Romanyshyn's ideas about the way we understand others make sense to you? Did your notes in the last activity express this idea of understanding a person by setting him or her in some kind of story? Bear in mind that characteristics and traits like 'jealous' and 'generous' carry within them implicit narratives of actions and experiences.

Looking back over Romanyshyn's analysis, it perhaps becomes more apparent now why phrases like 'personal worlds' and 'psychological life' are more appropriate than 'consciousness' to describe what we experience. The latter tends easily to locate our experience within us, whereas the former expressions accommodate more easily the idea of psychological reality depending, like a metaphor, on the deepening of our awareness *through* the things and people which make up our worlds.

3.3.3 Shared realities of reflection

Although one consequence of this analysis would seem to be that psychological realities will be constituted somewhat differently for each one of us, I think it is clear that there are also very definite limits to this variability. As we noted earlier, one is due to the fact that we are rooted in a physical body (*KF5*), that we have in common much of the sensory equipment, perceptual processes and physical environment on which our experience depends. Another is that we are also grounded in a social context (*KF6*). Within any one culture we share many of the concepts, narratives and feelings that are reflected through our experience of the world and imbue our realities with the particular qualities they have.

Such shared realities may be reflected in the way our physical environment is organized and constructed. For example, the way in which seating is arranged for a family, the kind of chairs used, and the way they are positioned, can reflect the shared realities – the roles, the attitudes of dominance and closeness – of that particular group of people (see Unit 2). Another illustration of the way in which 'matter mirrors man' is the traditional construction of the room used by the Japanese to perform their tea ceremony. This ceremony is conceived of as a poetic impulse which is manifested in the fragile, ephemeral nature of the room's structure (Okakura, 1964). It is symbolized too by a lack of symmetry which is reflected in both utensils and the design of the room, features which are often left deliberately unfinished. The notion of 'vacancy' is also important and this is expressed in the absence of ornamentation. The low door, not more than three feet in height, represents materially the attitude of humility with which the ceremony should be approached.

3.3.4 'Figuring' reality

Both between cultures and within cultures as individuals, our personal worlds can also be very different. Individual realities change too with time. I can remember as a child experiencing for the first time the horizon as curved, reflecting my new awareness of the world as a sphere. It was not just an idea but a new experience of reality. As we noted in our analysis of the 'Windows' in the last unit, each of us lives too in a world of *multiple* realities (*KF11 – Multiplicity*). This is not only because of the different social settings in which we live and the different frameworks of experience provided by our culture, but also because we are often capable of experiencing the same situation as a different type of reality at different moments in time. A simple example is the Necker cube (see Figure 1). If you look at it for long enough it can appear as one of two shapes. Given time the second one will seem to spontaneously emerge. We can also deliberately bring this about by deciding to and consequently fixating our eyes to produce the figure desired.

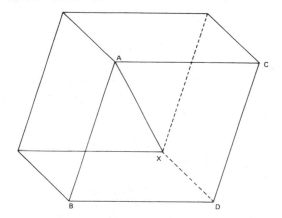

Figure 1   The Necker cube

ACTIVITY 6

On a clear evening stand on open ground at dusk and watch the setting sun. See it first of all as the sun going down. Then let your subjective experience (or, as Romanyshyn would say, 'reality') reflect the notion that the sun is stationary and it is the rotation of the earth that gradually obscures it from your view. As with the Necker cube, does the reality of your experience change?

---

figuring   The key to this analysis then is the notion that subjective experience is *figured*, i.e. it requires a perspective for its existence, and the subjective reality of our experience will be a reflection of that perspective through the phenomenon observed. Consider our reality as persons. We will be figured differently by each of the people who knows us and by ourselves. There is a sense in which, again to use a phrase of Merleau-Ponty's, we 'borrow' reflections of ourselves from others and in response to the way they behave towards us. We see ourselves through other people as we see others through ourselves. In experiencing ourselves, as with any other reality, we are not confined to one style of 'figuring'. There is that curious way in which multiple realities co-exist, as when Borges is aware of both his public and his private selves (see the discussion of *KF8 – sense of self* in section 1.2 of Unit 12). Each of these ways of figuring is a reality but a reality of reflection, a metaphor. We are each of them and yet we are not. They are neither fact nor yet are they fiction:

> I look at my friend and I say, 'Tom is a wolf.' This metaphor is neither factually true about Tom in himself nor merely my idea of him. On the contrary, like every metaphor, it says as much about the speaker as it does about the spoken. It says, implicitly if not explicitly, how to see in order to see that Tom is a wolf. To see what I say about Tom, I must look in a certain way. I must notice this and neglect that. But when I see in this way, I do see that indeed he is a wolf. The metaphor has a bite to it. It rings true. I can show another what to see by indicating how to look. Tom's wolfishness, like the increasing distance between horizon and sun, is originally a metaphorical reality. What is seen does reflect a way of seeing.

(Romanyshyn, 1981, p. 7)

Romanyshyn concludes the paper in which this example appeared:

> Psychological life understood on its own terms, *psychologically rather than scientifically or philosophically*, is neither thing nor thought, matter nor mind, fact nor idea. It is not either term of any of these dualisms, or any of these dualisms themselves. It is another reality. It is a metaphor. To appreciate the character of psychological life as psychological requires an eye and a heart for metaphor. To recover the originary metaphorical character of the world is to cultivate a psychological eye and heart.

(Romanyshyn, 1981, p. 19)

Perhaps now the question asked in section 1.3 of the previous unit as to why it is so difficult to tell apart accounts of worlds based on fictional characters and on those who have actually lived is becoming more easy to answer. Perhaps also more apparent are the implications of the aphorism with which this unit began. The problem with trying to find out how things really are is that all the time 'they aren't'.

3.3.5 Implications for psychology

Romanyshyn is not just concerned with the idea that subjective experience is best thought of as a metaphorical reality. He goes on to explore the implications for psychology of a point made in section 3.1 – that the growth of science as a way of making sense of the world is marked by a change in the kind of metaphors used to reflect reality. He points out that, although they may help us to manipulate and control the physical world, some of these metaphors are quite removed from our experience. To think of this table at which I sit as a moving mass of atoms or the light which permeates the room as a spectrum of unseen colours is to stretch the imagination. I certainly do not experience them like that. As Romanyshyn puts it, 'to do science is to turn one's back on the world in which one lives'.

Psychology is no exception. As was noted earlier, it seeks to progress by finding new metaphors, drawing these especially from physics and physiology. Romanyshyn adopts a historical perspective and traces how psychology as a science emerged in the sixteenth and seventeenth centuries and reflected the dominant 'physicalistic' metaphor of the intellectual thought of the period. This metaphor tends both to *literalize* the mind (i.e. conceive of it in terms of, potentially at least, tangible processes) and to *interiorize* it by locating it within the individual. It postulates both a dualism between a mind within and a world without, and that subjective experience is not just dependent on but can be reduced to material processes (e.g. the brain). Such a metaphor can provide us with new insights, but it is not to be identified as the way things are. It is a metaphor and, like any metaphor, while it may illuminate it also obscures, for it directs the reflection and in so doing creates reality in a particular way. Romanyshyn believes that the problem underlying much academic psychology is that it mistakes the 'scientific' metaphor for reality. The reflection of psychological life through this metaphor is taken as constituting empirical reality, while other metaphors are dismissed as subjective and therefore unreal. One unfortunate consequence is that the essentially metaphorical and elusive nature of psychological life is obscured. And the scientific metaphor's assumptions of an underlying tangible and immutable reality make it peculiarly inappropriate to deal with the subject-matter it seeks to understand.

Romanyshyn's approach is developed on the basis of phenomenological analysis – by appeal to introspection about the way we experience our worlds. He largely fails to acknowledge or realize how much evidence and theory has emerged from experimental psychology in line with his view. To seek such support is not, of course, inconsistent with Romanyshyn's notion of psychological life and understanding as realities of reflection. For, as indicated above, although experimental psychology may work from the standpoint of a different metaphor, this too, while it can obscure (particularly when it ignores the metaphorical nature of its subject-matter), can also offer us useful insights.

Can you think of any examples from the course so far of experiments consistent with Romanyshyn's line of reasoning?

In particular, as those of you who have done DS 262 or other courses in general psychology will be aware, experimental investigations in perception show very clearly how our perceptual experience is not just a question of an environment impinging on a passive perceiver. We construct our perceptions through our interactions with the world about us. We go beyond the evidence given, our constructions reflecting not just our past experience but also our values, emotions and attitudes. Perceptual experience is the reflection and deepening of ourselves through the objects we perceive.

In the preceding blocks, one example of an area of experimental research which has produced findings consistent with Romanyshyn's ideas is *attribution theory*. In Unit 9 you encountered numerous examples of experiments which illustrate the significance of inference and construction in the ways we make sense of the world. Our awareness is a product both of what we observe and the meanings we supply.

However, while it may be true that scientific psychology has produced results in line with the notion of the metaphorical nature of the psychological life, it could be argued that it has not followed through the implications of these in the way it conceptualizes its subject-matter, nor in terms of the methods it employs for investigating it. For example, the search for laws to explain behaviour presupposes a behaviour to explain, but, as we have seen, all we have is *experienced behaviour* which will vary according to the way it is 'figured'. The study of personality likewise presumes that there are 'personalities' to investigate. But if we accept Romanyshyn's idea, people as we experience them exist only as realities of reflection in their own or other people's world. The way they will be figured and the way they will figure themselves will vary from person to person and from situation to situation. No-one is the proud possessor of a neutral, objective and identifiable item labelled personality (see Metablock Paper 5).

What then are the implications of Romanyshyn's position for what he calls the *craft* of psychology, for what psychologists can do? First of all, the phenomenological psychologist tries to work with *psychological* reality – i.e. the phenomenal experience of the individuals being studied, not as this is reframed (i.e. literalized and interiorized) by the metaphors of the scientist. He or she adopts 'a practice of fidelity to experience as it takes place'.

imaginal reconstruction

Instead of explanation and the establishment of general laws, Romanyshyn emphasizes *imaginal reconstruction*. The psychologist's task is to deepen our imagination. We understand another when we can imagine him or her. To imagine or make sense of another or ourselves, we weave a story. *Psychological* understanding operates within:

> ... that domain of reality and that mode of understanding which lie between the divisions of fact and fiction, the empirically real and the rationally ideal.
>
> I am sitting in my office, looking out the window, thinking of this final paragraph, when suddenly I realize that for the last few minutes I have been watching a young woman cross the campus mall. It is a warm day and she is tired. Classes are finished, but she must still go to work for several hours, and later this evening there is an assignment to be completed. After that, however, there will be some time for friends and conversation. All of this is visible in her walk, in the style of her posture, in the manner in which she slowly passes by the things which compose her landscape. That girl, who is a stranger to me, is nevertheless known to me, and her behavior is visible and observable through my experience which imaginally weaves around the manner of her behavior a story. It is a rare occasion when we do not see in this way, imaginally. It is rare and perhaps even impossible, because 'everyone thinks of his life and all lives as something that can in every sense of the word be told as a "story"'. Stories imaginally understood belong to the character of human psychological life as much as facts empirically understood belong to the character of scientific life and ideas rationally understood to the life of philosophy. One's own life and the life of an other *make sense* psychologically as a story. They do not make sense because we know all the facts or because we have a rational idea of them. A *psychological* discipline needs to appreciate this difference.

(Romanyshyn, 1982, p. 89)

If Romanyshyn's conception of the craft of psychology seems strange to you, it is perhaps a measure of the hold on us which the metaphors of scientific psychology have exerted. It is difficult to fully apprehend the notion of psychological life as a reality of reflection and of the task of psychology as being imaginal understanding. Yet in everyday life, of course, this is precisely what we do. If I ask you to explain why you became an Open University student, you will in all probability weave a story for me. You will recount to me the thoughts, feelings and events which led up to your application. To the extent that I understand you, as one person to another, this will be because I can in turn weave a narrative around the event in question. The failure of scientific psychology to appreciate the metaphorical nature of psychological life may be the reason why so often its findings seem artificial, to fall short of what we desire, and why they play so little part in the psychological understanding we use to cope with everyday life.

3.3.6 The value of Romanyshyn's ideas

Whether or not you accept Romanyshyn's casting for the role which psychology might play, his analysis does draw our attention to several significant features about psychological life. His model of subjective experience as a metaphorical reality fits very well with and helps to make sense of several themes which we have encountered earlier in the course, particularly in Blocks 1 and 2:

1 By viewing social context, language and the unconscious as *sources* of metaphors which serve to deepen and transform our experience of the world, we, in turn, deepen and transform our conception of the process of social influence itself.

2 By demonstrating their reflective, metaphorical nature, Romanyshyn's concepts emphasize how psychological realities are intrinsically rooted in

interactions and relativities. Subjective experience emerges out of *the relationships between people, things and events.*

3   Romanyshyn's ideas make clear how our *psychological worlds are very much open to negotiation* rather than being fixed and immutable. Our social life revolves round the communication and demonstration of different ways of figuring reality. Humour in particular rests on the sudden transformation of the meaning of an experience by having it figured differently by the turn of a phrase or action. 'We all have to meet the Grim Reaper at some time in our lives', I've just heard Donald Sinden say wistfully on TV. 'You mean death?' his partner queries. 'No marriage!' he replies.

4   Frame analysis helped us to understand how social realities can be both stable and uncertain. The notion of subjective experience as a metaphorical reality gives us further insights into its *paradoxical qualities of at the same time having a stability and solidity and yet being variable and confused.* For, while the physical world of objects and events may itself remain much the same, the metaphors or comparisons we use to deepen and direct our apprehension of it may change. It also makes clear the elusive nature of consciousness and why it is so difficult to pin down and study.

5   Romanyshyn's model provides a way of understanding the *self-fulfilling nature* of *subjective experience* which we noted in the previous unit. For if it is a metaphorical reflection, then our expectations about the world and ourselves will be reflected in what we experience. We all too easily become, as Harré has put it 'what the best authorities tell us we are' because we have assimilated the metaphors they use.

Like any other theory, Romanyshyn's conception is itself a metaphor for psychological life. But its value is the degree to which it deepens our understanding of and is consistent with what we experience. Psychology has been slow to relinquish its apparently more solid 'scientific' metaphors of the mind as some kind of physical system. Paradoxically, the reluctance has often been because other approaches are thought too 'soft'. As Fernandez nicely puts it: 'One always feels a bit sheepish, of course, about bringing the metaphor concept into the social sciences and perhaps that is because one always feels there is something soft and woolly about it' (1972, p. 41). But 'soft and woolly' implies easy and comfortable to the touch. The problem of introducing the notion of psychological life as a metaphor-like reflection is precisely the reverse: its subtlety makes it difficult to grasp. But hold on to it as best you can for, although it may not have yet been properly assimilated by psychologists themselves, it has vitally important implications for the way we study and practise psychology.

PROGRESS BOX 4   Robert Romanyshyn: psychological life as metaphorical reflection

1   *Psychological life* is best regarded as *metaphorical* in nature. This means that:

(i)   Our experience of the world (both objects and people) is not in us or in them, but consists of the reflection of one through the other.

(ii)   Experience is 'figured' (i.e. constructed) from a particular perspective: it is open, therefore, to multiple interpretations depending on the perspectives adopted.

(iii)   Stability and communication are nevertheless possible because people share many metaphors derived from their common culture as well as having physical/sensory processes in common.

2   The *value* of regarding psychological life as metaphor (as a 'reality of reflection') is that it helps us to make sense of:

(i)   The process of social influence.

(ii)   How subjective experience is relativistic.

(iii)   How the way we make sense of the world is open to 'negotiation'.

(iv)   How subjective experience is stable yet variable.

(v)   The self-fulfilling nature of subjective experience.

3   Implications for psychology:

(i)   The need to realize that its scientific metaphors do not constitute empirical reality. They may obscure as well as illuminate.

(ii)   To understand someone is to set them in a *narrative*, not to explain in terms of causes and effects. The craft of psychology therefore becomes 'imaginal reconstruction'.

3.4   Personal construct theory revisited

Romanyshyn's rather sweeping strictures about 'scientific' psychology should not obscure the fact that many influential theories within social psychology are quite consistent with the notion that subjective experience has a metaphor-like nature. A notable example, discussed in detail in Unit 2, is systems theory. This makes no assumption of an objective, empirical reality. Its fundamental premise is that personal experience is continually open to change and redefinition depending on the patterning of relationships and meanings at the time. The method of reframing often used in family therapy essentially involves helping the client to make sense of his or her experience in a different way ('refiguring' the experience as Romanyshyn would say).

George Kelly's personal construct theory has been the most influential among those psychological theories which have tried to make sense of subjective experience. The only reason it is not examined in detail in this Unit is that this has already been done in Unit 8. To conclude this section it might be useful to review and supplement personal construct theory in the light of the notion of subjective experience as metaphor and the analysis of personal worlds presented in the preceding unit.

ACTIVITY 7

Try to recollect what you know about Kelly's theory (look back to Unit 8 if you need to). How far and in what ways is it consistent with the analysis of personal worlds and subjective experience presented so far in this Block?

Personal construct theory does seem to fit very well. As a therapist, Kelly appreciates the significance of coming to an understanding of the *personal worlds* of his clients. He also sees *time* as a fundamental dimension of our psychological worlds: for the primary function of constructs is to anticipate future events, and they are also seen as changing with experience over time. He postulates too a degree of *autonomy* in the way a person can employ his or her constructs: for there are usually alternative ways of construing open to us and, in this way, we have a part to play in determining what the nature of our experience will be. As Kelly expresses it: 'Man creates his own ways of seeing the world in which he lives; the world does not create them for him' (Kelly, 1955, p. 12). And later:

> the events we face today are subject to as great a variety of constructions as our wits will enable us to contrive. This is not to say that one construction is as good as any other, nor is it to deny that at some infinite point in time human vision will behold reality out to the utmost reaches of existence. But it does remind us that all our present perceptions are open to question and reconsideration and it does broadly suggest that even the most obvious

occurrences of everyday life might appear utterly transformed if we were inventive enough to construe them differently.

(Kelly, 1970, p. 1)

All this also seems highly consistent with both the features of *multiplicity* (KF11) and *reflexiveness (KF12)* which we identified in Unit 12 and the notion of subjective experience as a metaphorical reality which can be 'figured' in different ways. The language which Kelly uses may be different, but the ideas seem basically similar.

The idea of consciousness as metaphor is a useful way of viewing personal construct theory. The dominant metaphor underlined in his theory is, in fact, not metaphor itself but 'man the scientist': as individuals, we build up our personal understanding of the world by trying out various hypotheses (or metaphors we might say) to see how well they fit. But as scientific understanding is at least a part of our psychological reality, then such a metaphor seems more appropriate for getting at psychological experience than one taken from the physical world. This is perhaps one reason why construct theory so caught the imagination of clinical psychologists in particular, for they need an effective way of conceptualizing the personal experience of their clients, as they deal with this every day in their practice.

A further reason for Kelly's impact on academic as well as clinical psychology in this country is that he provided methods like the repertory grid technique (see the Kelly Project) to find out what kind of constructs a person uses. But this has its negative side, in that constructs elicited in this way can easily become reified (i.e. made a thing of). A person's subjective experience may then be regarded as made up of a system of constructs – which is not at all what Kelly intended. Thinking of subjective experience as metaphor-like provides a useful antidote to this. For if we think of constructs as metaphors and the elements as the aspects of the world to which they are applied, then conscious experience itself can be thought of as the emergent reflection resulting from their interplay, rather than as consisting of the constructs or the elements in themselves.

In trying to understand his patient's personal world, Kelly's preferred approach was in fact to ask the patient about his or her experience. One method he used to do this is described in Box 2.

self characterization

Box 2   Kelly's method of self-characterization

The client is instructed as follows:

> I want to write a character sketch of yourself, just as if you were the principal character in a play. Write it as it might be written by a friend who knows you very *intimately* and very *sympathetically*, perhaps better than anyone every really could know you. Be sure to write the sketch in the third person. For example start out by saying '(name) is . . .'

(Kelly, 1955, p. 323)

You might like to try this yourself sometime or get someone else to do it for you. Allow about twenty minutes for the task.

This way of eliciting understanding of a person is very similar to Romanyshyn's idea of making sense of a person by setting him in a story. Kelly suggests various ways of analysing self-characterizations, but the basic aim is to get a feeling for the way a person sees himself and the world about him or her – in other words to use the self-characterization to get at the metaphors which are reflected in his or her subjective experience.

Kelly found that a typical problem for many of his patients was that their constructs had become too fixed and rigid. The therapist's job then becomes to encourage new ways of construing which may 'work better'. One method which Kelly devised for this purpose is *fixed role therapy* (see Box 3).

fixed role therapy

Box 3   Fixed role therapy

1   The client is first asked to write a self-characterization.

2   The therapist then devises a 'fixed role sketch'. This is a characterization which he or she constructs so as to be different from the client's but not too much so.

3   This fixed role sketch is then discussed with the client, and changed if necessary so that the person it represents is seen as both believable and likeable.

4   The client is then asked to try to role play (i.e. to be and act like) that person for a specified period. The fixed role sketch becomes a hypothesis, if you like, for him or her to try out and see what it feels like. During this period, the therapist and client get together frequently to discuss what is happening. Fixed role therapy serves to help break rigid patterns of action and reaction in which the client may be locked. But its essential goal is to encourage the client into becoming aware of his or her capacity for self-creation.

Fixed role therapy fits in well with several of the key features in Unit 12: for example, the *multiplicity* of our personal worlds (*KF11*); our capacity to *reflect* on and look at ourselves, both as we are and could be (*KF12*); and our capacity for initiating change should we so choose (*KF9 – agency*). One is also reminded of Romanyshyn's notion of the psychologist's craft as being that of imaginal reconstruction.

The whole idea of fixed role therapy suggests that some ways of construing (i.e. some metaphors) work better for a person than others. Kelly encouraged his clients to explore different possibilities and would then discuss with them on the basis of that experience which seemed to be the best kinds of constructs for the individual to use. One might question, however, what basis the client (or indeed the therapist) can use to decide which constructs are best for him. His choice may merely rest on his usual way of construing, which is presumably precisely what he wishes to change. This alerts us to the very thorny question as to whether some metaphors and ways of construing are more likely to promote psychological well-being than others (rather as some diets are better for us than others), and, if so, what basis we can use to evaluate them. This issue of criteria for the 'quality of life' and 'psychoethics' (drawing implications from psychology for the way we should lead our lives) will be taken up in the conclusion to this Block (Part 2 of Unit 14).

PROGRESS BOX 5:   Personal construct theory

1   *Personal construct theory fits well with the analysis of personal worlds so far*: it is consistent with key features such as time, autonomy, multiplicity, reflexiveness and agency.

2   It is useful to view personal construct theory in terms of the idea of

---

consciousness being of a metaphor-like nature:

(i) The dominant metaphor of the theory is 'the person as a scientist'.

(ii) Regarding constructs as metaphors avoids reifying them.

3 Self-characterization and fixed role therapy are analogous to Romanyshyn's ideas of understanding by using a narrative, and the craft of psychology as being 'imaginal reconstruction'.

4 Given a degree of choice in the way we construct ourselves (see fixed role therapy), on what basis can we evaluate which constructs/metaphors to use? – the problem of 'psychoethics'.

4 THE SIGNIFICANCE OF IMAGINATION AND THE UNCONSCIOUS

'One's real life is often the life one does not lead' (Oscar Wilde).

By imagination I refer to the inner world of fantasy – our ability to create in our minds images and events with their associated feelings. Even in the brief glimpses into personal worlds afforded by the Windows in Unit 12, we saw the part played by fantasy. Liv Ullman in the plane circling over Hollywood, for example, imagines life back in Norway and the people she loves there. At times, for Leonard, fantasy seems even to dominate his consciousness, bringing alive the picture on his wall and peopling the blank television screen and his personal world with hallucinatory images. Capacity for fantasy also underlies some of the key features we abstracted from the accounts. A sense of *time* (*KF2*), for example, depends on remembered images of past events and on the ability to think of ourselves in the future. Imagined scenarios contribute to the *multiple* nature (*KF11*) of personal worlds, and *reflexiveness* (*KF12*) includes the ability to see in one's mind how one appears to be for others. Power of imagination also underlies existential issues: finiteness, for example, only takes on meaning if we can imagine our eventual death.

With important exceptions (such as Jerome Singer (1981) on daydreams and Joseph Campbell (1964, 1973) on myth) there has been relatively little research and theorizing by psychologists about the *content* of fantasy. Fantasy was touched on in the context of *frame analysis*, where it was seen as a form of keyed experience: but, if we are to begin to comprehend the nature of subjective experience, it is an area which we need to look at in a little more depth. It also provides an appropriate context for relating psychoanalytic ideas about unconscious meanings to personal worlds.

For children, fantasy clearly plays an explicit and important role: in their play they try out adult behaviours, create stories and scenes and attribute personalities and life to dolls and teddy-bears. As Erikson and others have pointed out, this is not just a question of amusement: for it is through play that children learn about the world, develop abilities and explore their needs and anxieties. To illustrate this, he quotes a delightful sequence from Mark Twain's *Tom Sawyer* in which Tom's friend Ben Rogers hove into view 'personating the *Big Missouri* . . .' and being 'boat and captain and engine-bells combined . . .'. In such ways, growing children explore, synthesize different aspects of themselves and their experiences and learn to become masters of themselves both in body and mind, while assimilating the metaphors of their culture:

> One 'meaning' of Ben's play could be that it affords his ego a temporary victory over his gangling body and self by making a well-functioning whole out of brain (captain), the nerves and muscles of will (signal system and engine), and the whole bulk of the body (boat). It permits him to be an entity within which he is his own boss, because he obeys himself. At the same time, he chooses his metaphors from the tool world of the young machine age, and anticipates the identity of the machine god of his day: the captain of the *Big Missouri*.
>
> (Erikson, 1950, p. 190)

(You might like to relate Piaget's concepts of *assimilation* and *accommodation* (see Unit 4, section 4.3) to this account of the function of fantasy and play. They could be regarded as providing both a way of adjusting to cultural images and models (i.e. accommodation) and also of making sense of the world in terms of pre-existing cognitive structures (i.e. assimilation).)

With the onset of adolescence, fantasy is expressed more through inner thought than explicit play. At such a critical time for identity formation (see Unit 12, section 5), one would expect a preoccupation with fantasy (both realistic and otherwise) about the multiple possibilities now opening up in personal development, relationships and work. As Singer (1981) has commented, given the likelihood that any request or remark by a parent is likely to interrupt an absorbing fantasy, this may be one reason at least for the reputed touchiness of adolescents.

We might assume then that fantasy has considerable significance for children and young persons, but what about adults?

4.1 The uses of fantasy

Most surveys have found that the majority of adults (regardless of intelligence) seem to engage in some form of 'day-dreaming' every day (Singer, 1981). To distinguish the various forms and uses of adult fantasies, I would like to suggest three broad categories: (A) fantasy which occupies the centre of consciousness as a *sequence* in its own right; (B) fantasy which *accompanies* an experience or action; and (C) fantasy which is *energizing*, i.e. which serves to guide and/or stimulate future action. This is not intended as a definitive classification but rather as a tool for unpacking some of the varied uses which fantasy serves:

fantasy sequences

(A)   Most people say that they enjoy their day-dreaming and it is not surprising that in this first category a common use of fantasy is as a *diversion*; as, for example, when we *replay* memories of pleasurable or significant events. Closely related to this are those sequences in which we rehearse in fantasy the scripts of *desire* – winning a marathon or the pools, for example, or becoming a politician, or marrying the person of our dreams. Also in this group comes what we might call *substitute* fantasy where the sequence is focused on a desired person who is absent or unobtainable. So a man whose wife has died or a wife whose husband is away might both fantasize their loved-one sitting in their usual chair or cuddling up to them through the night. In the final subcategory here are what I would term *working-through* fantasies: those times when people want to be 'left alone' to think through their recent experiences. This may involve 'replaying' the scene to try to digest and conceptualize in different ways what has happened; or it may mean musing on what might have been but was not done. To recall Eliot's lines quoted earlier (Unit 12, section 2.2):

Footfalls echo in the memory
Down the passage which we did not take
Towards the door we never opened
Into the rose-garden.

(Eliot, 1974, p. 189)

Although such sequences may be about pleasurable and exciting experiences, they may also represent efforts to come to terms with situations and actions which arouse shame or guilt.

accompaniment fantasies (B) Our second broad grouping is concerned with fantasy which *accompanies* ongoing experiences. This may be no more than those momentary *anticipations* as when the doorbell rings and a repertoire of possibilities as to whom it might be flashes through our mind as we go to answer it. Or it could be the inner, running *commentary* with themselves (or perhaps with God or with an imagined loved-one) which some people engage in as a way of coping with anxiety-provoking or difficult situations ('Now come on, old man, just three more miles to go!'). There are accompaniment fantasies also whose effect is to make mundane situations more exciting:

> While driving through Huddersfield recently a friend of mine was stopped by the police. 'Do you know how fast you were going?' he was asked. 'As a matter of fact I know exactly how fast I was driving,' replied my friend. 'I was doing precisely 38mph, in third gear at 2,850 revs per minute.'
>
> Suspecting a smart ass the police officer asked him how he could be so sure. 'Because I was pretending to take part in the Monte Carlo Rally,' said my friend, who will not see 50 again.
>
> 'You think I'm in Huddersfield but in my mind I'm in Grasse, looking forward to a quick spin down the Alpes Maritimes in time for an early supper in Antibes, and I know exactly how fast I have to go to get there before they take the last orders.'
>
> At this point my friend was invited to get out of his car with both hands showing. The police officer was taking no chances with a nutter in a 1965 Ford Cortina which had about as much chance of making it to Monte Carlo as my friend had of convincing the West Riding magistrate who was to fine him for breaking the 40mph limit.
>
> Unfortunately my friend happened to be telling the truth. In order to make his journey through the Pennines more tolerable he had invented a game for himself, complete with bizarre hazards like forest fires, Alpine avalanches, nubile Parisienne hitch-hikers, amphetamine-fired Tour de France cyclists and surly OAS-type gendarmerie. Like many of us he was living out a fantasy life, but, unlike most of us, he was honest enough to admit it, and attempt to use it as evidence in his defence.
>
> (Connolly, 1982, p. 7)

We see, in this extract, how such accompaniment fantasies could be regarded as being a form of sustained metaphor, reflecting through the events which are happening to transform them into a new and more exciting experience. Also included in this subcategory of *enhancing* fantasies is the use of imagination to intensify sexual feelings. In a study of women's sexual fantasies, Hariton and Singer (1974) found that sixty-five per cent of their 'normal' subjects engaged in 'moderate to high levels' of fantasy during sex. Such fantasies involved, for example, other lovers, multiple partners, different contexts such as being on the beach, or imagining resisting and being overcome. (Singer (1981) even cites an account of a pop group follower who had so often fantasized about the group's lead singer when she was making love with other men, that when the great day did eventually arrive and she found herself in bed with him, she had to continue to fantasize about him in the usual way in order to make the reality more satisfying!) In her collection of women's sexual fantasies, Nancy Friday (1976) also found it quite common for women to use fantasy while making love; and there is no reason, of course, to suppose that fantasy plays any less a part for men.

energizing fantasies

(C)   The third broad grouping consist of fantasies which serve in some way to *energize* and to stimulate the fantasizer into action (or at least into the active expression of an attitude); fantasies, in other words, which 'get us going'. These may take the form of either accompaniment fantasies (see category (B)) or sequences in their own right (A), As Yeats put it, the 'imagination has some way of lighting on the truth which reason has not, and . . . its commandments . . . are the most binding we can ever know' (Yeats, 1961, p. 65). It is through imagination that we are moved to create our futures. This is not just a matter of exploring alternatives, but of finding images which can precipitate us into movement, as when we suddenly see (and feel) how life could be. Like a metaphor, such images serve to transform experience and, in so doing, direct and sustain our movement into the future. Some people's lives are centred on some 'personal myth', seen by them, for example, as a way to salvation, or a hero's journey against adversity. Fantasy may be used to energize more limited sectors of one's life. In writing this section of the unit, for example, I see it at the moment as fighting a battle to gain command of a rather wild and difficult hump of ground.

Imagination then is a constant part of our personal worlds, serving to please and pain us, arousing hopes and anticipations and sometimes guiding us to new ways of doing things and living our lives. As suggested above, one way of regarding the role of fantasy in our lives (particularly in its enhancing and energizing forms) is as a type of sustained metaphor which allows a new reality to emerge from the reflection of itself through the experience with which it is associated.

4.2   Unconscious meanings

It might well seem that psychoanalysis should be of relevance to understanding fantasy. After all, dreams seem but one stage removed and, as we saw in Chapter 3 of *Freud and Psychoanalysis*, for Freud they offered an important way of finding out about unconscious meanings. Freud regarded fantasy ('primary process' thought) as one way of satisfying needs frustrated in reality ('secondary process'). But, while quite a few of our daydreams do seem to revolve around wish-fulfilment and sexual and even aggressive fantasies, in view of the very varied uses of fantasy which have been suggested, it would seem too limited a view to regard it as purely a process of drive reduction and/or catharsis (expression of repressed feelings). If we take a broader view of psychoanalysis, however, it can give us useful insights into the form taken by both fantasy and subjective experience in general.

ACTIVITY 8

Before reading further, you might like to think about or refer back to Chapters 3–5 of the Set Book *Freud and Psychoanalysis* which you read in the course of your work for Unit 4 (Chapters 6 and 7 which were optional reading are also relevant). What examples can you find there of ways in which unconscious meanings can affect fantasy and subjective experience?

---

transference

A useful notion here is *transference* (see *Freud and Psychoanalysis*, Chapter 7). This refers to the transferring into current relationships of feelings and 'scripts' which were originally experienced in relation to parents and other significant figures in childhood. The nature of such transference may well be more obvious in the fantasies which we weave round people than in the actual ways in which we relate to them. Underlying conflicts and needs may also show up in the form which recurrent fantasy sequences take (i.e. whether they are achievement-oriented or anxiety-related, etc.).

Again, if we go along with the idea of consciousness as a metaphor-like reality, which was put forward in section 3, then unconscious meanings might, like fantasies, be also regarded as a form of metaphor or construct which deepens and transforms subjective experience. The particular feature of unconscious constructs or 'metaphors', though, is the difficulty we have in becoming aware of them and their influence on the reflections which constitute our experience of the world.

Other ways in which unconscious meanings may be expressed through fantasy and subjective experience are given below. Some of these you may have already picked out yourself in Activity 8 above:

1   What we experience as enjoyable or unpleasant may be related to oral and/or anal tendencies (Chapter 4).

2   The form which sexual fantasies take may be due to infantile psychosexual fixations (Chapter 4).

3   Both our fantasies and feelings about other people may be influenced by our projections (Chapter 5).

4   Feelings about what is right or wrong (and what we get indignant about) may be based on the values introjected as a result of early identifications during superego development (Chapter 4).

5   The people we identify with and the kind of characters we like in films and literature may also be related to early identifications.

6   The general emotional tone of our fantasies and subjective experience (e.g. anxiety, feelings of hostility, the denial or isolation of feelings) may be influenced by unconscious conflicts.

4.3   Myth and archetype

myth
At the level of culture one might regard the place of fantasy as being taken by *myths*. Almost all cultures provide tales of the exploits of legendary figures, stories of gods and goddesses and saints and about the creation of the world. Our culture is no exception. Not only have we inherited a wealth of mythology from other times but, it might be argued, mythical characters and themes are continuously being both revamped and created anew in popular films, literature and television from Dickens to *Dallas*. Comedy and drama are the shared and structured public forms of the private fantasies already discussed.

In Chapter 9 of *Freud and Psychoanalysis* (which you might like to reread at some stage during your work on this section) there is a brief discussion of the psychoanalytic view of myth and fairy stories. Myths serve a similar function for adults, it is argued, as fairy stories do for children. Both play out fundamental conflicts experienced in the course of individual development and as part of human existence. I would suggest also that the mythology of a culture provides a rich source of personal myths and metaphors, the energizing symbols and images which carry the power to guide and generate our actions. Their power (e.g. the power of the flag, the cross, the heroic theme) cannot be underestimated. They inspired the building of the Pyramids and the cathedrals of the Middle Ages, they lead Hindus to die from starvation rather than slaughter the cattle around them and young Moslems to seek glorious death in battle as martyrs. Even as I write this, the three main items on the news are Mrs Gandhi's assassination (presumably by Sikhs outraged by what they regard as her desecration of the Golden Temple), the murder of a priest in Poland, and of a man in Northern Ireland. Each one of these murders was almost surely motivated not by ordinary personal gain but was an action fuelled by a clash of mythologies. Campbell argues that 'every little group is fixed in its own long-established, petrified mythology, changes having occurred only as a consequence of collision' (Campbell, 1973, p. 15). Campbell sees myths as serving important functions: (i) to stimulate 'a sense of awe before the mystery of being'; (ii) to offer a theory of the origins and the nature of the world; (iii) to provide a basis for morality, for choosing which actions to take; (iv) to 'initiate the individual into the orders of his own psyche, guiding him toward his own spiritual enrichment and realization' (Campbell, 1964, pp. 519–21). For Campbell though the problem is that what energizing myths we have today have been inherited from another time and culture. They fail to take account of or fit within the West's rational, science-based understanding of the world. What we need, he argues, are new forms appropriate to our time and understanding. As MacLeish has put it:

> A world ends when its metaphor has died . . .
> It perishes when those images, though seen,
> No longer mean.

> (MacLeish, 1952, pp. 173–4)

The problem though is (as discussed in Unit 12, section 4.3) can energizing myths or meaningfulness be constructed on rational grounds?

archetypes

While he agrees that contemporary Western culture 'suffers an unprecedented impoverishment of symbols', Jung has proposed that running through the mythologies of different cultures and the fantasies of different individuals are common themes. These emerge from *archetypes* in the 'collective unconscious' – images and constellations of feeling which crystallize universal human experiences and which have somehow been passed on through the generations (Jung, 1968). Such archetypes may express themselves as images which recur in mythologies and dreams (for example, the 'great mother', 'the wise old man', 'the wandering hero') or may take the form of dynamic process, i.e. a particular style of behaving in response to certain situations. Thus Jung might explain a person falling suddenly and irrationally in love as being precipitated by his *anima* or her *animus* – the archetypal image of the opposite sex within each of us. Jung is unclear about the actual nature both of archetypes and the collective unconscious itself (though this would appear to imply some form of inheritance of acquired experiences, thus running counter to accepted Darwinian notions of evolution – see Unit 3, section 4).

What is interesting about Jung's idea is that it views the unconscious not merely as a compendium of needs which demand expression but as a source of potential wisdom and energizing guidance in the business of life. (The topic of archetypes will be taken up in discussing Jung's idea of individuation in Unit 14.)

ACTIVITY 9 (optional)

1 *The place of fantasy in your experience*
Try to become aware of your own use of fantasy and imagination. How much of your time is usually taken up by fantasy? What forms does it take and what uses does it seem to serve for you? Do you want to expand or diminish the different kinds of use you make of it? You may find, for example, that, if you want to, you can deliberately encourage energizing fantasies and reduce the amount of time spent on fantasies which seem to depress or inhibit you.

2 *Dream diary*
If you would like to get more in touch with the role of unconscious meaning in your personal world, you might think of keeping a dream diary.

(a) Before going to sleep, tell yourself slowly at least ten times that you will remember whatever you dream when you wake up.

(b) Keep a pad and pen beside the bed. Try to write down the dream in as much detail as possible, as soon as you awake.

(c) After a few weeks, look back over your notes and try to pick out any key themes or content. Sort these in any way that seems meaningful to you.

(d) Try to critically consider the content and themes in terms of (i) Freud's ideas about the processes of dream-work discussed in Chapter 3 of the Set Book *Freud and Psychoanalysis*, and (ii) Jung's idea that dreams may offer guidelines for the way we live our lives.

PROGRESS BOX 6   The importance of fantasy and imagination in subjective experience

1   *Relevance* of fantasy and play for *children* (ego development) and *adolescents*.

2   Prevalence of fantasy for *adults*. Its *uses*:

(A)   *Fantasy sequences:* memory replays, wish-fulfilling, substitution and work-through (both positive and negative) types.

(B)   *Fantasies as accompaniment:* anticipatory, commentary and enhancement types.

(C)   *Energizing fantasies* and 'personal myth'.

The idea of fantasy as a 'sustained metaphor'.

3   *Psychoanalysis* in relation to fantasy and subjective experience. Transference. Expression of underlying conflicts and needs. Other areas of relevance – psychosexual development, projection, superego formation, identifications, unconscious conflicts influencing emotional tone.

4   *Myths* as structured, cultural forms of fantasy:

– like fairy stories, they represent fundamental themes and conflicts in human experience

– vital source of energizing metaphors for individuals

– the functions of myths (Campbell)

– lack of appropriate myths for contemporary culture?

5   *Archetypes* as a basic source of mythologies and personal fantasies and behaviours (Jung).

---

5   SUBJECTIVE EXPERIENCE IN EVOLUTIONARY, HISTORICAL AND CULTURAL PERSPECTIVES

So far, we have tried to make sense of subjective experience by looking at it directly. For the most part, you have been asked to take a phenomenological stance – to relate the ideas discussed to your own subjective experience. That is because this is the only *direct* contact you have with the subject-matter which concerns us. Now we step back to look at three approaches which, in very different ways, try to make sense of conscious experience by considering the *conditions which have made it possible* and have *shaped its present forms*. Our particular concern in this section is to gain more understanding of subjective experience by looking at its *origins*. How did it develop? On what does it depend? Why does it take the form that it does? Unit 1 on the family made clear the complexity of questions such as these. Social and psychological life has many roots – biological, social and developmental. Development in childhood of personal awareness and a sense of agency has already been dealt with in some detail in Block 2, so here we focus on biological and social roots. First we consider how and why consciousness might have evolved in the early phases of the development of the human species. Then we will examine a theory which suggests that human consciousness may have radically changed in much more recent historical time. Finally, we shall return to look in more detail at a theme already touched on – the way in which the nature of the society in which we live may influence the form and content of individual subjective experience.

Should you expect that, because we now adopt a more external stance, our feet will be on more solid ground, you will be disappointed. Unfortunately, the study of consciousness, from whatever perspective, does not permit such luxury. Many, if not most, of the ideas we shall consider here are speculative. But this does not undermine their value as a stimulus to thought. They offer a rich source of metaphors which have the potential to deepen and transform our awareness of the nature of the personal worlds in which we live.

5.1 The evolution of consciousness

As we saw in Unit 3, one way of getting to understand more about any aspect of human behaviour is to try to trace its evolutionary development and functional significance in the development of species. The primary sources of data for such theorizing are observations of the behaviour of other species living now but which are at different stages of phylogenetic development; and, to some extent, reconstructions of the life-style of animals of the past and early humans on the basis of fossil remains. This is a hazardous and speculative procedure at the best of times. The particular problem with consciousness is that, although we can observe an animal's actions, we have no access to whatever consciousness it might have. Nor is consciousness such as to leave traces of itself in tangible relics like the bones and fossils of early human beings. It is perhaps not surprising, therefore, that there are few contemporary theorists prepared to venture in this field. But, bearing in mind the limitations noted above, we shall look briefly at two theories which put forward some interesting hypotheses about the possible ways in which consciousness develops.

5.1.1 The social value of consciousness

In his book *Consciousness Regained* (1983) Nicholas Humphrey argues that consciousness is far from being an irrelevant epiphenomenon or mere reflection of the workings of the brain. He makes the case that, for a social species, consciousness has a very important biological function. In the distant past of humankind, living in social groups must have been vital to survival. Cooperative effort made food-getting, hunting and protection against predators far more effective. It also made possible a long period of protected development for children during which complex skills could be acquired: since, for humans, appropriate action is not programmed in but depends on learning, a prolonged childhood is essential. But the stable social system which makes all this possible requires people to live and interact with each other for sustained periods. This, in turn, requires natural psychological skills of a high order. For in social interactions each participant must always be ready to modify strategy, assumptions and even goals depending on the behaviour of the other(s). To engage in this successfully requires not just accumulated knowledge but the ability to understand the other person's intentions and to continuously reframe and readjust one's approach as required. Humphrey considers that the highly developed cognitive capacity of human beings evolved not only because of the need to cope with the ecological conditions in which they have had to survive but also because of the need to operate in the even more complex area of human relations. 'The chief role of creative intellect', he asserts, 'is to hold society together' (1983, p. 19).

Human beings need extraordinary skill as natural psychologists. We are capable of making all sorts of complex inferences from and predictions about the behaviour of other people. Although a high level of intelligence is necessary for this, it is not, Humphrey considers, sufficient. Some understanding and prediction of the reactions of others might be achieved by intelligent extrapolation on the basis of careful observation of the consistencies and patterns of their external behaviours. But a far more powerful method, he argues, is by recourse to the privileged picture we have of the workings of our own minds through introspection. This allows us to relate what we ourselves are conscious of to our own behaviours. We can then use this knowledge as a model for understanding others. In other words, we can put ourselves in their place. We know, of course, from experience that other people are not always like us. But there is sufficient consistency that, with appropriate adjustments, we can do a pretty good job of inferring their beliefs and feelings in this way and thus gain very useful insights into the ways in which they will react and behave:

> ... the introspectionist's privileged picture of the inner reasons for his own behaviour is one which he will immediately and naturally project on other people. He can and will use his own experience to get inside other people's skin. And since the chances are that he himself is not in reality untypical of human beings in general – since the chances are that ... from person to person there is generally no looking in the larder without hunger, no running away without fear, no rage without anger, etc. – this kind of imaginative projection gives him an explanatory scheme of remarkable generality and power.
> (Humphrey, 1983, pp. 53–4)

Because, for a social animal, both survival and sexual reproduction depend on gaining cooperation from other members of the same species, an attribute like consciousness which could significantly increase the ability to deal with other people would soon be selected for in the gene pool. This development would be intensified by the fact that this in itself would increase the complexity of the social environment (because other people would also possess consciousness) thus demanding ever higher levels of psychological skills in order to sustain the ability to be socially effective.

If Humphrey is correct in his argument that consciousness provides the means of modelling the feelings and reasons underlying other people's behaviour, then the more extensive one's conscious experience of different feeling and belief states is, then the greater the range of people and behaviours which can be understood. One of the functions of not only play and fantasy but also dreams, he considers, is to extend the scope of conscious experience beyond that possible in everyday actuality.

Humphrey summarizes the gist of his thesis thus:

> ... a revolutionary advance in the evolution of mind occurred when, for certain social animals, a new set of heuristic principles was devised to cope with the pressing need to model a special section of reality – the reality comprised by the behaviour of other kindred animals. The trick which nature came up with was *introspection*; it proved possible for an individual to develop a model of the behaviour of others by reasoning by analogy from his own case, the facts of his own case being revealed to him through examination of the contents of consciousness.

> For man and other animals which live in complex social groups reality is in larger measure a 'social reality'. No other class of environmental objects approaches in biological significance those living bodies which constitute for a social animal its companions, playmates, rivals, teachers, foes. It depends on the bodies of other conspecific animals not merely for its immediate sustenance in infancy and its sexual fulfilment as an adult, but in one way or another for the success (or failure) of almost every enterprise it

undertakes. In these circumstances the ability to model the behaviour of others in the social group has paramount survival value.

(Humphrey, 1983, pp. 30–1)

5.1.2 Possible origins of agency, identity and empathy

In his wide-ranging book *The Evolution of Human Consciousness* (1980) John Crook has approached the question of the origins of consciousness along similar lines. He accepts Humphrey's view (which had been expressed in a paper published by Humphrey prior to his book) that consciousness and creative intellect evolved because of their adaptive value for a species like humans who depend for survival on living together. But Crook goes on to make some interesting although speculative suggestions about possible evolutionary bases for specific aspects of consciousness.

He identifies three features which he considers to be especially characteristic of contemporary human consciousness. His aim is to speculate about the adaptive value which has led them to be selected for in the evolution of the human species. The three features he focuses on are all among those discussed as characteristics of personal worlds in the previous unit. One, for example, is *reflexiveness* – our capacity to become conscious of being conscious, to experience ourselves as having an experience. Another is *agency*, which he defines as the experience of the personal power 'to construct the future from a field of possibilities negotiated not at random but within a set of rules themselves often placed within a hierarchy of further rules' (1980, p. 271). Social interaction becomes a negotiation with other individuals who are perceived of as having a similar power of agency to ourselves. The third feature Crook identifies as crucial to human consciousness is a sense of *self-identity* – the capacity to 'present oneself to oneself'. Crook argues that the evolutionary origin of this appears to be very recent. If chimps get a smudge on their nose and then see their reflection in a mirror they touch their noses in acknowledgement of their awareness that the reflection is of themselves. Human infants acquire this ability at about fifteen months but rhesus monkeys never do. Crook regards some capacity for self-identity as crucial for the development of social life. Empathy – our capacity to attribute self-identity to another and 'take the role of that person' is essential, he argues, for coordinating our social relations, and the value judgements of a community have their effect because of their power to influence our self-esteem – which in turn depends on awareness of ourselves as individuals.

While a rudimentary consciousness may exist in other species, evolved consciousness with the distinguishing attributes noted above is confined to humans or at least to a few of the higher primates. How then and why did they develop? He accepts that these distinctive features of subjective experience are premised on a high level of intelligence and cognitive organization, but also suggests that their development may have been particularly encouraged by (i) the increasing use of tools and goods of various kinds, and (ii) the value of altruism in a primitive society and the cognitive abilities which this involved.

In the discussion of language in Unit 5, you may remember the idea was mooted at one point that the relationship between actor, action and object which seems to be found in all languages may have its roots in a 'universal conceptual structure'. Crook suggests that such a built-in mode of conceptual organization could have originated in the development of the idea of personal property which probably emerged with the use of tools and with cooperative activities in the life of early humans:

> The elaboration of a wide variety of tools for processes involved in self-protection, hunting, food-preparation, transport of materials, and building construction would mean that distinctions would have to be made between makers and users, between users and owners, between possessors and inheritors. In that some tools and goods are more valuable than others, their

possession and use became immediately associated with social contrasts in rank and in role. Tools became part of the matrix of society, markers defining categories and boundaries in an increasingly complex societal organization. We can therefore suggest that a linguistic provision for the naming of both tools and people underlies the evolutionary development of reference in human language and the emergence of grammatical structuring that provides the context in which the name plays its part in a meaningful communication.

(Crook, 1980, p. 134)

Crook goes on to argue that such developments in grammatical structure and naming would make it more possible to conceptualize oneself as distinct from others. The capacity to initiate change could thus have become ascribed to specific individuals, creating a sense of persons as agents.

In the past, evolutionary theory has had difficulty in explaining how any tendency for altruism and self-sacrifice could have evolved. On the grounds of Darwinian theory (see Unit 3) one might well have thought that it would have been selected out. For one would expect that individuals prone to sacrifice themselves would be less likely to reproduce and pass on their genes, in comparison with more competitive types. More recently though, sociobiologists have argued that altruism can have functional value in terms of biological 'fitness', i.e. the likelihood of passing one's genes to future generations. One variant of this argument is the notion of kin selection (e.g. Hamilton, 1972). If we sacrifice ourselves to ensure the survival of people to whom we are genetically related this can still serve to perpetuate our genes, and if we can help them without actually killing ourselves (for example, if we bring up our relative's children) this has even greater genetic advantage. Thus optimal fitness rests on a mix of selfishness (in the sense of ensuring direct propagation of our genes) and altruism.

reciprocal altruism

Robert Trivers (1971) has extended this idea by pointing out that altruism may have reproductive fitness value even when relatives are not involved. Saving someone now may encourage them to reciprocate by helping you or your children on some future occasion. Such 'reciprocal altruism' rests on the development of a capacity for communication, on being able to compute benefits and, in particular, to detect non-reciprocation or exploitation. As Crook points out, it would be reasonable to suppose that it provides a basis for the natural selection of the capacity for discrimination in relationships and for empathy – the capacity to put oneself in another person's place. Thus he argues that the monitoring of trustworthiness required by reciprocal altruism may well have played a critical role in the evolution of a sense of personal identity (i.e., awareness of oneself and others as different individuals).

5.1.3. Comment

This has been a very brief account of a set of subtle and complex ideas. The more specific links which Crook proposes are admittedly speculative and, even for Humphrey's more general thesis, it is not possible to provide decisive evidence for the reasons indicated in section 5.1. Nevertheless, their ideas do, I hope, give a flavour of the kind of arguments which have been put forward to account for the evolutionary origins of consciousness and may serve to stimulate your thinking about this issue. Humphrey's thesis, in particular, alerts us to the functional value of consciousness – what it helps us to do. His analysis supports the implication which has run throughout this Block that subjective experience is no mere concomitant of behaviour and the workings of the brain but plays an important role in its own right both in guiding our behaviours and in our relationships with other people. Like other theories presented earlier in this Unit, Humphrey's analysis also raises questions about the methods and approach used by psychology as a discipline. He argues that much of the history of experimental psychology reveals the difficulties that arise from working within an 'inappropriate framework'. Despite the great advantage of being able to carry out controlled experiments and to communicate with each other about their results, experimental psychologists have failed to come up with means for understanding and predicting individual behaviours any more effective (if indeed *as* effective) than the natural psychology which comes with everyday experience. This failure is precisely because they have tended to restrict themselves to objective observations and have deliberately not sought to develop the kind of modelling of their subjects' conscious states and behaviours on *the basis of their own introspective awareness.*

Natural psychology, as we have seen, involves 'constructing a model' of another person's beliefs and feelings on the basis of our own reflexive awareness. It is interesting that Humphrey calls this ability, which he regards as so effective, 'imaginative projection', as it does seem very similar to Romanyshyn's idea of imaginal reconstruction (see section 3.3.5).

If, as Humphrey asserts, reflexive consciousness is the primary source of psychological concepts, then our capacity for empathic modelling, and hence our skills as psychologists, can be increased by extending the range of situations and feelings that we are exposed to. This would imply that an important part of any psychologist's training should be to seek out different forms of human experience either in actuality or vicariously through, for example, fantasy and reading novels and autobiography. This issue will need to be taken up when we look, in the conclusion in Unit 14, at the implications of the Block for the practice of psychology.

PROGRESS BOX 7   The evolution of consciousness

1   *Problems of evidence:* consciousness leaves no solid traces. Theories in this area are inevitably speculative.

2   *Humphrey* – the adaptive function of consciousness:

(i)   It provides the capacity to model underlying feeling states of others and hence increases the capacity for effective social interaction.

(ii)   To increase one's capacity to understand others it is necessary to extend one's conscious experience (either directly or indirectly).

3   *Crook* considers:

(i)   *Property and tool use* led to grammatical structures and naming which encouraged a sense of agency and identity.

(ii)   *Altruism* may have played a role in increasing both the capacity for identity and also discriminating between the identities of self and other individuals.

4   The *implications* of Humphrey's ideas for *psychology*. The value of conscious modelling and 'imaginative projection' for understanding others.

5.2   Historical shifts in personal consciousness?

The human brain and our capacity for intelligence and creativity have probably remained much the same since the late paleolithic period (i.e. over about the last half million-years). Yet there is every reason to suppose that human consciousness has changed for, as Crook has expressed it, 'the history of human consciousness is the history of human social life'.

The only real evidence of human consciousness from the historical past (apart from the very barest glimpse afforded by cave drawings) lies in written documents. These do not go back very far – the earliest ones which can be interpreted with any confidence date only from about 3,000 years ago. In a detailed and fascinating analysis of early literature as well as archaelogical and historical evidence, Jaynes (1979) has put forward a controversial thesis that human consciousness at that time was fundamentally different from what it is today. In particular, he argues that *reflexive awareness* and a conscious sense of *individual agency* have only developed during the last few thousand years – very much later than Crook's analysis would imply.

5.2.1 Early Greeks – a different form of consciousness?

Jaynes illustrates his thesis by reference to the *Iliad* (most of which was probably written between 1,200 and 800 BC, i.e. about 3,000 years ago), analysing both its content and use of language. He argues that what is striking about it is the complete absence of references to mind, thoughts and feelings – anything that hints of consciousness, introspection or a sense of self. Words which in later Greek literature came to serve this purpose are used here in a very different and much more concrete sense. Thus *psyche,* later to mean mind or soul, refers in the *Iliad* to life-substances like breath or blood. 'When a spear strikes the heart of a warrior . . . his *psyche* dissolves, is destroyed, or simply leaves him or is coughed out through the mouth, or bled out through a wound . . .' (for each example Jaynes cites the relevant passages in the *Iliad*). The *thumos,* later to be emotions, here only means activity or agitation. The word *noos* (or *nous*) which was eventually to mean conscious mind seems only to indicate sight. Jaynes points out how difficult it is for us with our subjectivity to appreciate the nature of their experience.

> The characters of the *Iliad* do not sit down and think about what to do. They have no conscious minds such as we say we have, and certainly no introspections. (p.72)

> No one in any way ever sees, decides, thinks, knows, fears or remembers anything in his *psyche.* (p. 271)

In particular, Jaynes stresses the absence of any concept of individual *will.* Actions are not grounded in the conscious plans, reasons and motives of men, they are initiated by the voices and actions of the gods:

> When Agamemnon, king of men, robs Achilles of his mistress, it is a god that grasps Achilles by his yellow hair and warns him not to strike Agamemnon (1:197ff.). It is a god who then rises out of the gray sea and consoles him in his tears of wrath on the beach by his black ships, a god who whispers low to Helen to sweep her heart with homesick longing, a god who hides Paris in a mist in front of the attacking Menelaus, a god who tells Glaucus to take bronze for gold (6:234ff.), a god who leads the armies into battle, who speaks to each soldier at the turning points, who debates and teaches Hector what he must do, who urges the soldiers on or defeats them by casting them in spells or drawing mists over their visual fields. It is the gods who start quarrels among men (4:437ff.) that really cause the war (3:164ff.), and then plan its strategy (2:56ff.). It is one god who makes Achilles promise not to go into battle, another who urges him to go, and another who then clothes him in a golden fire reaching up to heaven and screams through his throat across the bloodied trench at the Trojans, rousing in them ungovernable panic. In fact, the gods take the place of consciousness.

> (Jaynes, 1979, p. 72)

It might be objected that all this represents is a trick of poetic style particularly suited for the oral presentation of the times: that the use of gods was merely a metaphorical device in place of the language we now possess for articulating volitions and feelings. But Jaynes rejects this argument. He points out that the idea of consciousness is totally alien to the nature of the poem. It is about actions, not the inner world of thoughts and feelings. He takes the controversial position that the statements in the poem mean what they say – that the protagonists actually hear the gods' voices which decide their actions and their fate. 'To say the gods are an artistic apparatus is the same kind of thing as to say that Joan of Arc told the Inquisition about her voices merely to make it all vivid to those who were about to condemn her' (p. 79).

bicameral mind

As Greek literature shortly afterwards becomes highly articulate about matters of consciousness, Jaynes sees the *Iliad* standing at a turning point in the history of the mind and as a window back into 'unsubjective times'. He argues that the *Iliad* is a manifestation of an earlier form of mentality which he calls the *bicameral* (literally 'two chambers') mind. It is at times of stress and when consequential decisions are called for that the difference between this and contemporary consciousness becomes apparent. A bicameral mind did not consciously deliberate what to do: the path to take was somehow intuited in the form of hallucinated voices attributed to the gods or perhaps mediated by the pronouncements of priests. On such occasions, decisions and the initiation of actions lay outside of conscious volition in some other part (or 'chamber') of the mind. Action was pursued without the direction of consciousness rather like the automatic driving of an experienced motorist.

If the idea of actually hearing voices of the gods seems a little far-fetched, Jaynes points to the evidence of such hallucinations even today in psychotic patients and in a fair proportion of normal people of good health. (One of the few surveys of this (Sidgewick, 1894) found an incidence of between 8–12 per cent in the normal population. See also the personal world of Leonard described in Window 3 in Unit 12, Part 1.) A factor in the instigation of such hallucinations, Jaynes suggests, could be *stress*, and those people who do experience them may just have a lower threshold than the rest of us. For the bicameral mind the stress involved in exposure to novel situations or conflicting alternatives (as in the dramatic situations reported in myth and story when the voices of the gods were most likely to have been heard) may have been quite sufficient to trigger an auditory hallucination. Hypnotic demonstrations can also provide us with present-day examples which illustrate how the personal initiation of action may be circumvented and replaced by a controlling voice.

5.2.2 Relation to organization of the brain?

Jaynes makes some attempt to link his train of argument with the organization and two hemispheres of the brain. He points out that unlike most other functions, the brain centres primarily involved in the *use* of language are usually (for right-handed people) located in the left hemisphere alone. He marshals a range of evidence consistent with the idea that the reason for this was that the equivalent areas in the right hemisphere were originally utilized for the internalized auditory control of volition he associates with the bicameral mind. For example, direct electrical stimulation of the right hemisphere in conscious patients often produces hallucinated voices (Penfield and Perot, 1963).

ACTIVITY 10

Look at the two faces in Figure 2. Stare at the nose of each. Which is happier?

He also refers to experiments on split brain patients (i.e. where the connections between the two hemispheres have been severed thus giving them 'bicameral' consciousness of the kind that Jaynes is postulating was prevalent in the past). These clearly indicate that the two hemispheres function in rather different ways and seem to possess the capacity for processing information independently of each other (see, for example, Gazzaniga and Le Doux, 1972). The way the right

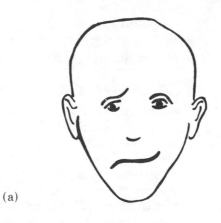

(a)

(b)

These faces are mirror images of each other. Stare at the nose of each. Which face is happier?

Figure 2
Source: from Jaynes, 1979, p. 120

hemisphere operates seems more in line with the 'role of the gods'. There is some indication that it triggers emotional reactions of displeasure from the lower brain. But in particular, it seems especially good at sorting and synthesizing experience. If you found the lower face (b) in Figure 2 to be the happier one you would be consistent with eighty per cent of right-handed people whom Jaynes has tested (and fifty-five per cent of left-handed people). This indicates, he argues, the more dominant role of the right hemisphere (at least, for right-handed people) in recognizing the emotional attributes of other people – quite probably an important basis for gauging responses in bicameral times. (This argument works on the basis that, if face (b) is generally perceived as happier than the upper one, then, because the upward smiling tilt of the mouth is on that side, the left visual field must be dominant in our recognition of emotion. If you bear in mind that the left visual field is represented in the right hemisphere of the brain and vice-versa, then you can see the reasons for assuming the importance of the right hemisphere in this respect.)

Even if we accept Jaynes's report of these results, can you see a flaw in the conclusions he draws from them?

While the results are consistent with Jaynes's thesis, they are open to alternative interpretation. Could they be due, for example, to the fact that we read from left to right, so the left-side information is registered first? (This explanation, though, would not account for why right-handed people show the effect more than left-handed ones do – but there *could* be further factors involved (as, for example, the possibility of a different incidence of reading difficulties between the two groups to account for this.) To test this idea against Jaynes's, we would need to check the finding with people from cultures where they read from right to left.

5.2.3 Further arguments from literature, archeology and history

In this account, I have had space only to indicate the way in which the *Iliad* might be considered to demonstrate the existence of the bicameral mind. Jaynes in fact brings to bear an impressive array of further support consistent with his thesis. For example, he compares Amos, probably the oldest book in the Old Testament, with Ecclesiastes, which has been dated as recently as the second century BC. He argues that they dramatically reveal the 'difference between an almost bicameral man and a subjective conscious man'. As both are fairly short, you might like to compare them for yourself. He makes a similar analysis of what has been deciphered of inscriptions from ancient Egypt and the Middle East. The pervasive and curious Egyptian notion of *ka*, which is often translated as spirit destiny or a double, he interprets as denoting a bicameral voice (an 'articulate directing voice heard inwardly'): it seems to direct action but the individual's attitude towards it seems entirely passive. He notes the tendency in Mesopotamia towards personal gods and intermediaries with whom a more intimate relation was possible, perhaps early versions of the multiple gods and voices of the Greeks (and perhaps also the saints of Christianity).

Jaynes suggests that many archeological findings are best interpreted in terms of a bicameral mind: for example, one reason for placing idols and temples in prominent positions was possibly to serve as a constant reinforcement to internal vocal dictates. Jaynes also applies his analysis to early civilizations in the Americas. Although he considers that the Incas were a culture partly in transition from a bicameral state, he suggests that the meeting with Pizzaro's men must have been one of the few in history where men with subjective consciousness came face-to-face with those of bicameral mind.

5.2.4 Development of the bicameral mind

But why should a bicameral mind have developed in the first place? What was the functional value of this kind of mentality? Jaynes considers that its emergence was probably associated with the gradual move from small tribal groups to large settled townships as a result of the development of agriculture, basic technology and a more settled existence. This brought with it a need for a form of social control which could be maintained without face-to-face contact between leader and led. Jaynes links this idea to what he regards as the final phases in the evolution of language. He points out that language must have only evolved its full complexity gradually over time. Each new phase of its development brought with it cultural changes reflected in the archeological record. One important side-effect which evolved by natural selection, he argues, was its use as a means of behavioural control. Language in the form of an internal 'verbal hallucination' would provide the kind of guidelines essential for an individual to sustain complex sequences of cooperative action. Auditory commands have a particular power because they cannot be easily ignored. (Jaynes points out that in several languages to 'hear' and 'obey' share the same root.) The final step to control by the voices of the gods was the invention of individuals' names. Jaynes suggests that this may only have occurred as recently as 10,000 years ago. But once a tribe member comes to have a particular name he can be recreated in his absence, invoked even if he is dead. Jaynes relates this phase to the emergence of elaborate funeral ceremonies. Auditory hallucinations could be recognized as the voices of ancestors and the gods and in this way they are enabled to play a powerful role in social organization and control.

5.2.5 Origins of subjective consciousness

Jaynes suggests several reasons to account for the gradual transition from a bicameral mentality to subjective consciousness. One was that the societies of bicameral man were too successful. They tended to increase in size so that the hierarchical pattern on which they depended was weakened and the rigid control collapsed, leading to breakdown of the community. He attributes the relatively sudden disappearance of several large cities in the millenium (thousand years) before Christ to this. Trading and travel played their parts also, undermining the monolithic belief and social structures on which the bicameral mentality depended. The introduction of writing, a series of major catastrophies (e.g. like the eruption of Thera – now the Greek island of Santorini – which produced a tidal wave which probably decimated Mediterranean communities) and resulting migration and conflict are also considered by Jaynes to have been factors involved. Given the turbulent nature of the times, subjective consciousness became a more flexible and hence more successful basis on which to survive.

Of course, Jaynes's argument implies that there has been a shift in the way the human brain has functioned during the last 3,000 years. Even if one accepts some role for natural selection for subjectivity, this is a difficult proposition to accept on the basis of Darwinian theory given such a brief span of time. However, Jaynes points out that the brain's most striking features are its plasticity and redundancy and how much of its development seems to take place in childhood and to depend on early experience: 'The function of brain tissue is not inevitable, and . . . perhaps different organizations given different developmental programs may be possible' (p. 125). Certainly Crook agrees that this is a possibility. Commenting on Jaynes's argument that people in 'bicameral times' made much greater use of the right hemisphere (i.e. were less 'lateralized'), he acknowledges that human consciousness has probably developed in stages along with the evolution of society and concludes that: 'It is indeed not implausible that a psyche dependent on intuitive, empathic understanding of others and of nature may have been much less lateralized or at least organized functionally in a different fashion from the cerebral structure guiding analytically verbalized action in modern people' (Crook, 1980, p. 275).

Jaynes demonstrates the distinction between the bicameral mind and subjective consciousness by comparing the *Iliad* with the *Odyssey*. (It should be mentioned that the origins of both poems and the identity of Homer, the author to whom they are attributed, are shrouded in uncertainty. Certainly, a number of commentators go along with Jaynes's assumption that the poems were the work of various contributors and that the *Odyssey* is later by a century or more.) Odysseus, for example, is the 'hero of the new mentality of how to get along in a ruined and god-weakened world . . .' and the *Odyssey*:

> . . . is a journey of deviousness. It is the very discovery of guile, its invention and celebration. It sings of indirections and disguises and subterfuges, transformations and recognitions, drugs and forgetfulness, of people in other people's places, of stories within stories, and men within men.

> The contrast with the Iliad is astonishing. Both in word and deed and character, the Odyssey describes a new and different world inhabited by new and different beings. The bicameral gods of the Iliad, in crossing over to the Odyssey, have become defensive and feeble.

> (Jaynes, 1979, p. 273)

The story of the Odyssey, he claims, is itself a story of identity, a voyage to the self. (A similar dramatization, I would suggest, can be found a few hundred years later in *The Oresteia*, initially performed in 458 BC. In the final play of the trilogy, Orestes is tried for the murder of his mother Clytemnestra. The trial revolves around the issue of responsibility. Can Orestes be held to blame for an action which, all agree, he did at the behest of the god Apollo? This might be regarded as, in some respects, representing the two modes of consciousness in opposition. In the bicameral mode, responsibility rests with the gods. If Apollo incited Orestes to murder, Orestes was not to blame. But if, as the mode of subjective consciousness would imply, a person is responsible and rules his or her own actions, then he was.)

But traces of the shift from the bicameral mind to subjective consciousness, Jaynes asserts, are not only to be found in literature. An increasing concern with making decisions and foretelling the future through divination and augury at that period in human history (100 BC to the time of Christ) is also an index, he suggests, of diminished reliance on the inner voices of the gods.

5.2.6 Our quest for authorization

Jaynes's argument is then that key aspects of present-day consciousness – introspective awareness or *reflexiveness (KF12)*, individual volition or *agency (KF9)*, and self-identity or *sense of self (KF8)* – are of relatively recent origin. But, while he presents an imaginative *tour de force* which is supported by more evidence than I have had space to marshal adequately here, the validity of his argument is not easy to assess. It is certainly open to question. It may be, for example, that the way people are described and references to the voices of the gods in the *Iliad* do merely reflect the poetic style of the time. And, as has been sometimes indicated, the other evidence which Jaynes brings to bear is usually explicable in alternative ways. And what status can we attribute to works like the *Iliad* and the *Odyssey* when we can only guess as their authorship? Why should we regard the former as looking back to bicameral times and the latter as representative of subjective consciousness when there may only have been about 100 years between them? At the most, we can only treat them as exemplars of the two styles of consciousness and not as demonstrative evidence.

But while we may dispute the particulars of Jaynes's argument, this is not to deny the more general thesis that the nature of consciousness may well have changed during the course of history and that 'psychological archeology' is a useful and necessary approach to understanding this.

One way of regarding the difference which Jaynes claims to observe between a bicameral mentality and subjective consciousness is in terms of the metaphors applied in the two cases to make sense of actions and events. It is notable that words like *psyche* (originally 'life substance'), *thumos* (originally 'movement'), etc., later became used in a more metaphorical sense to refer to mind and emotions. So also *noos* is later extended metaphorically from its original meaning of 'sight' to mean 'consciousness'. As discussed earlier in this Unit (section 3.1), our conceptualization of the world (both scientific and everyday) develops in this way by creating new concepts by means of metaphor. At the time of the *Iliad*, 'voices of the gods' was perhaps the only metaphor available to conceptualize the initiation of action. Today we have a broad range of concepts for introspective and volitional states developed over time by coining new metaphors. This is not to deny the subjective reality of either mentality. For, as argued earlier, the metaphors and concepts we employ condition the reality we experience. Metaphors are not only a way of representing experience, they are also capable of transforming it. This idea does alert us to the role of language and the range of metaphors it embraces in constituting the form which consciousness will take.

Jaynes's thesis does also have particular value in *provoking thought about the nature of contemporary consciousness*. The shift from bicameral to subjective consciousness may be reflected in the changing nature of our institutions – in Christianity, for example, in the movement away from reliance on the political authority of the church towards the individual authority of experience. Nevertheless, Jaynes argues, vestiges of the bicameral mentality remain with us today. Not only is it manifested under special conditions like hypnosis, possession or schizophrenia, but its residues permeate the fabric of everyday life:

> We have our houses of gods which record our births, define us, marry us, and bury us, receive our confessions and intercede with the gods to forgive us our trespasses. Our laws are based upon values which without their divine pendancy would be empty and unenforceable. Our national mottoes and hymns of state are usually divine invocations. Our kings, presidents,

judges, and officers begin their tenures with oaths to the now silent deities taken upon the writings of those who have last heard them.

(Jaynes, 1979, p. 317)

We still go in for idolatry, with a predilection for statues both secular to dead leaders and sacred to dead saints. The oscillation between bicameral and subjective mentalities shows itself in times of crisis. For many British and Argentinians the Falklands/Malvinas conflict of 1982 was quite sufficient to elicit a responsiveness to invocations of national honour which was able to overcome subjective awareness of what the tragic consequences must inevitably be. Bicamerality is authoritarian and absolute. Unlike subjectivity and rationality, it is uncomfortable with compromise. As Jaynes puts it: 'Even today, our ideas of nobility are largely residues of bicameral authority: it is not noble to whine, it is not noble to plead, it is not noble to beg, even though these postures are really the most moral of ways to settle differences' (ibid., p. 207). It was this inflexibility which resulted in the instability of bicameral regimes. No gradation of attitude was possible. Other societies were either friend or foe.

The need for the guidance of a divine voice is manifested today too in the popularity of astrology, fortune-telling and the search for gurus (and psychology!) to tell us the way. The growth of science is perhaps the clearest institutional expression of the shift from the bicameral mind. But, even here, 'for all its pomp of factness' science too can easily spawn its scientisms with their authoritarian assertion of infallible guidance towards the truth. At its heart, Jaynes claims, science like religion is a search for direction and understanding:

> The very notion of truth is a culturally given direction, a part of the pervasive nostalgia for an earlier certainty. The very idea of a universal stability, an eternal firmness of principle *out there* that can be sought for through the world as might an Arthurian knight for the Grail, is, in the morphology of history, a direct outgrowth of the search for lost gods in the first two millennia after the decline of the bicameral mind. What was then an augury for direction of action among the ruins of an archaic mentality is now the search for an innocence of certainty among the mythologies of facts.

(ibid., p. 446)

need for authorization Underlying much of contemporary life then is a quest for an authorization which we have lost. As we saw in Unit 12 (section 3.3), Erich Fromm, in different words, has put forward a similar position – that we seek escape from the freedom and uncertainty generated by the process of existence in the pseudo-certainties of ideologies, religion and conformity. We are reluctant to take the tiller in our own hands. Jaynes puts it this way:

> With consciousness we have given up those simpler more absolute methods of control of behaviour which characterized the bicameral mind. We live in a buzzing cloud of whys and wherefores, . . . And this constant spinning out of possibilities is precisely what is necessary to save us from behaviour of too impulsive a sort. [We] are always resting at the confluence of many collective cognitive imperatives. We know too much to command ourselves very far.

> Those who through what theologians call the 'gift of faith' can center and surround their lives in religious belief do indeed have different collective cognitive imperatives. They can indeed change themselves through prayer and its expectancies much as in post-hypnotic suggestion. It is a fact that belief, political or religious, or simply belief in oneself through some earlier cognitive imperative, works in wondrous ways. Anyone who has experienced the sufferings of prisons or detention camps knows that both mental and physical survival is often held carefully in such untouchable hands.

> But for the rest of us, who must scuttle along on conscious models and

skeptical ethics, we have to accept our lessened control. We are learned in self-doubt, scholars of our very failures, geniuses at excuse and tomorrowing our resolves. And so we become practiced in powerless resolution until hope gets undone and dies in the unattempted. At least that happens to some of us. And then to rise above this noise of knowings and really change ourselves, we need an authorization that 'we' do not have.

(ibid., pp. 402–3)

In these last two quotations, Jaynes is pointing to two fundamental issues for human beings of today. Firstly, we still demand 'the innocence of certainty' when, in subjective consciousness, no absolute, unchanging truths exist – only metaphorical realities of reflection, the 'mythologies of facts'. Secondly, we still crave guidance in the use of our new-found autonomy. For those contemporary people who, like most in our secular society, have no deep-rooted faith, the problem becomes what 'authorization' can they find for what they do. What definite guidance is there for the formidable task of creating their own lives? These vexed and paradoxical issues which we touched on in the previous unit are central problems for contemporary consciousness and ones to which we will return again in the conclusion to this Block.

PROGRESS BOX 8   Historical shifts in consciousness?

1   Jaynes's speculations about the *bicameral mind* (where volition is not subjective and individual but is exerted through the 'voices of the gods') and the *recent* emergence of *subjective consciousness* in the last 3,000 years.

2   *Evidence* for ideas:

(i)   *Literary comparisons:* e.g. *Iliad* vs. *Odyssey*; Amos vs. Ecclesiastes.

(ii)   *Archeological*: rise of elaborate funeral rites, forms of idols and position of temples, personal gods of Mesopotamia, Egyptian *ka*.

(iii)   *Organization of the brain*: evidence that the two hemispheres of the brain function differently.

3   Possible functional reasons for the *emergence of the bicameral mind* – it provides a means of social control in larger-scale societies.

4   Possible reasons for the *failure of the bicameral mind* and the *shift to subjective consciousness*. Bicameral consciousness undermined by:

– increase in size of societies

– increase in trade and travel

– development of writing

– migration and conflict as a result of natural catastrophies.

Subjective consciousness more adaptive in these changed conditions. But a problem for this explanation is that it assumes very rapid change in mental and, presumably, brain organization.

5   Question of *validity* of Jaynes's analysis – is he reading too much into what may be merely differences of expressive style?

6   A possible explanation of the development of subjective consciousness is as a result of the increased ability to conceptualize introspective states because of new and extended uses of *metaphor*.

7   *Value* of Jaynes's analysis is in alerting us to the problems of the vestigial *need for authorization*: for certainty and guidance in an uncertain world.

5.3 Society and subjective experience

When we contrast the accounts of different personal worlds presented in Part 1 of Unit 12 we can see how radical an influence social context has. It brings with it different physical environments – factory bench, hospital ward or a hotel room with flowers. It can determine whether life is a struggle for survival in a hostile world or a safe environment where the only need is to assuage boredom. We see also how powerfully it can constrain the kinds of behaviour and interactions we engage in. Contrast what Christopher the gardener does with his day and whom he meets, with, for example, her Ladyship (his employer) or Liv Ullman. Social context and the particular form of language which comes with it provide the metaphors which are reflected in our daily experience as well as the images which fuel our fantasy and goals. Society clearly influences the *contents* of subjective experience, the dominant metaphors we draw on and the ways we frame and key our experience. Does it affect our style of consciousness (i.e. the *way* we experience the world) as well? And, if, as has been suggested in the preceding section, modifications in consciousness have been brought about as a result of historical and social changes, in what ways might the circumstances of contemporary society condition the consciousness of persons in our *present* world?

One of the most assiduous explorers of this issue has been Peter Berger. In one study with his colleagues (Brigitte Berger and Hansfried Kellner) called *The Homeless Mind* (1974), he embarks on an analysis of the effects of modern life upon our consciousness. They single out three influences for particular attention – *technological production*, *bureaucratization* and the *pluralization of life-worlds*.

technological consciousness

5.3.1 Technological consciousness

Work, they argue, does not just demand a particular set of skills but it involves an attitude to the world, a particular way of organizing experience:

1 The fundamental feature of work in a technological society is its *mechanistic* character. What the worker does is tied into the operation of equipment.

2 A correlation of this is *reproducibility*. Any part of this process is standardized and in principle can be done by anyone else. There is nothing unique about it.

3 It also requires *participation in an organization* with many others (even though they may not actually be present).

4 Very possibly what the worker does is but one stage in a *sequence of production*.

5 His labours will be *measured* in terms of precise, often quantifiable criteria like amount produced and time taken to do it.

Work of this nature is clearly a relatively recent arrival in human society. It is very different, for example, from that of the hunter, farmer or even craftsman. Berger *et al.* argue that this pattern generates a 'cognitive style' of its own based on the logic of the machine process. It is not that this itself is necessarily directly apparent in the consciousness of modern workers but, if we can add to this argument by taking up again the notion of metaphorical consciousness, it serves as a set of metaphors to influence the ways in which they experience their world.

componentiality

One aspect of this cognitive style, for example, is *componentiality*. As the metaphor of the machine comes to dominate our underlying assumptions about the way things are, so the world is taken as being made up of definable, relatively self-contained and potentially interchangeable units rather than as an ongoing flux of unique experiences. There is a *separability of means from ends* (as in the factory where the same unit an operative is working on may be for a missile or a motorcar). It also leads to a quality of *implicit abstraction*: in other words, any experience or action is regarded from a specific and functional frame of reference

separability of means from ends
implicit abstraction

only, rather than as an experience in its own right. Thus, in a factory, aesthetic contemplation of the beauty of a gearbox is unlikely to be encouraged. (Some firms have tried to alleviate the more inhuman aspects of technological production. Volvo, for example, has encouraged working in teams rather than on the assembly line. But, in terms of the argument of Berger *et al.*, such practices could produce only cosmetic change. For they regard the features which they isolate as *intrinsic* to technological production. They will apply in whatever context or society that mode of production is found.)

Although such a cognitive style may be generated by working in a technological setting, Berger *et al.*, point out that it sets a general style of framing reality which will carry over to other aspects of the workers' world. Indeed, it will also underlie the way other members of modern society experience their worlds, even though they may not be directly involved in work of a technological kind. One consequence, Berger *et al.* suggest, is the tendency to *segregate* different areas of involvement, for example work from private life. Another is a shift to *anonymity in social relations,* with people coming to be regarded not so much as individuals but in terms of their work role. This may be accompanied by feelings of alienation because so much of a worker's sense of self is left outside the work process. Although there may be times when larking and joking are allowed, functional efficiency demands that emotions be 'managed' in the work situation. The operative has to control himself and accept both physical and temporal restraints. Such *emotional management* may be carried over into the private sphere. Feelings are kept under firm control and sexual and other relationships are characterized by coolness and restraint in emotional expression. There may be a carry-over too of the need to *measure* and *maximize* production: leisure activities being assessed by product or performance, sexual experience coming to be valued in terms of frequency and strength of orgasms. When problems arise in personal life, they may well be approached in the fashion of repairing a machine. There is a search for the right technology, the right procedure, the right replacement parts. The psychiatrist is regarded as just another specialist who should be able to solve the problem, to deliver the goods. Difficulties arise, however, in attempting such a transfer. Existential issues, for example, do not admit of pre-set solutions but demand an individual response. As has been argued in this Block, psychological life does not function like a machine. Psychology does not and cannot provide an analogous repair technology, and such expectations of psychotherapy are sadly misplaced.

segregation of life areas

anonymity in social relations

emotional management

measurement and maximization

BRING A REPLACEMENT!

primary and secondary carriers

While the technological production process is seen by Berger *et al.* as the *primary carrier* of such a constellation of consciousness, *secondary carriers* such as education and the media also play their part.

ACTIVITY 11

Spend a few minutes considering how far the aspects of the cognitive style of technological production apply to your experience of Open University studies. Does it involve separation into self-contained components, separation of means from ends, measurability, emotional management, etc.?

---

bureaucratic consciousness

5.3.2 Bureaucratic consciousness

Large-scale technological production almost invariably spawns bureaucratic agencies of administration. *Bureaucracy*, Berger *et al.* assert, carries a particular constellation of consciousness, in some ways related to technological consciousness but having special features of its own. It assumes that there are proper procedures and channels for dealing with any issue, and that people in an organization have defined and restricted spheres of competence. While it permits a degree of predictability, it also offers scope for considerable arbitrariness as to what procedures and requirements will be established. Unlike technological production, means are not separated from ends. Indeed the means may become an end in itself, and it has not been unknown for a bureaucracy to be devoted almost entirely to maintaining itself. Bureaucracy relates to people in terms of the roles they play or certain criteria which characterize them, like age and income, rather than as individuals. Such anonymity is not an unfortunate by-product of the bureaucratic process but is asserted as a moral principle. There is the general expectation of justice for all – that you will receive according to what is rightly due to you not because of the quality of your smile. But while such anonymity may be intended as a defence against corruption, it can have a depersonalizing effect on clients. They too easily become anonymous and passive recipients – people who are done to rather than who do for themselves.

The cognitive style which bureaucracy breeds is one of orderliness and organization. There is assumed to be a place and a pigeon-hole for everything. The solutions of both domestic and political problems are approached by trying to find the right procedure and the right agency.

5.3.3 Multiple life-worlds

The third major characteristic of modern society which Berger *et al.* focus on as having consequences for consciousness seems related to *multiplicity (KF11)*. It is what they call the *pluralization of life-worlds*. They argue that in traditional societies life had a cohesion. Institutions and activities were interrelated and fitted within a shared belief system. Contemporary life, in contrast, usually involves participating in several settings, each with their own pattern of activities and values. As Taylor has expressed it:

pluralization of life-worlds

> Within 'modern' societies we find by contrast separate institutional spheres which have developed their own ideologies, their own legitimations. The 'laws' of work and leisure and home are not now integrated, they are not aspects of the same belief system but have acquired an autonomy of their own. Work, leisure, private life, have become structurally separated; they occur in special places and at special times, and are attended to with different modes of consciousness, different expectations about their potentiality for self-fulfillment and self-realization. And we try to keep them structurally and experientially apart. We try not to 'take our work home', we expect to feel different when we are at work, at home, or on holiday. None of the life-worlds in themselves gives us the meaning of life. The office desk, the golf-club and the factory floor remain relatively

unrelated. They coexist but are not integrated. The beliefs that seem satisfactory at work, seem irrelevant at home, that which we regard as valuable at the golf-club becomes insignificant on the production line. Few people now experience religion as a cohesive force – an overarching vocabulary of symbols – which can correct this sense of living in different worlds.

For many of us, religion has now become one more life-world, a segmented aspect of existence:

> It occurs at certain times, on certain days, and in certain places. Religious programmes line up alongside programmes on hobbies, holidays, sport and politics. They are expected to keep within boundaries and those who periodically strike religious attitudes are called upon to recognize the distinction between such postures and those which are appropriate to their involvement in other life-worlds. (Cohen and Taylor, 1976, p. 217)

(The Open University, 1976, p. 28)

In public life, one way this pluralization manifests itself is in the multiplicity of different occupations. But even in private life there are many different possible spheres in both leisure activities and relationships. One effect on consciousness of such pluralization, Berger *et al.* suggest, is a sense of openness to alternative and potentially available possibilities. This sense of freedom is likely to be accompanied by anxiety about ensuring opportunities are not missed and quite probably also feelings of regret, frustration and confusion when desired options cannot be attained. Most people are also confronted with the need to plan and synchronize their activities and relationships – they need to construct some form **life plan** of life plan. Berger *et al.* regard the life trajectory as a major source of personal identity. One consequence of the need for such planning is that meaning often tends to be derived from future possibilities and hopes – when I pass my exams, get the right job, find the right partner, etc.

If the positive side of pluralization is the sense of autonomy and freedom it promises, its negative face is the rootlessness, anomie and distancing from immediate awareness which it can bring in its wake. A problem with living in many worlds is that we belong in none. The nomadic mind is a homeless one.

One further aspect of pluralization is the question of what effects different **occupational** spheres of life, e.g. occupations, may have on the consciousness of those who **consciousness** engage in these, over and above the general effects of living in modern society. Bensman and Lilienfeld (1975), for example, have looked at journalism to determine the particular cognitive style which it demands and how this might carry over into other areas of journalists' lives. They see the journalist's work as dominated by time, deadlines and the knowledge that yesterday's news is no news. He or she is required to select from events in terms of their newsworthiness or human interest value, and to transform experience by simplifying it, making it more dramatic and concrete, and, by rounding off the edges and closing gaps, to make it a coherent tale. Bensman and Lilienfeld suggest that journalists and their readers can easily come, over time, to see the world in overly dramatic and simplistic terms. Complexity may be disregarded and issues come to be seen in definitive tones of black and white. Any attempt to present a more subtle and many-sided picture may be considered as a deliberate and unnecessary attempt to be obscure.

ACTIVITY 12

How would you define *your* occupation in terms of the activities, relationships and cognitive style it involves? Think about what carry-over effects it may have on the way you experience and relate to your world in general.

5.3.4 Comment

This analysis by Peter Berger and his colleagues of modern consciousness and its influences is both general and speculative. Many details remain to be filled in. The authors make little attempt, for example, to explain *how* the cognitive style of technological production is carried over to people who do not themselves participate in such work. (Their ideas could be usefully supplemented, here, perhaps, by an analysis of the effects of the media and advertising.) Also, although technological and bureaucratic styles may predominate, what about alternative forms of consciousness? Given the varied subcultures in our society and the many life-worlds in which we live, could we not presume that, like occupations, these would also generate their own ways of framing experience? The analysis by Berger *et al.* does not really deal with this, nor does it make clear the limits of the technological and bureaucratic effects.

Finally, we might well wonder if it is not possible to bring to bear some evidence in support of the propositions they assert or to put some of them to some kind of empirical test.

ACTIVITY 13

Think for a few moments about why it is not easy to find a way of testing the ideas which Berger *et al.* put forward. Can you suggest a way of testing any one of their propositions?

The aim of this section has been to alert you to the idea that much of what we take for granted, of what we experience as 'reality', as the way things are, may rest to a considerable extent on the particular mode of socioeconomic organization which happens to characterize the society in which we live. It has also given us further insights into two at least of our key features of personal worlds. The quality of *multiplicity (KF11)*, the many ways in which it is possible to look at any personal world, may be, in part at least, a function of the fragmentation of the many life-worlds in which a modern person lives, each of which may be capable of generating its own perspective. Berger *et al.* indicate possible consequences of such multiplicity – a sense of freedom counterbalanced by anxiety and concern that desired options should be attained. They also suggest how a life plan – the future envisaged and aspired to – may represent an important aspect of a person's *sense of identity (KF8)*.

Although, as pointed out above, the analysis presented by Berger *et al.* is speculative, it would not seem to be entirely untestable. Did you manage to make any suggestions for putting their ideas to the test in Activity 13? As one possibility, it might be assumed that, although technological and bureaucratic consciousness pervade our society as a whole, they might have a special impact on those involved respectively in technological production and bureaucratic administration. Might we not expect then that civil servants as a group would possess a different cognitive style from, say, engineers and factory workers? An intriguing possibility perhaps, though not an easy project to design, nor one that, to my knowledge, has yet been tried.

ACTIVITY 14

Before reading on, look back at the list of features which Berger *et al.* suggest as characterizing technological society and its cognitive style. Are there any ways in which you can see them reflected in what you know of academic psychology?

To conclude this discussion of Berger *et al.*'s work, I would just like to raise the question as to how far the modern style of consciousness which they propose operates, not only in our experience of everyday realities but in scientific theorizing. It was pointed out earlier how metaphors and approaches in psychology are often assimilated from the dominant images of the day. In an interesting critique of positivist experimental psychology from a radical perspective, Heather (1976) has argued that the former both reflects and serves to maintain a technological society. Apart from its more obvious usefulness in areas like market research, Heather suggests that it does this most powerfully and in a more subtle way by influencing our conception of what a person is. In this respect it has what Ingleby (1972) has called a 'mythic' function in that people come to accept that they are what psychology represents them as. As we discussed earlier, the model of the mind which experimental psychology has been prone to present is, at least in Romanyshyn's view, essentially a 'physicalistic' one. Thus, persons tend easily to be reified (thought of as things):

> ... a reifying model of human nature, by definition, presents men as less than they really are (or could be): to the extent that a society requires men (or a certain proportion of them) to be thing-like in their work, orientation, thinking and experiencing, such a model will constitute both a reflection and a reinforcement of that society (reinforcing because men tend to become what they are told they *are*). If labour is mechanical, it is convenient that those who have to do it should think of themselves as a species of machine: if freedom of choice, imagination, the pursuit of untried goals and experiences are seen as threats to a sacrosanct 'social structure', then man should learn that he is a species of simple computer, a 'limited capacity information channel', incapable by definition of creating such goals and such meanings.

(Ingleby in Heather, 1976, p. 46)

Heather also discusses what he calls psychology's worship of normality. In other words, it takes present forms of society and human behaviour as the only possible ones. It is concerned with the way people *are*, rather than with the way they *could* be. It can thus have the effect of discouraging us from exploring our potentials. Yet another ideological reflection is experimental psychology's tendency to see people as isolated units and to fail to acknowledge the powerful influence of the social and economic contexts in which they live. (For a more general discussion of the way different approaches in psychology – including the phenomenological and humanistic views presented in this Block – are products of the cultural and scientific backgrounds in which they originated, see Metablock Paper 7).

Activity 14 asked if you could detect in academic psychology features which Berger *et al.* see as characteristic of technological society and its cognitive style. You might have suggested *componentiality* (breaking down subject-matter into component research areas like attitudes, person perception, developmental psychology, etc., which exist relatively independently of each other); *participation with others* (the notion of contributions from different research workers building up knowledge like bricks in a wall); *reproducibility* (the idea that psychological processes can be abstracted and described in general terms, and that the same process will apply to all other humans, even to other species).

One final word before leaving this discussion of the social construction of reality: I do not want to leave the impression that technological consciousness is necessarily a defective one. How it is related to the quality of life is a complex issue which is beyond the scope of the Block to pursue in any detail (though we will touch on it in Unit 14), but clearly technology has been highly successful in ensuring human material welfare at least. And, as we noted earlier, although the anonymity of bureaucracy may serve to intensify the alienation experienced by members of society, it also has the goal (and often the effect) of ensuring justice for all, regardless of who a person is.

PROGRESS BOX 9   Society and subjective experience

1 *Social context influences consciousness* through:

(i)   The physical environments it creates.

(ii)   The constraints it imposes on behaviour and experience.

(iii)   The metaphors and images it offers in language and culture.

2   The analysis by Berger *et al.* of the impact of contemporary society on consciousness:

(i)   *Technological consciousness.* Technological production is characterized by its mechanistic character involving reproducibility, participation in an organization, sequence of production, and measurement.

(ii)   This generates a cognitive style involving separation of means from ends, implicit abstraction, segregation of life-worlds, anonymity in social relations, emotional management, measurement and maximization. Technological work is the primary 'carrier' and education and the media are secondary 'carriers' of such a style of consciousness.

(iii)   *Bureaucratic consciousness*
– orderliness and organization
– proper procedures, spheres of competence, predictable yet arbitrary, no end product, anonymity.

(iv)   *Pluralization of life-worlds* and its effects.
– the life plan as source of identity.

(v)   *Other aspects*
– occupational consciousness, possible effects on scientific theorizing, and education.

PROGRESS BOX 10   Subjective experience from evolutionary, historical and cultural perspectives

General objectives. After reading Section 5 of this unit, you should be able to discuss the conditions under which consciousness has developed, and, in particular, to assess critically:

1   The problems of studying the evolution of consciousness.

2   Humphrey's theory of the biological function of consciousness.

3   Crook's ideas about the possible origins of our senses of agency and self.

4   Jaynes's thesis on the nature and rise of the bicameral mind and the evolution of modern consciousness, and the evidence on which this rests.

5   Ways in which the social context might be presumed to influence consciousness, including the particular significance of technological production, bureaucracy, pluralization of life-worlds and occupation. Also the relevance of social context to theorizing in psychology.

6   The values and limitations of the three kinds of analysis presented and their implications for our understanding of subjective experience.

EPILOGUE

The perspectives on subjective experience which we have considered in this unit have been varied and wide-ranging. Most of them, as might be expected, represent a phenomenological approach in that they have been concerned with analysing the nature of individual experience: these include Jaynes's and Romanyshyn's notion that consciousness is constituted like metaphor, Kelly's personal construct theory, the analysis which was made of fantasy, and William James's idea of consciousness (although the latter was referred to only briefly).

Two other theories looked at (Goffman's frame analysis and, in particular, Berger *et al.*'s theory of the social construction of contemporary consciousness), while being concerned with the way individuals make sense of their world, make a point also of linking this to the nature of society.

The remaining perspectives discussed (e.g. the evolutionary perspective of Humphrey and Crook and the attempt at a historical analysis of consciousness by Jaynes) have been further removed from direct analysis of subjective experience and have tended rather to analyse the conditions which help to make it what it is. It might be appropriate to include psychoanalytic theories about unconscious meaning in this category also for, although they try to make sense of how people see themselves, other people and the world around, they tend to interpret this in terms of how it has been conditioned by factors outside the conscious awareness of the persons concerned.

Why has such a range of perspectives been drawn on in this unit? The ideas about subjective experience which we have looked at, like any other theories, are constructions which look at their subject-matter from different angles and in different ways (see Metablock Paper 7). The ones presented were chosen because they covered different facets of the complexity of human experience and can therefore be regarded as complementary rather than contradictory. Taken together, they form a rounded and differentiated picture of the nature of consciousness.

Another reason for including a range of perspectives is that they can also serve to deepen and enrich each other. Thus, as noted earlier, the idea of consciousness as metaphor can be usefully applied to other types of analysis. Both personal constructs and unconscious meanings can be viewed, for example, as metaphors which serve both to represent and transform experience; and enhancing fantasies and energizing myths can be regarded as sequences of sustained metaphor which give new meaning to activities in which one is engaged.

Optional reading

Chapter 1 of the Set Book *Freud and Psychoanalysis* deals with the issue of the fundamentals (biological, social and individual-developmental) on which human experience rests, and the need to look at a person's behaviour and experience as an integration of these aspects. For this reason, you may find it worth looking at in the context of thinking about how the different perspectives on subjective experience presented in this unit interrelate. (Note, however, that this chapter does not deal specifically with consciousness. For that reason it is suggested here as optional rather than set reading.)

This unit has looked at several rather different ideas about the nature of subjective experience with the intention of stimulating your awareness and thinking about what it involves, how it might be conceptualized, its origins and the influences which shape it. But how can the ideas presented here be evaluated? In many cases they represent (as, for example, the idea of consciousness as metaphor) ways of conceptualizing subjective experience. The emphasis is on phenomenological analysis and on differentiation and it is not really appropriate or even possible here to bring empirical evidence effectively to bear (see Metablock Paper 10). But the analyses can be evaluated in terms of (1) their effectiveness and consistency in making sense of the subject-matter in question and (2) how far they match up with, help differentiate and provide insights into the nature of your own experience. Does the discussion of fantasy, for example, help you to become more aware of the place played by imagination in your own personal experience? The problem of effective validation of theories in this area is not to be underestimated. Because of the elusive nature of the subject-matter, the conceptualizations offered and the arguments by appeal to experience or rational inference are often themselves difficult to pin down. Nevertheless, I hope that you have found it a worthwhile topic to explore, that the analyses at least help you to differentiate more clearly the nature of subjective experience, and that they draw attention to some of the problems of existence for people in modern society.

In addition to methodological issues, a number of questions have been raised about the implications which these perspectives have for the way we live our lives. For example, it has been suggested that theories about human nature are often self-fulfilling; that there may well be different forms of consciousness; that it may be possible to encourage ourselves to make more use of particular kinds of constructs, metaphors or energizing myths. Such implications revolve round psycho-ethics: i.e. can some kinds of subjective experience be deemed as more desirable than others and on what grounds? Such ethical and practical implications, as well as the methodological issues noted above, will be looked at in relation to the Block as a whole in Part 2 of the next unit.

References

BATESON, G. (1972) 'A theory of play and phantasy', in *Steps to an Ecology of Mind*, New York, Ballantine Books.

BENSMAN, J. and LILIENFELD, R. (1975) 'The journalist', in Brown, H. and Stevens, R. (eds) *Social Behaviour and Experience: Multiple Perspectives*, Sevenoaks, Hodder and Stoughton.

BERGER, P. L., BERGER, B. and KELLNER, H. (1974) *The Homeless Mind*, Harmondsworth, Penguin Books.

CAMPBELL, J. (1964) *The Masks of God: Occidental Mythology*, New York, Viking Press.

CAMPBELL, J. (1973) *Myths to Live By*, New York, Bantam Books.

COHEN, S. and TAYLOR, L. (1976) *Escape Attempts: The Theory and Practice of Resistance to Everyday Life*, London, Allen Lane.

CONNOLLY, R. (1982) 'Sleeping partners', in *Observer Magazine*, February.

CROOK, J. H. (1980) *The Evolution of Human Consciousness*, Oxford, Oxford University Press.

ELIOT, T. S. (1974) *Collected Poems, 1909–1962*, London, Faber.

EMERSON, J. P. (1970) 'Nothing unusual is happening', in Shibutani, T. (ed.) *Human Nature and Collective Behaviour: Papers in Honor of Herbert Blumer*, Englewood Cliffs, New Jersey, Prentice-Hall.

ERIKSON, E. (1950) *Childhood and Society*, New York, Norton. (Reprinted in paperback (1977) by Triad/Paladin.)

FERNANDEZ, J. E. W. (1972) 'Persuasions and performances: of the beast in every body . . . and the metaphors of everyman', *Daedalus*, Winter.

FRIDAY, N. (1976) *My Secret Garden*, London, Virago.

GAZZANIGA, M. S. and LE DOUX, J. E. (1972) *The integrated mind*, New York, Plenum Press.

GOFFMAN, E. (1975) *Frame Analysis*, Harmondsworth, Penguin Books.

HARITON, E. B. and SINGER, J. L. (1974) 'Women's fantasies during sexual intercourse: normative and theoretical implications', *Journal of Consulting and Clinical Psychology*, Vol. 42, No. 3, pp. 313–22.

HAMILTON, W. D. (1972) 'Altruism and related phenomena; mainly in social insects', *Annual Review of Ecological Systems*, Vol. 3, pp. 193–232.

HEATHER, N. (1976) *Radical Perspectives in Psychology*, London, Methuen.

HUMPHREY, N. (1983) *Consciousness Regained*, Oxford, Oxford University Press.

INGLEBY, D. (1972) 'Ideology and the human sciences', in Pateman, T. (ed.) *Counter Course*, Harmondsworth, Penguin.

JAMES, W. (1950) *The Principles of Psychology*, Vol. 1, New York, Dover.

JAYNES, J. (1979) *The Origin of Consciousness in the Breakdown of the Bicameral Mind*, London, Allen Lane.

JUNG, C. J. (1968) *The Archetypes and the Collective Unconscious* (2nd edn), in *Collected Works*, Vol. 9, Part I, London, Routledge and Kegan Paul.

KELLY, G. A. (1955) *The Psychology of Personal Constructs*, New York, Norton.

KELLY, G. A. (1970) 'A brief introduction to personal construct theory', in Bannister, D. (ed.) *Perspectives in Personal Construct Theory*, London, Academic Press.

LAKOFF, G. and JOHNSON, M. (1980) *Metaphors We Live By*, Chicago, University of Chicago Press.

MACLEISH, A. (1952) 'Hypocrite Auteur', in *Collected Poems 1917–1962*, Boston, Houghton Mifflin.

MILGRAM, S. (1974) *Obedience to Authority*, London, Tavistock.

MURPHY, J., JOHN, M. and BROWN, H. (eds) (1984) *Dialogues and Debates in Social Psychology*, London, Erlbaum/The Open University (Course Reader).

OKAKURA, K. (1964) *The Book of Tea* (ed. by E. F. Bleiler), New York, Dover.

PENFIELD, W. and PEROT, T. (1963) 'The brain's record of auditory and visual experience: a final summary and discussion', *Brain*, Vol. 86, pp. 595–702.

PRATHER, H. (1970) *Notes to Myself*, Moab, Utah, Real People Press.

PRIBRAM, K. H. (1981) 'Behaviourism, phenomenology, and holism in psychology', in Valle, R. S. and von Eckartsberg, R. (eds) *The Metaphors of Consciousness*, New York, Plenum Press.

ROMANYSHYN, R. D. (1981) 'Science and reality', in Valle, R. S. and von Eckartsberg, R. (eds) *The Metaphors of Consciousness*, New York, Plenum Press.

ROMANYSHYN, R. D. (1982) *Psychological Life: From Science to Metaphor*, Milton Keynes, The Open University Press.

SCHUTZ, A. (1962) 'On multiple realities', in *Collected Papers*, The Hague, Martinus Nijhoff.

SIDGEWICK, H. *et al.* (1894) 'Report on the census of hallucinations', *Proceedings of the Society for Psychical Research*, Vol. 34, pp. 25–394.

SINGER, J. L. (1981) *Daydreaming and Fantasy*, Oxford, Oxford University Press.

STEVENS, R. (1983) *Freud and Psychoanalysis*, Milton Keynes, The Open University Press (Set Book).

THE OPEN UNIVERSITY (1976) D305 *Social Psychology*, Block 9, *Man's Experience of the World*, Milton Keynes, The Open University Press.

TOMKINS, S. (1963) *Affect – Imagery, Consciousness*, Vol. 2, New York, Springer.

TRIVERS, R. L. (1971) 'The evolution of reciprocal altruism', *Quarterly Review of Biology,* Vol. 46, pp. 35–57.

YEATS, W. B. (1961) *Essays and Introductions,* New York, Macmillan.

Acknowledgements

Grateful acknowledgement is made to the following sources for material used in this unit:

J. Jaynes, *The Origin of Consciousness in the Breakdown of the Bicameral Mind*, Houghton Mifflin, 1976, reprinted by permission of the author; R. D. Romanyshyn, *Psychological Life: From Science to Metaphor*, Open University Press, 1982.

Illustrations
p. *93* from M. Calman, *How About a Little Quarrel Before Bed?*, Methuen, London; p. *126* from Evans and Irons, *The Joke Works*, Larkham Printers and Publishers, 1981 (originally in *Socialist Worker* 28 June, 1975).

Index of concepts

UNIT 14
DEVELOPMENT AND CHANGE IN PERSONAL LIFE

Prepared for the course team by Richard Stevens

CONTENTS

Study guide

Unit 14 is in two distinct parts:
Part 1: The Life Cycle is concerned with the changing nature of personal worlds as we progress through life.
Part 2: Making Sense of and Managing Our Lives serves as a conclusion to the Block. It reviews the ideas which have been covered and discusses the methodological and theoretical problems which they raise, and what practical implications they might have for the way we live our lives.

Associated reading

In Part 1 you are referred to the brief section on Erikson in Chapter 8 of the Set Book *Freud and Psychoanalysis* (pp. 76–8). The set reading for Part 2 is Chapter 14 'Explorations in awareness' (pp. 143–9) from *Freud and Psychoanalysis*. It is suggested that you might also like to read the paper by Sarason in the Course Reader (optional).

PART 1: THE LIFE CYCLE

Objectives

By the time you have completed Part 1 of Unit 14, you should be able to:

1 Discuss the way personal worlds develop and change through life.

2 Give a critical account of Erikson's theory of ego development (the 'Eight ages of man') and show what he means by 'epigenesis' and 'crisis' and how his theory is both dialectical and psychosocial.

3 Give a critical account of the research by Levinson *et al.* into the 'seasons of a man's life', including the main phases and concepts which they postulate.

4 Provide a critique and comparison of phase theories in general (making reference to the work of Gould, Bühler, etc., as well as that of Erikson and Levinson *et al.*), discussing the assumptions on which they are based and showing the limitations as well as the value of this kind of analysis.

5 Consider possible sex and cultural differences in the pattern of adult development.

6 Discuss the notion of life contours.

7 Discuss the role of crisis in personal development.

8 Evaluate the arguments and evidence for a mid-life transition.

9 Describe Jung's theory of individuation.

10 Discuss the changing pattern of existential needs through the course of life.

1 INTRODUCTION

In the preceding units, we have seen how *time* is a fundamental feature of personal worlds. Subjective experience does not stand still. William James, you will remember, emphasized how consciousness is characterized by continuous flux. Personal life is structured by time: our sense of identity is rooted in a sequential narrative of experiences and events, of what has happened in the past and our expectations for the future. It was noted in Unit 12 that the way in which existential issues are experienced is likely to vary as a function of age. Time and awareness of personal finiteness, for example, may well be of more concern when most of life lies behind rather than ahead of one. We saw too how the search for meaningfulness may, for some people, only become insistent in later life. Clearly a person's experience of living cannot be regarded as static. Our task in Part 1 is to explore in what ways the nature and quality of our personal worlds change as we progress through life.

One problem in dealing with this issue is the vastness of the area, for we are talking about changes in behaviour and experience throughout the span of adult life. Central features like work and unemployment, marriage, having children, divorce, ageing and retirement, all play crucial roles in our changing and developing experience and each merits a separate thesis in itself. Throughout life there is constant shift in the structural features underlying any personal world. We have already noted how subjective experience is rooted in a body and this, in the course of living, matures and then ages. Typically, we become at first more agile, strong, physically capable and sexually excitable, and then slowly (or sometimes quite suddenly) we wane. Physical features – skin, hair, posture – change as we age, as do patterns of susceptibility to illness or injury. (Thus, for example, the risk of dying in a car accident is highest for young adults and old people, the likelihood of committing suicide reaches its peak in late middle-age, and the chances of being murdered steadily decrease as we get older.)

Personal worlds are also dependent on and constructed by the social context in which a person lives. Physical characteristics often have their major impact on our personal experience only because of the ways in which others react to them. Society tends to create different institutions, different social contexts and statuses for us depending on our age: school, university, the factory floor, the supervisor's office; parents' house, bachelor flat, our own home with mate and offspring; later the empty nest, perhaps a retirement home. Roles, relationships, the ways others react to us change as we grow older and with each new setting.

All of human life is here and it would be a mammoth task even to begin to sketch all these aspects of personal development. So our focus will be confined to the changing pattern of subjective experience: we can only bear in mind the possible effects of such structural changes as biology and society must produce as we grow through life.

Although psychologists have expended a great deal of effort on investigating and documenting the psychological changes which take place throughout childhood, the course of adult life has until recently been largely ignored. Apart from the problems of old age, the nature of adulthood was typically taken for granted and little change was assumed to occur with age once adolescence had been left behind. Although there have been notable exceptions, such as the work of Carl Jung and Charlotte Bühler, the major thrust of research and interest in the whole cycle of human life has come about only in the last few years. Some of these studies have been based on general and clinical observation (e.g. Erikson, 1950, 1980). Others have used more formalized research procedures based on sampling and the use of interviews and questionnaires. One approach has been the cross-sectional study in which development through the life cycle has been reconstructed primarily on the basis of comparing data from subjects at different ages (e.g. Gould, 1978; Nicholson, 1980). Another has been to develop a theory of life development by analysing biographies provided by individuals themselves (e.g. Bühler, 1968). A very few researchers have managed to carry out longitudinal research in which they have followed the same subjects through different stages of their lives (e.g. Vaillant, 1977).

A perspective on the course of life which has frequently been put forward in such studies is to view it as a series of *phases,* each relatively stable and qualitatively different from the others. Such phase or stage theories are, as you will probably have noted, commonly found in theories of child development. Piaget, for example, saw the growth of cognitive abilities and moral judgement in this way, and Freud postulated stages of psychosexual development (see Unit 4). As the social contexts of adults and the life tasks which they face typically change in a series of steps (e.g. first job, marriage, the birth of children, retirement, etc.) there would seem some reason to conceptualize the entire life cycle in a similar fashion. As we shall see in section 4, such phase theories of the course of adult life are beset by problems of interpretation. But they do offer us useful insights into possible ways in which personal worlds may change as we grow older. In this unit we will look at two such phase theories in some detail: first, in section 2, at the seminal theory of Erik Erikson in which he has tried to describe the essential features of ego development through the life cycle; then, in section 3, at the research based on interviews in which Levinson and his colleagues (1978) have attempted to piece together how men perceive changes in their lives. In considering some of the criticisms which have been levelled at phase approaches of this kind, we will discuss more briefly some other studies of the life course. Part 1 then goes on to look at specific issues like the continuity of life experience, transitions and the role of crisis, and concludes by drawing together the implications which the studies considered have for the changing pattern of existential needs and personal experience through life. Although some of the most important life developments occur in early childhood, this is an area which has already been dealt with in Block 2. Our main consideration in what follows will therefore be limited to growth and change in adolescent and adult life.

life course
life cycle
(In this unit, the term 'life course' is used to indicate generally the flow and development of an individual's life. The phrase 'life cycle' also refers to this but implies the idea that it takes the form of a sequence of relatively defined phases (cf. the cycle of the seasons).)

ACTIVITY 1

Find the line representing your life which you drew for Activity 5 in Unit 12 (or draw another one). Mark on it to scale the time and duration of key events in your past life (entering/leaving school, important relationships, marriage, jobs, etc.). Do the same for the probable events of the future (e.g. retirement). Spend four or five minutes jotting down some notes on what you consider might be key changes in the 'feel' of your personal world over the period of your life so far. Can you detect any noticeable *phases*, i.e. periods when relatively little change occurred, linked by transitions or 'crisis' times when quite a lot did?

> **PROGRESS BOX 1   Studying the course of adult life**
>
> 1   Time and change are central to personal worlds. Life is experienced as a sequential narrative over time with changing patterns of existential needs.
>
> 2   Studying the life cycle is made difficult because so many areas are involved (e.g. work, relationships, etc.): both biological ageing, and changing social contexts and reactions to these are intrinsic parts of personal development. The focus in Part 1 of this Unit is on changes in subjective experience.
>
> 3   Research into and interest in the changing pattern of adult experience are mostly relatively recent. Theories have been based on a variety of approaches including clinical analysis and interview and questionnaire studies (cross-sectional, biographical and longitudinal).
>
> 4   The idea of *phases* has been applied not just to childhood but to the whole life cycle.

2 EIGHT AGES – ERIK ERIKSON

By far the most influential conceptualization of the life cycle has been that of the psychoanalyst Erik Erikson.

Set reading

Read now pp. 76–8 in Chapter 8 of the Set Book *Freud and Psychoanalysis*, which give a brief account of Erikson's approach and work.

Although Erikson follows in the spirit of the Freudian approach, he extends psychoanalytic theory in a number of ways. In Unit 12, we noted some of his ideas about identity. His work has also been concerned with the related area of the development and functioning of the ego, which he describes as the 'inner synthesis which organizes experience and guides action' (Erikson, 1968, p. 154).

Erikson began as a child analyst and later worked with adults, as well as spending much of his life teaching undergraduate students. His clinical and life experience has therefore brought him into intimate contact with people of all ages. One of his most interesting conceptions has been his chart of the human life cycle in terms of eight ages or phases of ego development.

2.1 Ego development in childhood

As the first four stages are concerned with the development of the child rather than the adult, I shall deal with them only briefly for the sake of completeness. They will also serve to introduce some of the core features of Erikson's approach.

The first three stages follow closely Freud's idea of psychosexual development (see Chapter 4 of *Freud and Psychoanalysis*) but with the focus on its consequences for the ego.

1 Infancy

trust vs. mistrust ∴ hope

For the very young child at the oral stage, who is totally dependent on those who care for him, the critical issue becomes one of *trust/mistrust*. Depending on how the child's needs are satisfied at this stage will be laid, Erikson asserts, the basis for the ego quality of *hope* – whether that child will later come to take a basically optimistic or pessimistic view of life.

2 Early childhood

autonomy vs. shame and self-doubt ∴ will

The critical issue at the anal stage, as the child begins to be capable of independent action, revolves around his first attempts at self-assertion. Again, depending on the way this stage is handled by the parents (or caretakers), so the seeds are sown for a later sense of *autonomy* as opposed to feelings of *shame and self-doubt*. What is crucial is balance and the ability to ensure cooperation without dominating the child's desire for freely chosen action. Successful navigation of this phase lays the basis for the ego quality of *will*.

3 Play age

initiative vs. guilt ∴ purpose

By the phallic stage, children are capable of planning and initiating actions to get what they want. But this, as you will remember, is the time of the Oedipus complex. The child's capacity for *initiative* may be counterbalanced by fear of negative consequences or by *guilt*. A balanced outcome to this crisis can lay the basis for a sense of *purposefulness* – 'the courage to envisage and pursue valued goals' (1964, p. 122).

Erikson sees these early stages of development, then, as being the time when the bases are laid for the ego qualities of trust, self-confidence, and faith in one's own actions.

4   School age

For his account of ego development beyond the age of five, Erikson moves outside the framework provided by Freudian ideas. Although the early school years coincide with the latency period when Freud believed that the stormy emotions of the younger child become subdued, in social terms, as Erikson points out, this is a very decisive phase. Recognition now begins to rest on the exercise of skills, and children may become aware of being judged on their performance in comparison with their peers. Where children feel inadequate to their task, a *sense of inferiority* may be the result and they may be deterred from testing out what they can do. But if a child is encouraged and given confidence, the ego quality which can emerge is a sense of lasting *competence*. A danger of overemphasizing competence at this stage, though, is that a person later comes to place too great an importance on work and achievement, resulting in 'constriction of his horizons' so that 'he may become the conformist and thoughtless slave of his technology and of those who are in a position to exploit it' (1950, p. 234).

industry vs. sense of inferiority ∴ competence

2.2   Erikson's scheme

I have now briefly sketched how Erikson conceives of ego development during childhood or the first four phases of life. Before going on to consider how it continues through adult life – our subject of primary interest – let me clarify some basic features of the scheme:

dialectical   1   It is essentially *dialectical*. By that, I mean that instead of postulating certain characteristics of experience as typical for each age, he conceptualizes each phase in terms of the interplay between a pair of alternative orientations or attitudes. From the way the growing person is able to resolve each issue emerges a 'virtue' – a word used in its original sense by Erikson to denote a strength or quality of ego functioning. Thus, as we saw, the very first phase of life is characterized by the polarity of *basic trust versus mistrust* from the resolution of which emerges the ego strength of *hope*. His use of the word 'versus' to link each polarity 'suggests a dialectic dynamics, in that the final strength postulated could not emerge without either of the contending qualities; yet, to assure growth, . . . the one more intent on adaptation must absorb the [other]' (1976, p. 23).

epigenesis   2   Erikson describes ego development as an *epigenetic* process: that is, the growth of the ego involves a progressive differentiation or unfolding. It is not that each polarity or virtue is significant only at that particular phase, but that is the time of its special ascendancy – when it becomes of especial concern to the individual. What Erikson is suggesting then is an inner process of maturation for each person which creates a 'succession of potentialities for significant interaction with those persons who tend and respond to him and those institutions which are ready for him' (1968, p. 93). Different qualities of ego strength arise at different stages of a person's life.

crisis   3   Erikson applies the term *crisis* to the stages to indicate that each involves a fundamental shift in perspective which, although essential for growth, leaves the person vulnerable to impairment of the quality concerned. He is not implying any catastrophe, but rather that the phases represent (as in the essential meaning of the term 'crisis') crucial developments in which 'a decisive turn one way or another is unavoidable'. Each phase represents 'a crucial period of increased vulnerability and heightened potential, and therefore, the ontogenetic source of generational strength and maladjustment' ('ontogenetic' here means 'developed within the individual').

He calls the whole sequence the 'life cycle' to indicate not only that each individual life has its own overall pattern but also that, at the same time, it forms a link in the continuous sequence of generations.

2.3   Ego development after childhood

We now go on to consider the final four stages in Erikson's scheme. These concern adolescence and adult development.

5   Adolescence

The phase which has perhaps most fascination for Erikson is adolescence. It is not surprising that he should regard this as a crisis stage. Then, more than at any other time in life, we experience radical changes both in body functioning and social role. We noted earlier that Erikson regards adolescence as the critical time for the development of *identity*. The young person is confronted with the need to make decisions as to what he or she is and will be. What job should he take? What attitudes should he hold? What kinds of relationship should he pursue? Who is he? How should he dress, behave, react? The boundaries which hitherto have kept him or her firmly in place now one by one dissolve. He is confronted by the need to re-establish them for himself and to do this in the face of an often potentially hostile world. Creating his or her own identity may require reacting negatively. It may mean actively denying those attributes and roles thrust upon him or her by other people like parents and teachers. As Erikson points out, so much of the phenomena of adolescence is concerned with this establishing of identity – a search for people and ideas to have faith in, idolizing heroes, going together in groups, adhering to special styles and conventions of behaviour and dress (think of punks, teds, mods and rockers, and the loyal fans of pop groups) and rejecting deviants from their norms. It is also a time of self-consciousness and concern with how they appear to other people. First relationships are not just a matter of re-emergent sexuality. They are concerned with finding oneself through being reflected in the eyes of an intimate partner, which is 'why so much of young love is conversation' (Erikson, 1968, p. 132). The problem of adolescence is one of *role confusion* – a lack of awareness of who one is, and a reluctance to commit oneself which may haunt a person into his mature years. Given the right conditions (and Erikson believes these are essentially having enough space and time, a 'psychosocial moratorium' when a young person can freely experiment and explore) what may emerge is a firm sense of *identity*, an emotional and deep awareness of who he or she is.

identity vs. role confusion ∴ fidelity

Dependent on this stage is the ego quality of *fidelity* – the ability to sustain loyalty to a person, idea or set of values.

6: Young adulthood

This is the first of three broad phases into which Erikson segments adult life. Following close on the heels of the identity concerns of adolescence, comes – usually in the early twenties – the need to develop the capacity for *intimacy*. The essence of intimacy is being able to commit oneself to 'concrete affiliations and partnerships and to develop the ethical strength to abide by such commitments, even though they may call for significant sacrifices and compromises' (1950, p. 237). Intimacy may be sought in friendship, inspiration and love. It tests the firmness of the identity established, for deep involvement with another demands the strength to put one's own individual identity at risk.

While sexual relations may be involved, the key issue, Erikson believes, is the mutual search for a shared identity, 'finding oneself as one loses oneself in another'. This can develop as easily between friends, or, say, two soldiers fighting as comrades together, as between sexual partners. He argues that it is only at this stage that what he calls 'true genitality' can develop, for up until this time sexual relations are more likely to have been in the service of the search for individual identity, or a kind of proving ground for sexual prowess, rather than a true intimacy.

intimacy vs. isolation ∴ love

From the interplay of polarities at this stage comes the capacity for *love*. The counterpart of intimacy is a growing sense of *isolation* and *self-absorption*.

7: Maturity

The theme of Erikson's seventh age is *generativity versus stagnation*. As children are dependent on us so we are on them, for mature adults 'need to be needed'. The essence of generativity is 'the concern in establishing and guiding the next generation'. This may not necessarily imply caring for one's own offspring, although this is the prototypal form. Adults may give of themselves by passing on to others their skills and knowledge and the products of their work and creativity. What is important is the sense of giving of oneself without expectation of return.

generativity vs. stagnation ∴ care

While becoming a parent may make generativity more likely, in itself it by no means guarantees this. An adult who does not develop generativity, Erikson asserts, retreats instead to a stagnating and eventually boring preoccupation with self in which 'he becomes his own infant and pet'. For couples this is likely to take the form of regression to an obsessive need for 'pseudo-intimacy' in which they indulge themselves and each other as if they themselves were their children. Erikson labels the ego quality which emerges from this stage as *care* – 'the widening concern with what has been generated by love, necessity, or accident' (1964, p. 131).

8: Old age

ego integrity vs. despair ∴ wisdom

The polarity of the final stage of life is between what Erikson calls *ego integrity* and *despair*. While Erikson hesitates to define *ego integrity*, he indicates the kind of attributes it embraces – the quiet certainty of the ego's strength, accepting the nature and inevitability of the pattern of one's life and not seeking desperately for last-minute restorations. While appreciating the richness of the many ways in which life can be lived, and while realizing that 'an individual life is the accidental coincidence of but one life cycle with but one segment of history' (1950, p. 241), such a person is ready to stay with and assert the particular pattern which has come to characterize his own life. Lack of ego integrity is marked by *despair* – by agonized concern in the shadow of impending death over unrealized goals and unfulfilled potentials, sometimes expressed in disgust with life and other people. Only 'integrity can balance the despair of the knowledge that a limited life is coming to a conscious conclusion, only such wholeness can transcend the petty disgust of feeling finished and passed by, and the despair of facing the period of relative helplessness which marks the end as it marked the beginning' (Erikson, 1964, p. 134). From the interplay of ego integrity versus despair come the fruits of our final years – the ego quality of *wisdom*.

2.4   Comment

A summary of Erikson's scheme is given in Figure 1. This represents a conceptualization of the stages of ego development through life. The chart brings out the epigenetic nature of Erikson's theory (see section 2.2). It shows how, although each polarity and its emergent ego quality has its particular time of ascendance, it is not restricted to that stage and that alone. So, for example, once the capacity for hope has emerged, it is likely to persist through life, though it will be modified according to the nature of the needs and conflicts which are dominant at any particular time. The scheme is intended to be more flexible than may appear from the diagram. Thus, Erikson did not intend that an individual should be thought of as 'located' only at one stage. It is more likely that there will be an oscillation between the conflicts characteristic of more than one stage, and a person is likely to move fully into a new phase only when the crisis of a yet higher one begins to come into play.

Erikson is very concerned to refute the idea that his scheme represents some kind of achievement scale. All that he will commit himself to is the desirability of establishing a 'dynamic balance' or 'favourable ratio' of the positive to the negative pole. Essentially, as we have seen, it is a dialectic conception. The poles at each stage represent dynamic counterparts, each tendency playing a part in

	1	2	3	4	5	6	7	8
H old age								Integrity vs. Despair, Disgust: **WISDOM**
G maturity							Generativity vs. Stagnation: **CARE**	
F young adulthood						Intimacy vs. Isolation: **LOVE**		
E adolescence					Identity vs. Role Confusion: **FIDELITY**			
D school age				Industry vs. Inferiority: **COMPETENCE**				
C play age			Initiative vs. Guilt: **PURPOSE**					
B early childhood		Autonomy vs. Shame, Doubt: **WILL**						
A infancy	Trust vs. Mistrust: **HOPE**							

Figure 1   Erikson's life stages (based on Erikson, 1976)

The stages are charted in this fashion to indicate the 'epigenetic nature' of Erikson's scheme. Each polarity and ego quality comes to the fore at the stage indicated. Each, though, exists in some form at the stages both before and after its 'crisis' time (see discussion in the text).

fostering the development of ego strength. So, for example, too firm a consolidation of identity at adolescence may close off the possibility of later flexibility and openness to change which may have to be paid for at maturity by painful readjustments.

Although Erikson's theory is focused on personal development, it is premised on the idea that this is intrinsically interwoven with patterns of biological functioning and social context: it is, therefore, what we might call an 'integrative bio-psychosocial' scheme. Thus, as with childhood development, each adult stage can be considered also to be underpinned by biological maturation. The heightened reflexiveness and working through of multiple possibilities which characterizes the identity explorations of adolescence, for example, are made possible only by the attainment of the cognitive stage of formal operations (see Unit 4, section 4.2.4), itself based on biological maturation. The search for intimacy might, in part, be considered to be stimulated by intensified sexual interest; generativity may be related, if only indirectly, to childbearing; and the conflict between despair and ego integrity is likely to be precipitated by awareness of the looming approach of death.

Each stage is set also in an appropriate social context. Having just left school, the adolescent is confronted with the identity-related tasks of job choice and what he or she is to make of his or her life; the prospect of marriage comes traditionally during those years which Erikson assumes to be the stage for conflict between the need for intimacy and isolation; and the possibility of parenthood and bringing up children is likely to be associated with the time of generativity versus stagnation. Society demands of most of us that we retire and this may, in itself, also help intensify or precipitate in a reflective person the conflict between integrity versus despair which Erikson proposes is typical of the eighth and final age.

Both crisis and developmental process, then, emerge at each stage out of the interactions between the biological, the social and the personal. As Stevens-Long has expressed it:

> ... children develop because they experience biological growth, which confers new psychological status and a new sense of mastery. Growth also influences how people react to the developing child. The entire environment is transformed by biological growth; at the same time, the environment is an important predictor of the extent and timing of such physical development. Growth and a changing environment produces a succession of imbalances within the child and between the child and the outside world. As the child tries to adjust the imbalance, personality structure changes. The child begins to interact with the environment differently, expressing adaptation and sowing the seeds of new conflict.

(Stevens-Long, 1983, p. 73)

triple book-keeping

Throughout Erikson's work we see a fascination with the interplay between social context, biological factors and individual development. To understand the course of personal development, he argues, it is necessary to view each aspect in relation to the others and over time: he calls this 'triple book-keeping'. To give flesh to this idea he has presented detailed 'psychobiographical' studies of Luther (1959) and Gandhi (1969) in which he traces the development of their lives and experience against the social and historical background of their times. (If you are interested in these, see the 'References' section for details of the books concerned, or for a briefer summary and discussion of them in the context of Erikson's work as a whole see Stevens (1983a).

There is no doubt that Erikson's scheme has had very considerable influence on thinking about adult development. One reason for this may be that there is no other theory which differentiates psychological development right through the life cycle in such a distinctive, comprehensive and plausible way. Nevertheless, the scheme does have its drawbacks. For a start, the formulation of the phases is not always very precise: what is involved at each stage in terms of behaviour and experience, for example, is often unclear. The account is given in very general terms: there is little detail about what actually happens in the dialectical process of conflict between polarities which he postulates. (It is true, though, that Erikson does provide illustrations of it by means of his clinical and historical case studies.) Furthermore, although the scheme may be anchored in Erikson's observations of his patients and other people, we are offered no evidence, apart from such case studies, in support of its propositions.

What criticisms Erikson's theory has attracted have been largely centred on the question of universality. Apart from some attempts to apply his ideas to personal development in the different social context of India (see his study of Gandhi, 1969), Erikson takes relatively little account of possible uii. rences between cultures, the sexes and classes. A number of critiques have pointed out that the course of *identity* development at least may well be different for boys and girls. One suggestion has been that, for girls, the capacity for intimacy precedes identity concerns and that identity consolidation may typically be postponed until after the experience of sustained relationships such as marriage. Certainly Gilligan (1982) has found, in a series of interviews with both sexes, that women, when asked to describe themselves, were much more likely to fuse identity with intimacy. The twenty-seven-year-old women she interviewed typically expressed their identity not in terms of achievements or activities but in relation to other people. As one subject, Claire, expressed it: 'it's hard for me to think of myself without thinking about other people around me that I'm giving to' (Gilligan, 1982, p. 158). Gilligan concludes that 'in all of the women's descriptions, identity is defined in a context of relationship and judged by a standard of responsibility and care' (ibid., p. 160).

Erikson has been accused not only of ignoring possible differences between the sexes but also of being too ethnocentric and uncritical of the pattern of contemporary life and of tending to support and confirm the values of male-oriented development and institutions in Western society (see, for example, Buss, 1979).

The scheme is best regarded, to adapt Erikson's own phrase, as a 'tool to think with' rather than a 'prescription to abide by' (1950, p. 243). It serves to draw our attention to the changing pattern of needs, interests and psychological capacities as we mature and age. It can be usefully applied in considering the nature of personal worlds and how they change over time. The model would tend to suggest, for example, that the origins of several aspects of a personal world lie in childhood. We might presume that *emotional tone (KF4* – see Unit 12, section 1.2) would depend in part on the basic trust versus mistrust stage; that the confidence reposing in the *sense of self (KF8)* would be related to the second stage of autonomy versus shame; that variations in capacity to exert *agency (KF9)* may have some source in the stage of initiative versus guilt.

It is interesting to speculate on the implications of the scheme for the changing pattern of existential needs through life. Although Erikson does present us with a fixed progression, he does not tie the stages to precise chronological ages. While his scheme suggests a degree of determinism, it does allow scope for individual autonomy: for the way individuals cope with the various crises plays an important part in determining the course of future development. It would seem reasonable to suppose that it is during adolescence that existential needs first come to the fore, for it is then that the flowering of cognitive ability and the gradual release from the social constraints of childhood open up the realms of possibility in imagination and action. According to Erikson, as noted earlier, there is a preoccupation at this time with forging an *identity*. Although the basis for agency has been laid in childhood (see Unit 7) only now is the young person in a position to fully exert the power of *choice*. For the first time, perhaps, he or she may also begin to think deeply about the implications of *time* – the finiteness of life and the prospect of eventual death. There is likely to be a concern with *meaningfulness* – with making some kind of sense of life, perhaps through exploring ideologies or values. As the person grows older, the arena in which meaning is sought is likely to change. In young adulthood (Erikson's sixth age), the existential emphasis would seem to shift to a concern with overcoming isolation (which may well have been exacerbated by the focus on the self in later adolescence): the search for meaningfulness is now more likely to be diverted into relationships. It is in mature adulthood (the seventh age) that we might expect the scope for personal autonomy to reach its optimum. If a person develops through the generativity versus stagnation stage as Erikson suggests, then it would seem likely that, at this stage, meaning comes to be sought more through altruism, giving and care for others rather than just a concern with intimate relationships in themselves. It is also at this time, perhaps, when the 'dark at the end of the tunnel' begins to appear, when the issue of finiteness begins to assert itself more strongly. The awareness of closing options may stimulate a sense of identity reappraisal and an attempt to redirect one's life along different lines (see the discussion of mid-life crisis in sections 3.2 and 5.2). Finally, in the closing years of life, when for most people the power of agency begins to wane (at least in terms of what we can *do*), Erikson's scheme would seem to suggest that attaining a sense of meaningfulness depends on some kind of acceptance and coming to terms with life, and, for some people perhaps, on finding some way of making sense of it all.

ACTIVITY 2

The power of the scheme as a tool to think with is beautifully revealed in Erikson's analysis (1976) of Ingmar Bergman's film *Wild Strawberries*. This narrates the long journey of the ageing Dr Borg from his home to the University of Lund where he is to receive an honorary degree. On the way, he encounters members of his family and acquaintances of different generations and muses on his dreams and on recollections of the past. Erikson takes the scenes from the film and shows how they can be seen to reflect the critical phases in the old man's life – 'his own terminal conflicts open up all his earlier ones, as personified by the younger persons who confront him (in fact or in fantasy) on his journey' (1976, p. 24). So, for example, his son's resistance to his daughter in law's desire for a child opens up his own unresolved conflict over generativity versus stagnation; and his reveries about his past, as well as the quarrel of a middle-aged couple picked up on the road, re-awaken awareness of his own problems over intimacy.

Try thinking about Erikson's 'eight ages' in relation to your own life cycle and those of other people of different ages whom you know well. How well do his ideas seem to fit?

PROGRESS BOX 2   The 'eight ages' proposed by Erik Erikson

1   *Erikson:* extends Freudian theory; is particularly concerned with identity; and has worked with people of all ages.

2   *Phases of ego development:*

(i)   *infancy:* trust vs. mistrust ∴ hope.

(ii)   *Early childhood:* autonomy vs. shame and doubt ∴ will.

(iii)   *Play age:* initiative vs. guilt ∴ purpose.

(iv)   *School age:* industry vs. inferiority ∴ competence.

(v)   *Adolescence:* identity vs. role confusion ∴ fidelity.

(vi)   *Young adulthood:* intimacy vs. isolation ∴ love.

(vii)   *Maturity:* generativity vs. stagnation ∴ care.

(viii)   *Old age:* integrity vs. despair and disgust ∴ wisdom.

3   *Characteristics of scheme:*

(i)   A *dialectical* conception.

(ii)   Ego development is seen as an *epigenetic* process.

(iii)   Ego development is also seen as a series of *crises* or turning points.

(iv)   *Integrative* and bio-psychosocial in approach (psychobiographical studies of Luther and Gandhi illustrate this 'triple book-keeping').

4   *Limitations:*

(i)   Generalized nature: no independent supporting evidence.

(ii)   Male-oriented? In girls, intimacy stage may precede identity.

(iii)   How far limited by culture and class?

(iv)   Too ethnocentric and unquestioning of social patterns of Western society?

5   The scheme is a *'tool to think with':*

(i)   It offers insights into personal worlds – possible sources of emotional tone and sense of self.

(ii)   It implies a *changing pattern of existential needs* through life: *adolescence* – existential needs (e.g. concern with identity and meaningfulness, finiteness, and scope for exerting choice) come to the fore; *young adulthood* – meaning sought through relationships; *maturity* – the time of maximum autonomy, meaning through care, personal concern with time and identity; *old age* – autonomy reduced, meaning through acceptance.

3 RESEARCH STUDIES OF THE LIFE CYCLE

Erikson has put forward a stimulating theory which has influenced many psychologists' thinking about the course of adult life. But what about *empirical* research in this area?

3.1 The development of life course studies

One of the first people to engage in empirical studies of the course of human life was Charlotte Bühler in the 1930s in Vienna. (Erikson also happened to be resident there at that time, though Bühler's initial work pre-dated publication of his theory by more than a decade.) Like Erikson, Bühler emigrated to the USA and she continued to work and develop her ideas there. Also like him, she is one of the few theorists to have presented a conceptualization of the whole span of the human life cycle from birth to death (Bühler, 1968).

Bühler and her co-workers collected and analysed more than 400 biographies drawn from both ordinary individuals and people known for their creative work. On the basis of this, she suggested that there are five distinct phases of human development through life:

1 Age 0 to 15:   The period of childhood.

2 Age approximately 15 to 25:   The second phase of life is characterized by expanding experience and by experimentation. There is often a provisional quality about the choices made about career and relationships. It is at this stage that the young person may come to be aware for the first time that 'one's own life belongs to oneself and represents a time unit with a beginning and end' (Bühler, 1968, p. 74).

3 Age approximately 25 to 45 or 50:   More definite attitudes and specific goals are being decided on and this is the time for expressing and implementing these.

4 Age approximately 45 to 65:   The beginning of this phase is the turning point of life when most biological powers have reached full development and have begun to wane. There is still, though, much room for psychological expansion. This period is likely to be dominated by self-assessment of life so far. There is concern in particular about how fulfilling it has been and the prospects for the future.

5 Age approximately 65 on: In this phase, Bühler points out, there is considerable variation between individuals. Some continue to engage actively with life: others withdraw and adjust to a much more restricted style of living. There is quite likely to be a re-emergence of short-term goals. Although her team did not find much evidence of despair, there did seem to be reduced scope for fulfilment and often a kind of resignation to this.

Bühler is concerned to emphasize the biological underpinning and social context of individual development. There are broad parallels, she suggests, between the course of life and the pattern of biological growth, culmination and decline. There is a similar pattern too in the psychological sphere, with gradual development and expansion of social involvements of various kinds to a maximum in middle life, usually followed later by a decline in old age. However, Bühler stresses that individual variations can often occur in this linking of phases. Sometimes, for example, personal development will lag behind biological changes, as when a person remains fully active and involved even when his or her physical powers have begun to fade. Some creative individuals continue their accomplishments at the highest level well after the time when many people have retired.

Particularly in her later work, Bühler has adopted a humanistic orientation. She focuses, for example, on the capacity for self-determination – for setting one's own goals and evaluating the fulfilment received from different styles of living. She has pointed out how one way in which the phases of life differ is in the typical style of setting goals, ranging from the long-term aspirations often typical of early adulthood to re-evaluation of goals in middle life and the gradual constriction to more immediate goals in old age.

The next major empirical study of note was not until the mid-1950s when Bernice Neugarten and her team studied over 700 people of different ages in Kansas City over a period of seven years (Neugarten *et al.*, 1964). They used interviews supplemented with projective techniques (for example, the Thematic Apperception Test where subjects are presented with pictures and asked to tell a story about what might be happening: their responses are then interpreted for prevailing themes, etc., which they may 'project' into the material).

Thematic Apperception Test

The focus was on the mid-life period and, like Bühler, they found some evidence of a major shift in perspective at this time. The typical pattern was increased introspection and reflectiveness about personal life and a move towards concern with 'interiority' rather than with outward events. Neugarten also suggests that there is often a reversal of directionality at about this time: life becomes 'restructured in terms of time-left-to-live rather than time-since-birth' (Neugarten, 1968, p. 97). While not denying the significance of biological ageing, Neugarten emphasizes age-group identifications and the internalization of social norms about what is appropriate and expected for different stages of life. As she points out, the biological events which may lead to significant shifts in attitudes and behaviours may, in fact, be those which happen to other people rather than the person concerned (e.g. becoming a grandparent or widow).

In the late 1970s came a flurry of publications of research studies about people's experience of change through the life cycle, notably those by Roger Gould, Daniel Levinson and colleagues and George Vaillant. All of these are American studies and were published in 1977–78. There has also been a book based on interviews by a journalist, Gail Sheehy (*Passages*, 1976) and a study in England in conjunction with a television series by John Nicholson (1980). Although there is something of an incestuous quality about this area (for both Levinson and Gould admit to the influence of Erikson, and Sheehy acknowledges her debt to the work of Levinson and Gould), each of the studies has come up with a different kind of analysis. None can be easily condensed into a brief summary as they are based on qualitative data from interviews and case histories.

In the next section, we will look in some detail at the work of Levinson *et al.* (1978). This study has its limitations. Levinson acknowledges that there are likely to be differences in the development of men and women and, in order not to make his subject sample so small as to be unrepresentative, he chose regretfully to confine the initial research to the study of men alone. This means that his findings at best can apply to no more than fifty per cent of the population. Nevertheless, I have selected this study for detailed presentation as an example of research into the phases of life because it was not only carefully carried out and analysed over several years but is also the best presented and articulated of the studies available, particularly in terms of its discussion of the kind of general issues about personal change and development which concern us in this unit.

3.2 The seasons of a man's life

This is the title of the book published in 1978 by Daniel Levinson and his co-workers Charlotte Darrow, Edward Klein, Maria Levinson and Braxton McKee. The subjects were forty men aged between 35 and 45 at the start of the research project in 1968, ten from each of four occupational groups selected for study – industrial workers, executives, biologists and novelists. Although the sample was quite diverse in terms of education, class, ethnic and religious background and included five black respondents, it was tilted towards the upper end of the socioeconomic spectrum. Levinson chose occupation as a primary basis for selection in accordance with his belief that 'a man's work is the primary base for his life in society' (p. 9).

biographical interview

The research method used was essentially 'to elicit the life stories of forty men, to construct biographies and to develop generalizations based upon these biographies' (p. 16). This was done primarily by means of the biographical interview. Each subject was seen during the initial phase of study between five and ten times for a total period of between ten and twenty hours. The interviews covered the life of each individual as a whole and as he experienced it. The interviewer's approach was essentially exploratory though every now and again he or she would attempt to pull the material together and to structure it with the respondent's help. Interviews were supplemented by use of the Thematic Apperception Test (see section 3.1), interviews with the subjects' wives and, where appropriate, visits to the subjects' place of work. There was a 'quasi-anthropological' attempt to establish a picture of each man's social context as well as his personal experience. A supplementary sample of biographies in published form of men like Gandhi and Bertrand Russell was also collected. In view of the point made in section 1.3 of Unit 12 about the often indistinguishable quality of representations of actual and fictional personal worlds, it is interesting that this secondary sample also included characters from fiction like King Lear and Willy Loman from Arthur Miller's play *Death of a Salesman*.

Levinson had been inspired to investigate the life cycle by the realization that, while a lot was known about development up to the age of twenty, very little work had been done on life thereafter. Although we have a mass of statistical information about life expectancy, occupation, income, marriage and divorce, etc., there is limited understanding of the *experience* of adulthood. The questions which his team sought to answer were:

> What does it mean to be an adult? What are the root issues of adult life – the essential problems and satisfactions, the sources of disappointment, grief and fulfilment? Is there an underlying order in the progression of our lives over the adult years, as there is in childhood and adolescence?

(Levinson, 1978, p. ix)

life structure

A central concept in Levinson's approach is the *life structure*, 'the basic pattern or design of a person's life at a given time' (p. 41). Interview data is analysed in terms of the choices made and any clear themes, in order to construct a biography. This biography will reflect the interaction between a person's actions as a creative agent and events in his social background. Levinson is concerned not only with those aspects of the self which are expressed in overt behaviours but also those which may be neglected or inhibited. He pays attention to fantasies, anxieties and feelings, to unconscious as well as conscious events. He looks for the possibility that 'old scripts' learned in earlier life are being played out in contemporary experience. He is particularly interested in the way a person participates in the world, how he uses or is used by other people. The life structure is seen as being constituted by key components – in particular, occupation, marriage and family, friendships and relations with peers, ethnic identifications and religious beliefs, leisure activities and the use of solitude. An individual's relationship with each of these components is 'like a thread in a tapestry; the meaning of each thread depends on its place in the total design' (Levinson, 1980, p. 278). One or two threads are likely to be central (for most of the men in this study these proved to be family and work), others are more peripheral, some are detached and isolated from the overall pattern.

On the basis of analysing the life structures of their subjects, Levinson and his co-workers came to share Erikson's view that not only can the life cycle be considered as a relatively ordered and predictable progression, but that it is broken up into distinctive 'seasons', each, like spring and summer, with its own time and character. They propose that the life cycle is best conceptualized as a sequence of four broad and overlapping *eras* (0–22: childhood and adolescence; 17–45: early adulthood; 40–65: middle adulthood; 60–85: late adulthood). It is the two middle eras of adulthood which are their primary concern. Each era subdivides into an alternating sequence of 'periods' usually lasting between five and seven but no more than ten years. There are structure-building periods concerned with establishing life in a particular fashion and extending what has been attained. Each of these is followed by a transitional period which serves a review and exploratory function and is a time of movement to the next phase. The sequence of periods during the two eras of early and middle adulthood are portrayed in Figure 2.

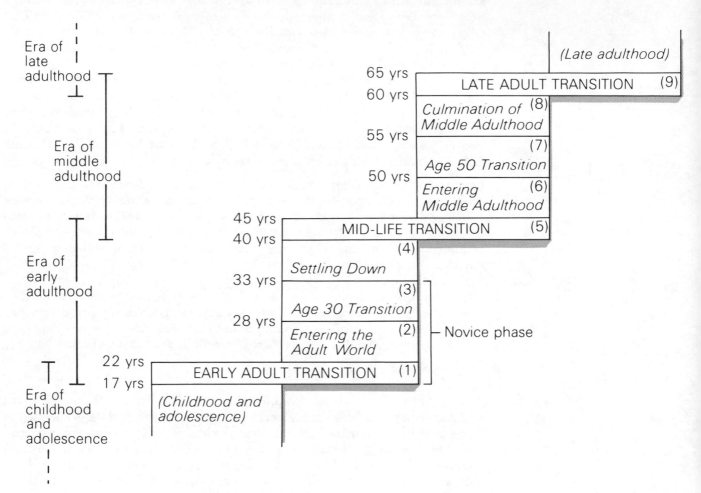

Figure 2 Developmental periods in early and middle adulthood (based on Levinson *et al.*, 1978)

Each period has *key tasks* associated with it which Levinson sees dialectically as having an antithetical quality: thus, in the period he calls *Entering the Adult World*, men between 22 and 28 are concerned both with freely exploring and with establishing stability; and in the *Settling Down* period in the late thirties there is a concern both with gaining recognition (and therefore becoming open to social pressure) and with being true to one's self. Every transitional period involves the complementary activities of terminating the old phase and commencing a new one. Levinson regards personal growth as intrinsically related to separation: in order to grow, some kind of separation is invariably required. Usually though such a separation is partial: thus, a young adult needs to reject certain aspects of his bond with his parents by changing rather than completely destroying it.

154

3.2.1 Era of early adulthood (approximate age 17–45)

era of early adulthood

This, the second of Levinson's life eras (after childhood and adolescence), is the time both of 'greatest energy and abundance, and of greatest contradiction and stress' (Levinson, 1980, p. 282). Biological capacity rises to its peak and patterns of living, loving and working become established for better or worse. While there is scope during this era for rich satisfactions, there can also be much stress: in particular, there is the possibility of conflict between personal aspirations and desires and the pressures caused by lack of money and the demands of work and society.

Period 1: Early Adult Transition (age 17–22)

Early Adult Transition

The first major transition Levinson deals with is from adolescence to early adulthood and comes between the ages of 17 and 22. This period involves two primary tasks. One is to separate from home and dependence on the family. The roles offered by society can be of help in this. Sixty-five per cent of Levinson's sample did military service during this time and seventy per cent completed college (NB, this is an American study). The other task is to form some kind of direction or basis for living as an adult.

Period 2: Entering the Adult World (age 22–28)

Entering the Adult World

Next there usually follows a more stable period from about 22 to 28 which Levinson calls *Entering the Adult World*. Here, as we have noted, the primary tasks are antithetical – to explore possibilities and what options are open, while at the same time making the commitment required to build some sort of stable life structure.

Period 3: Age 30 Transition (age 28–33)

Age 30 Transition

At the age of 30 or thereabouts, according to Levinson, there is likely to be another transitional period. This is a time for reflection and results either in the choices made being confirmed or a search for a new style of life. The life-structure has always changed in some key way, Levinson claims, by the end of this period. Though for some of his subjects this transition was smooth, for most it was a time of crisis as they struggled with the questions: 'where am I going, and is this where I really want to be?'

novice phase

Levinson regards the time until the early thirties as a *novice* phase. Even though they may have got married, had children and developed successful careers by that time, his subjects still felt themselves engaged in finding out what life is about. In the *novice phase*, which runs from age 17–33 approximately and covers the first three periods of early adulthood, Levinson identifies four major tasks:

1 Following a *Dream* and giving it a place in the life structure (see Box 1).

2 Forming *mentor* relationships (see Box 2).

3 Developing an *occupation*.

4 Forming *love relationships, marriage and family* (see Box 3).

The Dream

> **Box 1 The Dream**
>
> It has the quality of a vision, an imagined possibility that generates excitement and vitality. At the start it is poorly articulated and only tenuously connected to reality, although it may contain concrete images such as winning the Nobel Prize or making the all-star team. It may take a dramatic form as in the myth of the hero: the great artist, business tycoon, athletic or intellectual superstar performing magnificent feats and receiving special honors. It may take mundane forms that are yet inspiring and sustaining: the excellent craftsman, the husband-father in a certain kind of family, the highly respected member of one's community.

Whatever the nature of his Dream, a young man has the developmental task of giving it greater definition and finding ways to live it out. It makes a great difference in his growth whether his initial life structure is consonant with and infused by the Dream, or opposed to it. If the Dream remains unconnected to his life it may simply die, and with it his sense of aliveness and purpose.

(Levinson *et al.*, 1978, pp. 91–2)

For the biologists and novelists in Levinson's sample, the Dream was intimately connected with their work: this was true for only a few of the executives. Their Dream was more likely to centre on family and community life. None of the industrial workers lived out an occupational Dream. Several of them had begun their Early Adult Transition with fantasies about exciting kinds of work and accomplishment but this incipient Dream could not be developed and so faded in the light of hard reality and immediate problems of survival. For those who still retained a Dream, this was likely to be a vision of the good life as a mixture of work, family and community involvement. For two men, it was to be a star athlete.

We can link Levinson's concept of the Dream to our discussion in Unit 13, section 4, of the importance of fantasy and imagination. The Dream could also be regarded as a kind of superordinate metaphor serving to direct and orient us to the world.

ACTIVITY 3

Do you have a Dream? What it it? If you have the opportunity, discuss with someone else whether the idea of having a Dream is a meaningful notion to them and, if so, what form theirs takes.

mentor

Box 2   The mentor
Levinson regards this, when it occurs, as one of the most important relationships in the novice phase:

> The mentoring relationship is often situated in a work setting, and the mentoring functions are taken by a teacher, boss, editor or senior colleague. It may also evolve informally, when the mentor is a friend, neighbour or relative. Mentoring is defined not in terms of formal roles but in terms of the character of the relationship and the functions it serves. A student may receive very little mentoring from his teacher-adviser, and very important mentoring from an older friend or relative . . .

> What are the various functions of the mentor? He may act as a *teacher* to enhance the young man's skills and intellectual development. Serving as *sponsor,* he may use his influence to facilitate the young man's entry and advancement. He may be a *host and guide,* welcoming the initiate into a new occupational and social world and acquainting him with its values, customs, resources and cast of characters. Through his own virtues, achievements and way of living, the mentor may be an *exemplar* that the protégé can admire and seek to emulate. He may provide *counsel* and moral support in time of stress.

The mentor has another function, and this is developmentally the most crucial one: to support and facilitate the *realization of the Dream.*

(Levinson *et al.,* 1978, p. 98)

Levinson emphasizes that, although a mentor is usually a little older than the protégé (by about 8–15 years), the relationship is not that of a substitute parent. The mentor is perhaps more like an admired, older sibling. A crucial aspect of the relationship is that, as the protégé's skills increase, so the relationship gradually attains a status of equality. In this way it provides an indirect means of coming to terms with and transcending the child-parent feelings embedded in us all.

In the mentor relationship all is not necessarily sweetness and light. Mentoring relationships can be both partial and ambivalent:

A relationship may be remarkably beneficial to the younger person and yet be seriously flawed. For example, a teacher or boss cares for and sponsors a protégé, but is so afraid of being eclipsed that he behaves destructively at crucial moments. A relationship may be very limited and yet have great value in certain respects. Some men have a purely symbolic mentor whom they never meet. Thus, an aspiring young novelist may admire an older writer, devour his books, learn a great deal about his life, and create an idealized internal figure with whom he has a complex relationship.

. . . the young man feels admiration, respect, appreciation, gratitude and love for the mentor. These outweigh but cannot entirely prevent the opposite feelings: resentment, inferiority, envy, intimidation.

(ibid., p. 100)

Levinson sees mentoring as a form of love relationship, unlikely to last more than at the most ten years; its real value being perceived only after it is over.

Box 3   Special woman (or special man)
Levinson regards one form of love relationship as of particular importance in the life-structure. This is where one partner experiences the other as the 'Special Woman' or 'Special Man':

This is a unique relationship that ordinarily includes loving, romantic, tender and sexual feelings, but it goes beyond this. The special woman is like the true mentor: her special quality lies in her connection to the young man's Dream. She helps to animate the part of the self that contains the Dream. She facilitates his entry into the adult world and his pursuit of the Dream. She does this partly through her own actual efforts as teacher, guide, host, critic, sponsor. At a deeper psychological level she enables him to project onto her his own internal feminine figure – the 'anima,' as Jung has depicted it – who generates and supports his heroic strivings. The special woman helps him to shape and live out the Dream: she shares it, believes in him as its hero, gives it her blessing, joins him on the journey and creates a 'boundary space' within which his aspirations can be imagined and his hopes nourished.

Like the mentor, the special woman is a transitional figure. During early adulthood, a man is struggling to outgrow the little boy in himself and to become a more autonomous adult. The special

special woman/man

woman can foster his adult aspirations while accepting his dependency, his incompleteness and his need to make her into something more than (and less than) she actually is. Later, in the Mid-life Transition, he will have to become a more individual person. With further development, he will be more complete in himself and will have less need of the actual and the illusory contributions of the special woman.

A couple can form a lasting relationship that furthers his development only if it also furthers hers. If his sense of her as the special woman stems mainly from his wishful projections and hardly at all from her own desires and efforts, sooner or later the bubble will burst and both will feel cheated. If in supporting his Dream she loses her own, then her development will suffer and both will later pay the price. Disparities of this kind often surface in transitional periods such as the Age Thirty Transition or the Mid-life Transition.

(Levinson *et al.*, 1978, p. 109)

The special woman or man may be a person's spouse. On the other hand, the choice of spouse may be (probably unconsciously) antithetical to the Dream and may get in the way of rather than facilitating its attainment: when this is the case, such a contradiction will surface and have to be dealt with in time.

Levinson acknowledges that his account is given from the perspective of his male subjects (and, of course, he is describing it in terms of what these men may think and feel rather than what necessarily is the case) but the same kind of considerations are presumed to apply to women. The problem in most contemporary marriages (especially where the wife is also seriously involved in an occupation) is how to support and nurture together their mutual Dreams.

Period 4: Settling Down (age 33–40)

Settling Down

After the Age 30 Transition and graduation from the novice phase, most subjects in Levinson's group seemed to settle down in what he calls the 'second life structure'. In most cases, this continued in a fairly stable fashion until about age 40. For most, this was a time when they felt their feet securely on the ladder of life and their primary concern was to climb it. The specific tasks of the period are to create a niche in society for themselves and, in so doing, to 'make it'.

Becoming One's Own Man

Toward the end of this phase, Levinson identifies a particular kind of attitude which he terms 'Becoming One's Own Man' – the desire to be independent, 'more true to himself and less vulnerable to pressures and blandishments from others'. This attitude can run in opposition to the contradictory aim of seeking *affirmation* from his work or social context:

Speaking with his own voice is important, even if no one listens – but he especially wants to be heard and respected and given the rewards that are his due. The wish for independence leads him to do what he alone considers most essential, regardless of consequences; the wish for affirmation makes him sensitive to the response of others and susceptible to their influence.

(ibid., p. 144)

Levinson continues:

A man is likely to be rather sensitive, even touchy, about anything in the environment or in himself that interferes with these aims. Since the successful outcome of this period is not assured, he often feels that he has not accomplished enough and that he is not sufficiently his own man. He

158

may have a sense of being held back – of being oppressed by others and restrained by his own conflicts and inhibitions.

(ibid., p. 145)

Levinson points out that 'these concerns reflect external realities and internal processes'. The external reality is that organizations are often so rigid that self-assertion by an employee and a desire for independence may create problems. The internal process, which Levinson asserts is part of normal psychosocial development, is that:

Becoming One's Own Man represents a peaking in the aspirations of early adulthood. A man wants to become a 'senior' adult, to realize the fruits of the labors of the past fifteen or twenty years, to accomplish goals that in turn will provide a base for his life in the years to come. He wants, in short, to become manly in a fuller sense than ever before. The urgency of the desires for manhood, however, bring about a resurgence of the *little boy* in the adult.

(ibid., pp. 145–6)

It is at this time that mentor relationships are likely to founder. As one of the novelists in the sample expressed it:

Randall gave me tremendous support and encouragement. I was very close to this man – enormously, deeply committed to him in fact. He had a wonderful quality, but I later realized that this quality was good only if you were very young, and once you became a man yourself it almost became a matter of competition. I had to break, and it was too bad because there was a lack of insight on his part, I think.

(ibid., p. 148)

3.2.2   Era of middle adulthood (approximate age 40–65)

Period 5: Mid-life Transition (age 40–45)

For Levinson, this is a period of particular interest. He began the study intending to chart development in the mid-life decade between the ages of 35 and 45 years. He was himself 46 at the time and a major stimulus to his research was his concern to understand better what he had just gone through himself. It was only the research team's early realization that to understand this phase it was necessary to look at the experiences which lead up to it that encouraged them to **era of middle adulthood** extend the project to cover the whole of early and middle adulthood.

Like Bühler and Neugarten before him, Levinson claims that, for most of his subjects, there comes a fundamental shift in life pattern at around the age of 40. This **Mid-life Transition** is the transition from the era of early adulthood which we have just considered to the beginning of middle adulthood (the years from 40–65).

According to Levinson, for about the next four years, a man is likely to be working through three major tasks:

1   One is to *review* his life so far. How has it been? Is it the kind of life he wants? He is now no longer a novice. He feels himself able to make judgements. This task **de-illusionment** essentially involves what Levinson calls *de-illusionment*. He points out the vital role which illusions play in life – for good in that they may inspire us to achievement of actions of a positive kind, and for bad in that they may foster inappropriate expectations and lead to destructive behaviours. Losing one's illusions is part of the process of maturity but this may be painful – it may induce feelings of sadness and loss or it may bring with it a sense of joyful liberation; or both.

2   The second task is to revise and *modify the life structure* in the light of this review. This may involve external events (eg. job change, separations, changing

159

the pattern of leisure activities), or it may be entirely internal (a gradual shift in attitudes to work and/or relationships).

individuation

3 The task which Levinson makes the most of is what, drawing on the ideas of Carl Jung, he describes as the *individuation process*. Basically, Jung proposed that there is a fundamental difference between the first and second halves of life. The first is concerned with establishing oneself and involvement in the outside world, with 'making it' in whatever context you have chosen. In the second half, in contrast, people are likely to turn inward; in particular, to strengthen those aspects of themselves which have been subdued, the 'dark' unacknowledged side of their personalities. Levinson, following Jung, takes the task of later life as being to *'confront and re-integrate' the polarities or oppositional tendencies within our being.* Levinson singles out four such polarities whose resolution he regards as the 'principle task of mid-life individuation' (see Box 4).

Box 4 Four polarities to be worked through in the Mid-life Transition

Young/Old polarity

legacy

1 The primary polarity to be confronted is *Young/Old*. A person of this age has to come to terms with the paradox of beginning to feel old in some respects and yet still having the experience of being young in others. He needs to find ways of experiencing and being able to express both. At this age comes a growing sense of vulnerability, brought on by waning physical vigour, perhaps the onset of illness, and the death of parents, even of a friend or colleague. Such a sense of vulnerability brings to the surface what Levinson regards as a fundamental human desire – longing for immortality. One result will be the feeling that there is not much time left. Another may be to direct attention to the *legacy*. What will be left to posterity in the way of reputation, material possessions, creative work or influence on other people's lives?

Masculine/Feminine polarity

anima/animus

2 A second polarity to be confronted at this age is between the *masculine and feminine* sides of self. Levinson sees society as offering particular psychological stereotypes (or metaphors we might say) for the two sexes. At the extremes, the masculine is concerned with doing things, toughness, power, thinking, assertion; the feminine is sensitive, submissive, feeling. While these qualities are open to all of us, our culture, he argues, encourages us to emphasize the pattern considered appropriate for our sex, and to stifle expression of the other side. Mid-life is the time to redress the balance. It becomes important for men to express the hidden feminine side of themselves (in Jung's terms, the *anima*) and presumably for women (though Levinson does not say this directly) to open up to their masculine side (the *animus*).

One consequence of this change, Levinson asserts, is that a man becomes more capable of loving a woman for what she is rather than seeing her through the projections of those sides of himself which he is unable to accept and integrate (presumably a similar situation applies to women in relation to men).

Destruction/Creation polarity

3 A third resolution is concerned with what Levinson describes as the *Destruction/Creation* polarity. By this he refers to a person's need to come to terms with the inevitability of destructive impulses and effects (even where these are not intended) both in his own life and in human society, and the guilt and remorse he may feel over this:

> Much of the work on this task is unconscious. What is involved, above all, is the re-working of painful feelings and experiences. Some men articulate their new awareness in words, others in the esthetic terms of music, painting or poetry. Most men simply live it out in their daily lives. In any case, a man must come to terms with

160

his grievances and guilts – his view of himself as victim and as villain in the continuing tale of man's inhumanity to man. If he is burdened excessively by his grievances or guilts, he will be unable to surmount them. If he is forced to maintain the illusion that destructiveness does not exist, he will also be impaired in his capacity for creating, loving and affirming life.

(ibid., p. 224)

Attachment/Separateness polarity

4 The final polarity which Levinson discusses is that of *Attachment/Separateness*. By attachment he means the many ways in which we are involved in life and with others, prompted by needs like dependency, sexuality, aggression, ambition and affection. Separateness is where we turn inwards, temporarily withdrawing from the environment and focusing on our inner experience. The balance between attachment and separateness, he claims, changes as we progress through life. During early adulthood our orientation is primarily outwards, and thus to attachment to career, marriage and family. At the Mid-life Transition, there is a marked compensatory shift towards separateness, to establishing a greater equilibrium between these two aspects. (As an example of such a balance, a creative artist or scientist (or psychologist, we could add) must be engaged with what is happening in the world, both to understand and produce, and yet also needs time for separateness so that reflection and creativity become possible.)

Levinson, then, regards the Mid-life Transition as a time of profound change. While not all his sample went through obvious turmoil at the time, for eighty per cent of them, he claims, it was a time of 'tumultuous struggle'. Change may also occur, Levinson believes, quietly and gradually, but where there is no change at this time, the price is paid by a 'withering' of personality in later life. For this transition prepares the ground for new growth. The conflicts can generate patterns of behaviour which may seem irrational to others. Part of the struggle may be due to changes necessary to the structure of life (e.g. career and marriage) in order to accommodate the revisions, inner conflicts and changes which are taking place. These are also likely to lead to a modification of the Dream. Its hold may be reduced or, alternatively, if it has been betrayed in early adulthood, this may be the time for its resurgence. This is the theme of a novel by Elia Kazan called *The Arrangement*. Levinson quotes from a review of this by James Baldwin, the Black American novelist:

Though we would like to live without regrets, and sometimes proudly insist that we have none, this is not really possible, if only because we are mortal. When more time stretches behind than stretches before one, some assessments, however reluctantly and incompletely, begin to be made. Between what one wishes to become and what one *has* become there is a momentous gap, which will now never be closed. And this gap seems to operate as one's final margin, one's last opportunity, for creation. And between the self as it is and the self as one sees it, there is also a distance, even harder to gauge. Some of us are compelled, around the middle of our lives, to make a study of this baffling geography, less in the hope of conquering these distances than in the determination that the distance shall not become any greater.

(ibid., p. 250)

Levinson believes there are many gains to be made at this time. The rounding of personality opens up the possibility of a richer, more aware style of existence. It also brings with it the qualities and strength which now give a person the capacity to be a good mentor him or herself (cf. Erikson's notion of generativity). With the increased reflectiveness and the attempt to confront conflicts and destructiveness in the self, comes also a greater concern for *meaning* and *identity*. What is life about? What sort of person have I been and do I want to be? How am I to lead what is left to me of my life?

Periods 6–9 and later life (age 45 on)

The focus of Levinson's study is on early adulthood and the Mid-life Transition. The age of even his oldest subjects at the end of the eight-year project was not much over 50. He has no research data to work from for adult life beyond that age. He does, though, offer a cursory and openly speculative preview of the later periods (see Figure 2). For example, he postulates that, as in early adulthood, there is a settling down period into middle adulthood (Levinson calls this period **Entering Middle Adulthood**). A revised life structure begins to be established. In some cases, there are clear marker events like separation or a change of job. In other cases, there may be no conspicuous change. Levinson suggests that there is substantial individual variation in the quality of the life structures which are evolved at this time. Some men never quite make it and face a middle and late adulthood 'of constriction and decline'. For some, however:

> ... middle adulthood is often the fullest and most creative season in the life cycle. They are less tyrannized by the ambitions, passions and illusions of youth. They can be more deeply attached to others and yet more separate, more centered in the self. For them, the season passes in its best and most satisfying rhythm.

> (ibid., p. 62)

Around the age of 50, there is a minor transitional period analogous to the Age 30 Transition of early adulthood (**Age 50 Transition**). At this time, there may be further changes if those made during the Mid-life Transition have not proved sufficiently satisfactory or radical. This is followed by the period which he calls the **Culmination of Late Adulthood**. The major shift comes with the **Late Adult Transition** in the early sixties to the **era of late adulthood**. Here, a person has to come to terms with the idea of retirement, of stepping from centre stage and negotiating a new balance of involvement between himself and society. Anxieties about this may be exacerbated by marked feelings of bodily decline. The inner issues become ones of formulating an effective personal style and image to fit 'being old' and coming to terms with the proximity of death. Levinson follows Erikson's suggestion that the basic polarity to be worked through here is that of *integrity versus despair*. Levinson asserts that this can be as much a time of development as decline, and he points to examples of the flowering of creativity in old age both in work produced and (perhaps more importantly) in the way that life is lived.

PROGRESS BOX 3   Research studies of the life cycle

1   The work of Bühler and her team:

(i)   Based on analyses of biographies.

(ii)   Five phases of the life cycle are proposed.

(iii) Emphasis on biological and social underpinning of personal development.

(iv)   Humanistic emphasis on goal setting and self-determination.

2   Neugarten study:

(i)   Primarily based on analysis of interviews with people of different ages.

(ii)   Focus on mid-life period. Neugarten claims that there is a shift of perspective:
    (a)   to more introspective concerns; and
    (b)   a reversal of the way in which the life span is conceived.

(iii)   Emphasis on the effects of age-related social norms on behaviours and attitudes.

3   Several studies of the life cycle were published in the 1970s.

4   Levinson *et al.'s The Seasons of a Man's Life* provides an illustrative example of research on life phases:

(i)   40 subjects: diverse backgrounds but men only, plus a secondary sample drawn from published biographies and fiction.

(ii)   Analysis based primarily on a series of intensive *biographical interviews.*

(iii)   Key concepts: the *life structure, developmental tasks.*

(iv)   They propose four overlapping *eras*, and focus on two – early and middle adulthood.

(v)   Eras subdivided into an alternating sequence of *structure building* and *transitional periods.*

(vi)   Era of early adulthood:
   (a)   *Four periods:* Early Adult Transition, Entering the Adult World, Age 30 Transition (these three periods make up the novice phase), Settling Down.
   (b)   *Key tasks* of novice period: the Dream, establishing mentor and love relationships (especially with the 'special woman'), forming an occupation.

(vii)   The era of middle adulthood begins with the *Mid-life Transition:*
   (a)   This is Levinson's primary *focus of interest.*
   (b)   Almost all subjects undergo a *major shift* at this stage but there is not necessarily turmoil. Where there is no change, however, there will be disruption or a withering in later life.
   (c)   *Three key tasks* of this period: life review, modifying the life structure, individuation process (to confront and re-integrate four polarities in particular – Young/Old, Masculine/Feminine, Destruction/Creation, Attachment/Separateness).
   (d)   Increased reflectiveness about the meaning of one's life and identity.

(viii) *Later periods of middle adulthood* are less well-documented. Levinson suggests that they are: Entering Middle Adulthood, Age 50 Transition, Culmination of Middle Adulthood.

(ix)   Late Adult Transition to the *era of late adulthood* involves a major readjustment to becoming old.

4   VALUES AND LIMITATIONS OF PHASE THEORIES

The study by Levinson and his colleagues on the seasons of a man's life was intensively and carefully researched over a period of years. It offers an interesting and articulate theory of the phases of the life cycle which is empirically based, enriched by subtle interpretation and well supported by illustrative case studies. Nevertheless, the work has its limitations. In discussing these and the many questions which the study raises, I will look briefly at some other phase theories and open up more general consideration of the values and limitations of this kind of approach.

4.1　The nature of Levinson's theory

What is it then that this theory offers us? Levinson describes it as an 'overarching conception of development' (1978, p. 8). It is concerned not just with each individual's experience of development but with the ways in which this is intrinsically linked with biological growth and changing social contexts. It is a schedule of the kind of changes which every man can expect to pass through as he grows through life. In particular, the periods which are postulated indicate the 'tasks' which have to be worked through if an appropriate mode of living is to be established both for that time of life and as a satisfactory basis for future development.

It is, then, a theory which claims to describe the typical pattern of phases through which men make their way in the course of adult life. The researchers found that these appear to be remarkably tightly tied to specific ages:

> One of our greatest surprises was the relatively low variability in the age at which every period begins and ends. It was not a prediction we made in advance, not a predisposition in our thinking. This finding violates the long-held and cherished idea that individual adults develop at very different paces.
>
> (Levinson *et al.*, 1978, p. 318)

But Levinson does concede that, although the periods are age-linked, there will be some individual variation depending on 'the biological, psychological and social conditions of a man's life' (p. 319). What was invariant in his sample, though, he claims, is the order in which the phases occurred.

None of this is to deny, Levinson asserts, the unique character of each individual life. The periods prescribe the developmental tasks which predominate at that time not how each person will deal with them. He is concerned to make clear that 'our theory of life structure does not specify a single, "normal" course that everyone must follow. . . . Rather than imposing a template for conformity, it increases our sense of human potentialities and of the variousness of individual lives' (1980, p. 289).

In evaluating the Levinson study, it is worth considering in what sense his analysis can be considered empirical. Extensive interviews and observations were used as a rich source of ideas and hypotheses. The form in which the theory is presented is an account of the phases of early and middle adulthood, copiously illustrated with detailed examples and case studies. But although the propositions about phases are well-supported by the interview material, they are not *explicitly* derived from it. Indeed, it is difficult to see how they could be, for interviews and observations have to be structured and interpreted in some way. Pre-existing ideas must therefore come into play to some extent in constructing and generalizing from the biographies of his subjects. Levinson makes no bones about the fact that his research was fuelled by personal interest: we might perhaps consider it as part of the reflective process of his own Mid-life Transition. The theory of phases was evolved through seminars and discussions among the team (including invited colleagues) in which personal experience as well as the data collected were brought under scrutiny. Although this must mean that the research may reflect the researchers' life experiences as well as that of their subjects, it could be argued that this approach is also likely to have added depth to the theory which emerged. Levinson's view of the product of their labours is that: 'the validity and usefulness of this particular theory remains to be determined. No doubt it will change considerably as a result of further research and experience. I present it as empirically grounded theory, not as demonstrated truth' (1980, p. 289).

4.2 Are there differences between the life cycles of men and women?

Even if we accept Levinson's theory of phases as having some validity as a description of the development through early and middle adulthood of the men in his sample, a major question which the study raises is how far we can generalize the theory to the population at large. To what extent can we regard it as universal?

One acknowledged limitation arises from the fact that the selection of subjects was confined to men. Can we assume that the same pattern of development applies to women as well? A problem in considering this question is lack of evidence about the life cycle of women. In their book Levinson *et al.* mention that a study of women in their mid-thirties by Wendy Stewart confirmed that 'all of them went through the same developmental periods as our men, though some of the specific issues were different' (p. 9), but no details of this are given. There have been one or two relatively small scale studies of aspects of the female life cycle: Livson (1976), for example, investigated the mid-life transition of a group of 50-year-old women. Several life course studies have included women as well as men among their subjects (e.g. Gould, 1978) and two popular books, by Nicholson (1980) and, in particular, by Sheehy (1976), have made some effort to compare the life development patterns of men and women. But, as yet, there has been no published research on the life cycle of women comparable in depth and approach to *The Seasons of a Man's Life*.

In considering possible differences between the life cycles of the two sexes, one important consideration is the effects which age- and sex-related social roles and expectations can have upon behaviour and experience. The life styles open to women have become much more variable in more recent years (for example, in respect of whether they are centred on work or in the family). It would seem a reasonable assumption that personal development is geared, to some extent, to the style of life adopted. Where a woman's way of living is similar to the pattern which is typical for males, is there any reason to suppose that her life cycle would be particularly different, in broad outline, from that of a man? There are, in fact, at least two features which might be considered as a source of variation.

One is *having children*. For most women this would appear to occupy a more central place in the life structure than it does for men. Judith Bardwick (1971) has suggested that it is their most important developmental task. While having and bringing up children may be a fundamental source of fulfilment for both sexes, it is more likely, in the case of women, to be a significant distraction from her occupation and career.

In their studies of the life cycle, both Sheehy and Nicholson claim that life structure differences between young men and women are relatively small and that the developmental patterns are pretty similar also in later life. It is in the middle years where sex differences in development and life structures are most pronounced. Nicholson's team interviewed some 600 men, women and children in Colchester in 1979–80. One interesting sex difference was that men were much more likely to identify the thirties as being the 'prime of life'. When subjects in their forties were questioned, women were about eight times as likely as men to report that they considered their prime as still to come. After exploring with his subjects possible reasons for this difference, Nicholson comments:

> Their answers leave no doubt that the thirties and forties are the period of life when the two sexes have least in common, and they suggest that it's parenthood rather than marriage or work which makes the lives of men and women so different. For women of all ages, the most frequently mentioned marker-event of the prime of life is freedom from the responsibility of looking after children. For men, this was rarely a consideration.

> (Nicholson, 1980, pp. 126–7)

A second possible source of variation in the life cycles of the sexes is that women may have a greater concern with *attachment* than men. Both Levinson and Nicholson report that men appear to have fewer close friends than women and Gilligan (1982), on the basis of her study of identity and moral development in young women which was mentioned in section 2.4 has concluded: 'the elusive mystery of women's development lies in its recognition of the continuing importance of attachment in the human life cycle' (p. 23). She argues that, in the face of men's celebration of separation and autonomy, it is essential that women protect this recognition.

We noted earlier in the comment on Erikson's theory that Gilligan considers that there is an important difference in the developmental pattern of young men and women in that, for the latter, a concern for caring and intimacy is likely to have precedence over identity concerns. Horner (1972) has observed that women often experience anxiety about achieving success in competitive situations. This may well be due, Gilligan suggests, to the capacity of women, with their propensity for attachment, to feel sympathy with the losing side.

If there is a particular concern for attachment among women, then one might well expect that marriage would represent an even more important event than it does for men: particularly so because of the greater implications which it is likely to carry for a women's sense of identity (symbolized by the fact that she usually adopts her husband's name). Bardwick comments on the significance of marriage for women: 'Because of their investment in the relationship, because of their history of assessing themselves by others' responses, and because they really do perceive reality in interpersonal terms, they overwhelmingly define and evaluate identity and femininity within the context of this relationship' (Bardwick, 1971, p. 211). Correspondingly, should there be a separation or divorce, this is likely to be more devastating for a woman than a man. She is faced not just with restructuring her relationships but her identity as well.

We saw that Levinson *et al.*, in keeping with many other studies, found that mid-life was a time for many men to begin to open up to those sides of themselves which had been neglected hitherto. But, as Gilligan somewhat wryly puts it: 'the discovery now being celebrated by men in mid-life of the importance of intimacy, relationships and care is something that women have known from the beginning' (1982, p. 17). Might we then expect the converse – that there will be a tendency for women at this time of life to move towards a more assertive, dominant, even achievement-oriented style (particularly in view of the novel sense of freedom which many women experience as a result of children leaving home)?

cross-over effects There is some evidence that there is a change with age in both men and women towards greater similarity in personality style, or even a 'cross-over' to the style more usually associated with the opposite sex. For example, in Neugarten's study (1968) which was referred to earlier (section 4.1), it was found that women as well as men demonstrated a shift towards greater 'interiority' in mid-life: in other words, they seem to become more introverted and less concerned with external events. In another study using a version of the Thematic Apperception Test in which subjects were asked to describe figures of different ages shown in the picture, the findings suggest that both men and women perceive themselves differently as they grow older (Neugarten and Guttmann, 1958). Older subjects of both sexes described the older woman depicted as more dominant than did younger subjects, and the old man in the picture as more submissive. The investigators concluded: '. . . women, as they age, seem to become more tolerant of their own aggressive, egocentric impulses; while men, as they age, of their own nurturant and affiliative impulses . . .' (Neugarten and Guttmann, 1958, p. 89). This would seem to be supported by a more recent study by Lowenthal (1977) who found a tendency among older respondents not only for interpersonal relationships to feature more in the lives of men but also for women to become more assertive. In a cross-cultural analysis, Guttmann (1977) suggests that such cross-overs with age may not just be a feature of our culture. Among both the Navaho Indians and the Lebanese, for example, he claims that there is a tendency for men to adopt a more passive, 'contemplative' role as they grow older: women, on the other hand, are more likely to become assertive and dominant, particularly in the sphere of family affairs.

In view of the significance of having children, one might have thought that the menopause might constitute an important transitional event for women. The evidence is difficult to assess and indicates that women respond in varied ways (e.g. Neugarten, 1967). Neugarten found that about half the women in her study felt that the menopause signified a decrease in attractiveness. But it was seen to bring benefits too, such as not having to worry about periods or getting pregnant any more. Most women did not identify it as a particularly negative feature of middle age or feel that it produced fundamental changes of a psychological kind.

What some women writers (e.g. de Beauvoir, 1972 and Sontag, 1982) consider a problem for all the women, however, is what they see as a 'double standard' of ageing. As Sontag puts it: 'Aging is a man's destiny, something that must happen because he is a human being. For a women, aging is not only her destiny. Because she is that more *narrowly* defined kind of human being, a woman, it is also her vulnerability' (Sontag, 1982, p. 327). Both writers consider that it is in the arena of sexual relations where the double standard particularly applies. Even given the changing attitudes in contemporary society, they argue it is still less acceptable and more difficult for a woman than for a man to seek out and find a younger sexual partner (a problem which is exacerbated, of course, by the fact that women tend to live longer than men and so there are more of them at older age levels). One might consider that Sontag takes too sanguine a view of ageing for men, but it would be hard not to concur with her exhortation to women not to accept the status quo: 'Women have another option. . . . They can let themselves age naturally and without embarrassment, actively protesting and disobeying the conventions that stem from this society's double standard about aging . . .' (ibid., p. 333).

The data available do not permit this to be more than a few comments on possible differences between the life cycles of the two sexes. The issue is complicated by the possibility that there is greater variability of life structures among women. There are sufficient indications, however, that it would be unwise to assume that the findings of Levinson's study (or indeed that of any research using male subjects alone) apply, except in the broadest outline, to women as well.

4.3   The possibility of cultural variation

Although, as we have seen, Levinson and his colleagues deliberately drew their sample from varied backgrounds, in effect their subjects could still be regarded as a fairly homogeneous group. All the executives and industrial workers (fifty per cent of the total sample) worked for two companies. All the subjects were not only American but from a particular area of the USA (the north eastern coastal area). We noted also that they included proportionately far more middle-class respondents than would be found in the general population. How far, therefore, might this study be subject to criticisms which Kimmel has levelled at Erikson and other theories of the life cycle? He argues that:

> they do not give very much indication of the ways in which cultural differences, sex differences, or social class differences interact with this general developmental progression; and they describe a process of development that leads toward the ideal of 'human fulfillment' or 'successful aging' as defined in the middle class in our society. For other persons, fulfillment or successful aging may mean physical survival and providing one's offspring with at least a reasonable chance for survival; for others, aging means illness, poverty, and isolation with little opportunity for fulfillment or success.
>
> (Kimmel, 1980, pp. 19–20)

Levinson admits that without cross-cultural studies and a much more extensive sample than he used, it is not possible to assess the universality of his scheme. But, briefly referring to historical and literary comments on the life cycle, he is prepared to hazard the hypothesis that the broad plan of development is much the same: 'If we place the timetable of our eras and periods over each of the ancient accounts, like a template, they show a remarkably close fit' (1978, p. 324).

It seems quite plausible that there would be a core of similarity. We can think of psychological growth through life as the confluence of three broad and interrelated themes. There is biologically generated change (e.g. hormonal changes at puberty, waning physical vigour and sexual drive in middle and old age). Secondly, there is the context which the society and people among whom we live provide (what jobs are or are not available, what kinds of relationships a person is encouraged to form, etc.). There is also a third dimension which represents the cumulation of experience, the ever-changing balance, rather like that between the two halves of an egg-timer, between the past which has been lived and the future to come. One would anticipate universality in the first dimension. There must also be some communality across cultures for the third. Even in terms of social context, many of the reactions and institutions which societies and subcultures offer at different periods of life are quite likely to form a similar kind of pattern.

But, while one might expect a *broadly* similar shape to development through the human life cycle, there is no evidence to suggest that the specific detail of Levinson's scheme is to be found in other cultures. There are clearly limits to the generalizability of any theory of adult development from one culture or from one historical period to another. The *average* length of life has increased substantially in contemporary society. Tomb inscriptions suggest that it may have been little more than thirty years in ancient Greece. Even in the UK at the turn of the century, it was below 50 compared with 73 today. Although there were many people in earlier times who lived to a ripe old age, the general pattern must have been considerably different from what it is now. If he had lived today, would Napoleon have become, as he is reputed to have, an army captain at 16 and an emperor at 32?

4.4 Phase studies compared

Although there may be little in the way of cross-cultural research available for direct comparison, there have been, as we have already seen, several relevant studies conducted in contemporary Western societies. These provide some support for the broad outline of adult development indicated in Levinson's study. So, for example, Bühler and Neugarten confirm that a major developmental transition occurs in mid-life. But even if we limit the comparisons to studies carried out in the USA, the results could not be regarded as providing solid confirmation for the *specific* pattern of phases which Levinson proposes and of concepts such as the Dream which he regards as central.

longitudinal study A limitation of the Levinson study, in common with most research in this area, is that it was not a longitudinal study in the sense of following up the same men from 22 till old age. Levinson largely relied on comparing men of different ages in his sample (and hence men who, because they were born in different years, had lived through somewhat different social-historical periods), and on the older respondents' memories of their earlier life. In contrast, George Vaillant (1978) studied 94 men (initially selected for testing in 1937) over a period of about 25 years, analysing interviews, questionnaire and physical and psychological assessment data taken at least bi-annually. It is not easy to make a direct comparison with the Levinson results, but many of the distinctions made in the latter study did not seem to be apparent. The period between 20 and 40 years of age, for example, is seen by Vaillant as a relatively homogeneous phase where the essential tasks are establishing intimate relations and consolidating career. Vaillant did detect somewhat similar changes to those in Levinson's account during the Mid-life Transition period, but without much evidence of turmoil or radical revision of lifestyle.

One problem in comparing the findings from different studies is the different ways in which researchers interpret their findings. One apparent difference, for example, between Vaillant's and Levinson's research concerns the degree of emotional turbulence experienced at mid-life. Such an assessment involving interpretation of data must inevitably be to some degree subjective.

As another example, Nicholson claims to find little support in his study of Colchester adults for Levinson's idea of a mentor figure. It turns out, however, that more than half his subjects did in fact mention such a person as playing a significant role in their lives, but that, because this was very often a parent or relative, Nicholson considered that they 'failed to match the definition of a mentor provided by Levinson' (Nicholson, 1980, p. 112). Levinson does, though, specifically allow for the possibility that an older relative may fill the role of mentor, and an uncle who taught his nephew to fish or repair a motor-cycle could presumably be regarded as such. If the examples which Levinson gives tend to be teachers or senior colleagues, this reflects more his subject sample than his conception of the role. We see how comparisons may be muddied by different interpretations made and the different samples of subjects selected for investigation.

Another problem in comparisons of life span studies and in seeking consistencies or contradictions among their results is the fact that they often involve very different kinds of enquiry. Compare, for example, the Levinson study with the approach and way of conceptualizing development in the study of life phases by Roger Gould which is briefly described in Box 5.

Box 5   Roger Gould's study (1978) – *Transformations: Growth and Change in Adult Life*

In a cross-sectional study, Gould compared subjects from a large sample in seven age groups across the life span. In a first study, observations of psychiatric outpatients were collected by a team which included an anthropologist as well as pychologists and psychiatrists. In a follow-up study, questionnaires were administered to over 500 non-patients.

The major emphasis of his analysis is placed on the slow and painful process in which the individual gradually attempts to free him or herself from the unconscious myths and fears originating in childhood. One of these, for example, is the need to be cared for and dependent. Another is the need to be the greatest and most important being. Gould documents this evolution through four phases between the ages of 16 and 45, each of which he sees as characterized by certain 'major false assumptions which we use defensively in order to avoid facing the difficult transformations which development requires'. Thus, the false assumption of the first period (ages 16–22) is that 'I'll always belong to my parents and believe in their world'. And in the early thirties, it is that 'Life is simple and controllable. There are no significant coexisting contradictory forces within me'. (It is not that people at these ages necessarily believe these ideas to be literally true but that such assumptions have an emotional hold on them which needs to be challenged if life is to be lived in a realistic fashion.)

The pattern of Gould's analysis has broad features in common with Levinson's. For example, the mid-life period is seen as a time of opening up to the 'dark side' of the self, with the eventual outcome of becoming more inner-directed and in possession of oneself. The issue of striving to assert separateness he found was a particular problem for women. Generally, however, because of the very different ways in which their analyses are presented, effective cross-comparisons are difficult to draw.

That different studies should ask different kinds of question and should conceptualize development and interpret their findings in various ways is not surprising (nor unusual in psychology – see Metablock Paper 2). What we are inevitably dealing with here are different constructions of the life cycle generated by the particular goals, theoretical constructs and investigating techniques used by the researchers.

But although there is considerable variety in description and detail between theories, when we compare the number and timing of the phases of adult development which are proposed, it is possible to detect some broad overlap. Four of Erikson's eight ages refer to adult development (these, you may remember from section 2.3, are focused respectively on identity vs. role confusion, intimacy vs. isolation, generativity vs. stagnation, and ego integrity vs. despair). Bühler also suggests four developmental phases after childhood (youth: 15–25 years; early adulthood: 25–45/50 years; mature adulthood: 45/50–65 years; old age: 65 years onwards – see section 3.1). The first and last of these would appear to match Erikson's scheme. Although Erikson does not give chronological ages, the middle two stages of both schemes also roughly coincide, though probably the onset of generativity-isolation concerns comes for most people a little earlier than 45, the age at which Bühler places the beginning of mature adulthood. Bühler's phases also fit quite well with Levinson's four overlapping eras of: (1) childhood and adolescence up to 22 years (this encompasses most of Bühler's two separate phases of childhood and youth); (2) early adulthood lasting from 17 to 45 years; (3) middle adulthood from 40 to 65 years; and (4) late adulthood from 60 years onwards.

Levinson, as we have seen, subdivides his eras into shorter periods. Even here we can find consistency with other theories. Although Gould conceptualizes the content of the periods differently, with a focus on the illusory, unconscious assumptions which emotionally dominate a person's attitude to life, the ages at which he sets the periods of early and middle adulthood match closely those of Levinson. Thus the years from 16–22 Gould describes as the phase of 'leaving one's parents' world' (cf. Levinson's theory where 17–22 is the Early Adult Transition). From 22–28 years is the period he describes as 'I'm nobody's baby now' (cf. for Levinson 22–28 years is the period of Entering the Adult World). From 28–34 years is the time of 'opening up' (for Levinson 28–33 is the Age 30 Transition). Only then do their subdivisions notably diverge, as Gould regards 35–45 years as one phase – what he calls the mid-life decade (cf. Levinson: 33–40 – Settling Down; 40–45 – Mid-life Transition).

It is true, nevertheless, that the way in which other theorists and researchers break up the life span can be quite dissimilar to the examples cited above. Nicholson, for instance, divides it into childhood (0–11 years), adolescence (11–17 years), young adulthood (17–25 years), parenthood (25–38 years), early middle-age (38–48 years), later middle-age (49 to retirement), and the retirement years (60 or 65 years onwards). As the naming of some of these phases suggests, his divisions are based on the principle of tying them to life events (like being a parent or retirement) rather than, as in the case of Levinson, Gould and Erikson, seeing them as phases which evolve as part of human development and which are qualitatively distinct in terms of psychological experience and approach to life.

The different approaches and ways of conceptualizing adult development used by different theories may tend to give the impression that there is little if any consistency between them, and that the nature and number of the phases which they propose is pretty much an arbitrary affair. However, as we have noted, there is some broad agreement about the general outline of human development. Taken as a whole, phase theories offer a varied but overlapping account of growth through adult life.

4.5   The value of Levinson's contribution

Levinson's theory is a good example of what phase theories can offer. Like Erikson's scheme, it is best regarded as a tool to think with. He gives us a way of thinking about the qualitative changes likely to occur in personal worlds as we grow older. It makes fascinating reading, in that it raises questions and our consciousness about both our present life development and the possibilities open to us. It is of value in drawing our attention to the fact that adult experience does not stay constant through life, and in helping us to understand the personal worlds of people of different ages. It alerts us to how others cope with change and crises. We may also come to see more clearly the pattern of our lives and the stages we are at: we may become more aware of the problems and transitions **anticipatory socialization** which we may have to face in the future. Such 'anticipatory socialization' can help us come to terms more effectively with change. This is particularly relevant in the contemporary world where styles of living are changing so rapidly that traditional patterns no longer always provide a useful guide. In this way, Levinson's theory and others like it, rather than presenting us with a standard blueprint for life, stimulate our capacity for shaping our development along lines which we choose.

Like many other phase theories, Levinson's study also emphasizes the psychosocial nature of development – that it rests on complex interactions between biological growth, social context and individual accumulation of experience. Levinson is concerned not just with the way individuals can shape their own lives but with the role which social context and institutions play. He tries to stimulate our thinking about whether these might be modified to offer more adequate support for the changes brought about in the normal course of human development.

PROGRESS BOX 4

An evaluation of phase theories, in particular that of Levinson *et al.*:

1   The nature of Levinson's theory:

(i)   A *schedule* of typical *changes* and *tasks* arising in adult development.

(ii)   These are tied to particular *ages*.

(iii)   It allows for *individual variation* and uniqueness.

(iv)   How far is the theory *empirically based?*
  (a)   The propositions are not explicitly derived from data.
  (b)   Personal concerns were involved both in starting and in conducting the study.
  (c)   'Empirically grounded' not 'demonstrated truth'.

2   Does Levinson's theory apply to women?

(i)   The problems of *lack of data* about the female life cycle.

(ii)   Women's life style is likely to be more individually *variable?*

(iii)   *Possible source of variation* between men's and women's life cycles:
  (a)   *Giving birth to and rearing children* usually plays a more significant role for women.
  (b)   Women have a greater concern with *attachment?*

(iv)   *Cross-over effects* at mid-life?

(v)   Does the *menopause* have any effect?

(vi)   A double standard of ageing?

3   The possibility of cultural variations in adult development:

(i)   The *subjects* in Levinson's study were fairly homogeneous.

(ii) The life pattern and values described are essentially *Western and middle-class* as well as male.

(iii) There is little cross-cultural data on the life cycle but Levinson claims that the *broad pattern of human development* is probably much the *same* in other cultures and was similar in earlier historical periods also.

(iv) But there are *limits to generalizability*, e.g. the effects of differences in average life span.

4 Comparisons between the findings of Levinson's and other life-phase research:

(i) The *problems of comparing studies:*
  (a) There are different *interpretations* of findings, e.g.
    – Vaillant's longitudinal study shows more homogeneity of development between 20 and 40 years and less sign of turmoil at mid-life.
    – Nicholson finds little evidence for the role of 'mentor' but seems to be interpreting the concept differently from Levinson.
  (b) Problems in comparing studies also result from *different ways of conceptualizing development*: cf. Levinson and Gould.

(ii) Although the ways in which development is described may vary, there is nevertheless some *consistency* in the number and timing of the broad phases (and even specific periods) of adult development proposed by different theories: e.g. Erikson, Bühler, Levinson and Gould.

5 The *value* of Levinson's contribution:

(i) Stimulates thought about personal change and development.

(ii) Increases awareness of possible differences of attitude and experience of people of different ages.

(iii) Serves as anticipatory socialization to help us deal with transitions in our own lives.

(iv) Draws attention to the need to modify social institutions to accommodate better the changing pattern of needs with age.

5 GROWTH THROUGH LIFE

I would like to conclude this discussion of change and development in adult life by considering three issues. To provide a contrast to the phase approach, I shall first discuss briefly other ways of conceptualizing the course of life, particularly those which stress its continuities. I shall then look at the role played by crisis and transition in the shaping of individual lives. Finally, I shall try to relate what we have learned in this unit about adult development to the discussion of personal worlds in the previous two units, considering in particular the ways in which existential needs change as we grow through life.

5.1 Continuities and contours

One feature of life as we experience it is its sense of continuity. Each of us is still likely to consider him or herself as fundamentally the same person as twenty years ago, in spite of the fact that we no longer look or sound the same and even though our attitudes and fund of experience may be very different. The central aspects of our world are likely to share this sense of continuity. Relationships which are important are, for most of us, more or less enduring ones. Values and beliefs do not usually change from year to year but remain much the same for considerable stretches of our lives. Even today, this is often true of work as well once a career has been established, and quite a number of people remain in the same job, or at least occupation, for the whole of their working lives. Life may be punctuated by events, some recurring like Christmas, others less predictable or novel like falling in love or taking one's first parachute jump; but these are woven into a fabric of continuous flow. As at New Year, we may try to establish frontiers of time, but these are somewhat arbitrary and artificial. In terms of ongoing experience, New Year's Day is unlikely to be intrinsically different from any other new day. It is only when we stand back to look at our life in retrospect, or at someone's else's, that we can segment it into distinctively different phases.

The alternative to conceptualizing adult life as a cycle of phases is to think of it as an unfolding pattern or life course marked by events but essentially characterized by a sense of personal continuity. In fact, rather than viewing each person's development as a single life course, it may be more useful to think of it as a set of multiple but interrelated courses. Smelser (1980) has suggested the term **life contours** 'contour' to designate the pattern of each continuously changing thread.

One contour, for example, is the *historical time* in which a person lives: the major events, perhaps war or economic depression, which dominate the period, and the *Zeitgeist* ('the spirit of the times') which conditions prevailing attitudes and feelings. In writing his psychobiographies of Luther and Gandhi, Erikson was very concerned to explore the role which this historical background played in the developing attitudes and actions of his subjects and in other people's reactions to **psychohistory** them (Erikson sometimes refers to these books as studies in *psychohistory*). He argues, for example, for the influence of the Renaissance on Luther, and that both British and Hindu cultures were important in determining the course and style of Gandhi's life.

Closely related to historical time is the patterning of *social context*. As we grow older, so the social settings in which we find ourselves change. Often these are thrust on us as when we start school, begin a job or face retirement. Such settings play an important role in determining and giving meaning to the roles we play and the ways in which we behave and relate with others. One of the critical problems of unemployment is finding that a whole segment of our usual means of engaging with the world is suddenly missing. Not only do the settings which are available to us change as we grow older but so also do the assumptions which others make about us. There are influential stereotypes and normative expectations of the life style and behaviours of people of different ages. These are often an important source not only of the identities ascribed to us by others but also of the changing view of ourselves as we grow older (see, for example, the discussion of the double standard of ageing in section 4.2). The significance of social context **rites of passage** and changes of role and setting are made explicit in rites of passage. These are formal and informal ceremonies, such as religious confirmation, a twenty-first birthday celebration, graduation day, a wedding or a retirement presentation, where a new-found change of social status is marked by a social occasion. They serve to make clear the enmeshing of the personal in the social by reaffirming the importance of social role and the identity conferred by it. In some cases (such as a wedding or confirmation) they may also help to strengthen a personal commitment by making it a public reality. Although such a ceremony may signify change, it also serves to assert continuities by explicitly linking a person's previous state to his or her new one.

Another major thread is the *biological underpinning* of personal development. In itself this may bring about major modifications in life style and experience, as when behaviour becomes constrained due to the effects of sensory, cognitive or physical deterioration. But, as we noted earlier, biological changes as we grow older may take on significance only because of the ways in which they lead other people to react to us.

The historical, social and biological contours focused on so far suggest that much of the course of life and the contexts and events which dominate it are imposed upon us and lie outwith our control. Yet, as discussed in Unit 12, there is a very real sense in which we *actively create* what we are and what we may become. We are likely to monitor what is happening to us and use the feedback to stimulate ourselves towards renewed efforts to bring about what we desire, attempt radical changes, or perhaps resign ourselves to what may seem to be our inevitable fate. Plath (1982) has emphasized the interactive nature of this contour by referring to it as 'a collective fabricating of selves, a mutual building of biographies' (pp. 115–16).

Almost all theories of the life span, certainly the phase theories which we have considered in this unit, acknowledge that personal development represents the confluences of such interacting contours. The problem is that none (apart from possibly the example of Erikson) analyse in detail the ways in which the different strands interact. Clearly we are presented here with the kind of paradox which we encountered in Unit 12 (see section 3). On one hand, the patterning of significant contours is largely determined for us. On the other, in important respects, we can and often do feel that we have the scope to create life along lines which we choose. The idea of the life course being a form of 'personal career' captures this paradox, for it implies to some extent that it is open to our own direction and efforts but also that it is governed by chance, opportunity and the reactions of others.

self

convoy

pathways

In analysing the dynamics of the life course, Plath (1982) uses three core concepts. One is the *self*, by which he denotes the sense of continuity and the capacity for reflexiveness and initiation of change which characterize us as persons. Another is the *convoy*: 'the circle of others who share in the actions of the self and who have the power to decide which actions are culturally "authorized"'. His third concept is the *pathways*, the 'long-term guidelines that self and convoy initially apply to their actions as they pilot their collective course down the biographical current' (Plath, 1982, p. 116). This trilogy of concepts emphasizes the complexity of the interactions which shape the course of life. This is generated not only by our own self-direction but by the autonomous actions of others as well as the more impersonal forces which have their source in our biology and in the social and historical context.

Awareness of one's own personal biography is an important basis of individual identity. It is worth reiterating, though, that any account of the life course, from whatever perspective and based on whatever method, can only be a construction. We may conceptualize it as phases or as intersecting contours or plotted as a series of significant events: but how we will construct it will depend on the ideas and theories we have been exposed to and the needs and values which underlie our effort. Any account, whether of our own life or someone else's, will also be influenced by what Plath has called 'cultural archetypes'. He points out that every cultural heritage offers ways of making sense of and symbolizing the self, the convoy and life-course pathways. Often these are incorporated into popular sayings and philosophy. He contrasts, for example, the Western focus on 'individualism' with the Japanese archetype of growth which centres, he claims, on 'the cultivation of personal capacities for relatedness' (p. 119): 'The Western archetype . . . seems more aimed at cultivating a self that feels secure in its uniqueness in the cosmos, the Japanese archetype to a self that can feel human in the company of others' (p. 120).

In the last analysis, any biography or autobiography is a personal affair. As Jung comments on undertaking to tell his 'personal myth' in the book *Memories, Dreams and Reflections*: 'I can only make direct statements, only "tell stories". Whether or not the stories are "true" is not the problem. The only question is whether what I tell is *my* fable, *my* truth' (Jung, 1977, p. 17).

5.2 Crisis and transition

Another approach to the study of adult development is to focus neither on phases nor on contours but on times of change or transition. One feature of Erikson's theory, as we saw earlier, is that he conceives such transitions in dialectical terms – that development emerges from the interplay of oppositions. He also makes the point that it is in times of crisis, when a person is vulnerable, that shifts of direction and personal growth are likely to occur. Riegel (1975) is one of a number of psychologists who have emphasized the importance of crisis for growth. He sees conflict and contradictions as 'the basis for any innovative and creative work' (Riegel, 1975, p. 101). Gilligan has described crisis as the 'harbinger of growth' (1982, p. 108) and Ferguson (1980) has stressed that, in order to bring about personal transformation, it is necessary not to sidestep crisis but to confront it.

When we consider the role of crisis in adult development, it is worth distinguishing between two types – 'scheduled' or 'normative' changes which come about as part of the normal sequence of development, and those unscheduled events which often create major stress and are imposed upon a person without warning (e.g. accidents, unemployment or the break-up of a relationship).

A crisis is essentially a turning point. Although it is likely to produce personal change of some kind, this, as shown by Gilligan's (1982) study of young women who decided to undergo an abortion, can be experienced as either deterioration or growth. A positive outcome can occur when the difficulties experienced lead a person to deal with blocks in his or or her development. Coming through a crisis may shake up one's usual attitudes and approach to life and may generate a sense of direction and meaning. The most dramatic examples of this are accounts of near-death experiences (these were briefly discussed in section 2.3 of Unit 12).

Whether experiencing a crisis encourages growth or deterioration will depend on the nature and degree of the stress involved and on the coping strategies which an individual adopts. Given the importance of work as a source not only of income but of structure, social contacts, identity and often status, challenge and involvement, it is not surprising that losing one's job should usually be experienced as profoundly disturbing and stressful. However, the research of Fryer and Payne (1984), which was referred to briefly in section 2.1 of Unit 12, suggests that some people can find ways of coping with unemployment which make it at least tolerable and, at best, a time of opportunity for development and change. The essential characteristics held in common by their sample of subjects, selected for their ability to cope with unemployment in a positive creative way, seemed to be their capacity to act as autonomous agents who choose:

> ... to take the lead, initiate and intervene in situations to bring about change in valued directions rather than responding to imposed change passively and/or revising expectations and requirements of life correspondingly downwards. This may involve actually changing the situation to produce opportunities or creatively re-perceiving it in ways which reveal previously unseen opportunities and then exploiting them.

(Fryer and Payne, 1984, p. 17)

This attitude reflected these subjects' usual way of dealing with life situations and seemed often, the researchers claim, to be related both to parental models and firmly held personal values. Another relevant factor was the support of friends or relatives for the attitude which they had adopted.

In a major study of life crises and coping behaviour, Pearlin and his co-workers (see Pearlin, 1980) interviewed over 2,000 subjects aged between 18 and 65, re-interviewing the same subjects four years later. They were particularly interested in finding out about problems in their subjects' experience of work, marital relationships and parenthood. They also gathered information about the ways in which they coped with crises and the degree of emotional distress they experienced. One of their major findings was that the key to coping with stress is the manipulation of meaning: 'The most common mode of response to life strains is the employment of a large inventory of perceptual and cognitive devices enabling one to view one's... problem in a manner that reduces its threat and consequently minimizes its stressful impact' (p. 185). Popular philosophies according to which, for example, 'things always work out for the best', or which urge us to 'count our blessings' or 'look on the bright side', help us in this. Another technique is to place a lower value on an area in which stress is being experienced (work for example) and to give greater priority to a role in which satisfaction can be obtained (for example, being a devoted father). Such selective commitment is greatly aided by the complexity and fragmentation of much of modern life into relatively separate areas (see Unit 13, section 5.3.3).

A point which Pearlin emphasizes is that both stress-inducing circumstances and support and the means of coping with them tend to be unequally distributed in our society. For example, younger people, they found, were more likely to encounter difficulties in working life, although the stresses experienced by older people (e.g. serious illness) tended to be more difficult to reverse. The amount of stress and the resulting emotional upset, Pearlin argues, are particularly related to one's position in society. People lower down the socioeconomic scale are not only more subject to stresses of various kinds but are less likely to have the personal resources which enable them to deal with such situations effectively. He found, for instance, that they are less likely to have a developed sense of mastery and self-esteem, both of which he claims are key attributes for successfully coping with stress.

Because of his emphasis on the significance of stress and its unequal distribution, Pearlin has criticized the notion that life patterns are as universal as Levinson claims. He emphasizes that:

> ... development should not be construed as a single course universally followed by all people. It would perhaps fit reality better if we were to assume that there are many developmental patterns, each shaped and channelled by the confluence of the social characteristics of adults, their standing in the social order, the problematic experiences to which they must adapt, the social contexts and situations in which they are embedded, and the coping resources with which they are equipped.

> (Pearlin, 1980, pp. 176–7)

Some crises or transitions are brought about in the normal course of development. Often they are precipitated by a shift in one life contour to which it is then necessary to re-align other aspects of the life structure. Thus, physical illness may require a person to adopt a more restrained life style, and retirement from work may require a radical revision of interest and the use of leisure time. The alternating pattern of transitions followed by periods of relative equilibrium where a revised life structure is then developed is, as we saw, a feature of Levinson's theory.

mid-life crisis The transition which has received perhaps most attention in the research literature (apart possibly from adolescence) is what is often termed the 'mid-life crisis'. We noted earlier (see section 3) that almost all the research on adult development through the life span has indicated that there are likely to be significant changes occurring at mid-life. There are, however, substantial variations in the way this transition has been conceptualized, in estimations of its onset and duration, the significance and degree of the changes involved and the extent to which they are to be found in the population at large.

Jung was among the first to discuss the nature of the psychological changes which take place during mid-life (see, for example, his paper 'The stages of life', first published in 1931). According to Jung, the key feature of 'the psychic revolution of life's noon' (i.e. mid-life) is a turning inward – a gradual movement away from active involvement with external events towards a greater reflectiveness and exploration of inner life. As Jung puts it: 'After having lavished its light upon the world, the sun withdraws its rays in order to illuminate itself' (1969, p. 399).

individuation (Jung)
The mid-life transition can involve what Jung calls 'individuation' or 'self-realization'. The essence of this process is to give greater expression to those aspects of self which are unconscious and undeveloped, which have been ignored or repressed. If the task of young adulthood is to establish a place in the world, to succeed in making a living and possibly bringing up children, the task of middle life is to develop and round out the whole personality, particularly those potentialities which have been suppressed in the pursuit of the goals of younger life. Individuation involves becoming aware of archetypes from the collective unconscious (see Unit 13, section 4.3) and incorporating them as part of the individual self (which is why Jung calls it 'individuation'). This includes con-
shadow
frontation with the *shadow*, the dark unrealized side of ourselves, and also learn-
soul image – anima/us
ing to give greater expression to the *soul image* or *anima/animus* which is the representation of the opposite sex which Jung claims each of us carries within our unconscious (see Box 4 for discussion of this in the context of Levinson's theory). There is also a concern with developing spiritual understanding. If a person is able to assimilate this rich mine of experience, the result will be a new balance in
self-realization
personality, a higher synthesis or *self-realization*.

Another classic study after Jung which explored the idea of a mid-life transition is Elliott Jaques' paper 'Death and the mid-life crisis' (1965), which was based on clinical experience and also analysis of the lives of artists and writers. Jaques pointed out that it is at mid-life (the onset of which he placed as early as the mid-thirties) that a person stops 'growing up and has begun to grow old'. He argued that at the core of the crisis is the need to confront the fact of finiteness and eventual death in order to liberate energy for new growth. Those creative people he studied who managed to do this produced their most profound work in later life. Vaillant (1977) though has disputed the significance of fear of death at this stage, preferring to stress the often euphoric sense of liberation which may be felt as the responsibilities and burdens of young adulthood begin to be alleviated.

Jung's ideas about development in mid-life seem quite consistent with the findings of the research studies which we have already examined. Indeed, Levinson openly acknowledges Jung's influence on his thinking. It is interesting that the conceptualization of the life span into four eras (childhood, early adulthood, middle adulthood and late adulthood, each linked by a transitional period) had earlier been suggested by Jung. There is also a clear echo of his ideas in Levinson's conception of the key tasks of mid-life. These include, you will remember, working through a set of polarities (Young/Old, Attachment/Separateness, Masculine/Feminine, Creativeness/Destruction), a task which involves coming to terms with aspects of the self which may not hitherto have been acknowledged or expressed. Almost all researchers agree that at mid-life there is likely to be some kind of turning inwards – a move to a more reflective and introspective approach to life than before. As we saw in section 4.2, there is some evidence too of 'cross-overs', of developing more of the attributes of the opposite sex during the course of middle life. There is inconsistency, though, among theorists and researchers about the likely time of onset of the mid-life crisis. Levinson sees it as beginning around 40, for example, Neugarten at around 50. Lowenthal and Chiriboga (1972) suggest that the real crisis does not arrive until the sixties. They claim to find no evidence of it in mid-life. There is not only disagreement then about how far a mid-life crisis is a contemporary middle-class, Western phenomenon and when it starts, but also about whether it makes sense to talk of one at all. Certainly there are middle-aged people in our culture who claim that this has no meaning in their experience. Nicholson (1980), for example, found that less than seventeen per cent of his women subjects aged between 45 and 58, and even fewer of the men, reported that the forties had been a difficult time. But again we encounter the problem of what is meant by the concept 'crisis' and also the possibility (as Farrell and Rosenberg (1981) have suggested) that some people may repress mid-life concerns because of the anxieties which they arouse.

*"Now, see here, Harley. I was forty once, and I never
went through any mid-life crisis!"*

Crisis, as noted earlier, means turning point. Mid-life is clearly a time of many changes both biologically and in terms of one's social situations. The precise form which these changes and subsequent personal development will take depends on each individual and the style of his or her life. As Kimmel (1980) has observed after reviewing studies of the mid-life transition, if they generate emotional turbulence this may well result from:

> . . . a growing awareness that one's life, or style of living one's life, has become more and more out of step with one's inner characteristics, wishes, desires, goals, needs, and feelings. It is as if, early in adulthood, one followed the well-worn footpath through the dense forest in pursuit of a distant mountain and for the next 10 or 15 miles (years) the climb was so difficult that one never looked back or paid attention to all that was being ignored along the way. Perhaps not until the summit is reached does one realize that the path led to the wrong mountain. Or perhaps it is the first cool day of autumn that reminds one to smell the flowers because soon they will be gone.

(Kimmel, 1980, p. 108)

5.3 A changing sense of being

The discussion in this unit of development through adult life carries many implications for the ways in which the features of our personal worlds (see Unit 12) change and evolve as we grow older.

ACTIVITY 4

The commentary earlier on Erikson's theory included some speculations about ways in which existential needs assume different significance and salience as we progress through life (see near the end of section 2.4). Take a few minutes to recall the points made there. If you find it difficult to remember them, you might like to look back at that section before proceeding.

In the light of the ideas covered in subsequent sections of this unit, are there any further suggestions you can make about ways in which existential needs might change over time?

One implication which seems to emerge from theory and research about the life cycle is that it is especially during *transitional* stages such as adolescence, mid-life and retirement that existential issues are likely to preoccupy a person. Transitions also seem accordingly to be the times of maximum reflexiveness.

The experience of *time* underpins and permeates development as a central contour running through life. Time is what the life course is about. Slowly, gradually, almost imperceptibly, we move from a situation where most of life lies ahead of us to one where almost all lies behind. The passing of time is marked as much by social events (the 'social clock' is Neugarten's phrase) as by inner feelings or biological change. Neugarten (1968) claims, as we noted earlier, that at mid-life there is quite likely to be a reversal of directionality', in which life is restructured in terms of how much time there is left rather than as a sequence of events since birth. Concern with one's finiteness and eventual death is not the preserve of later life – it seems also likely to be a feature of transitional times, especially at mid-life. In the final years, it may not necessarily become a major concern, even for those not convinced that there is existence after death. As Jung put it towards the end of his own life: 'the last steps are the loveliest and most precious, for they lead to that fullness to which the innermost essence of man is born' (Jung, 1973).

Although there is continuity in each individual's sense of *identity*, there is also evolution and change. One root of identity is in the cumulative pattern of experience. Another lies in one's awareness of one's body, of the way it feels and functions. It also depends, of course, on the reactions of others towards us. All of these change with age. So too does the extent to which we are influenced by how others see us and the characteristics which we assume that they ascribe to us. The self-consciousness of adolescence can be a painful affair, and one of the joys of maturity for many people is the gradual freeing from concerns about what others think. Because life is limited it becomes too precious to spend it in any way other than that which we ourselves think is appropriate for us.

As we progress through life, both the need for finding some *meaning* in life and the arena in which it is sought are likely to change. There is the burning idealism of youth with exploration of values and ideologies; then early adulthood when it is particularly achievements, doing things and forming relationships which are likely to give a sense of meaning to life. Both theories and research suggest that in later life comes a greater reflectiveness and concern with (given the necessary energy and strength) exploring unrealized possibilities: perhaps also for a few people there may be a search for meaning of a more metaphysical and spiritual kind which may involve reviewing one's life and trying to make sense of it within the wider context of human existence.

Life is not lived passively. We may be confronted with particular problems and tasks at different stages of life, but the outcome will be, in part at least, determined by how we respond. There are no ways to make definite predictions of the course of any particular individual's life. The significance of *autonomous action* and the variability of individual responses is stressed even in theories like Levinson's which describes life as a series of more-or-less predictable phases. For Bühler, life goals and personal intentions are central concepts.

Humanistic psychologists have theorized about what are likely to be central life goals for people in our culture. Rogers has argued, for example, that a major need is self-acceptance. White has suggested that it is also important to people to increase their competence in dealing with the world. Maslow stresses that, once physiological needs and needs for security, self-esteem and love have been satisfied, the fundamental concern becomes to actualize one's potentials. It is on measures such as these that we may assess ourselves in the accounting at mid-life and in the final struggle between ego integrity versus despair.

Autonomy is exercised in a social context. The complexity and fragmentation of contemporary society leads to a particular emphasis being placed on personal autonomy. This may be a confusing and often difficult burden to bear. But it does allow opportunity to transcend standard roles and to create our own variants in style of living. Autonomous acts are also related to personal values and the meanings assigned to life. The enterprise of living is thus both a social and a moral affair:

> The human life course entity in transition is both an *individual*, a mortal center of initiative and integrity, and a *person*, a moral actor in society's dramas. Aware of morality, we are under a biographical imperative: to own responsibility for a line of continuity that connects our conduct – our efforts and rewards – past, present, and potential. Aware of mortality, we are under an existential imperative: to sustain hope that despite the probability of decline and the certainty of death we may nevertheless achieve a fair share of 'the promise of adulthood'.

> (Plath, 1982, p. 116)

As noted earlier, each of us can only make sense of our own lives in our own way. In doing so, we are likely to draw on the cultural 'archetypes' of our time. As life-course theories have permeated people's consciousness, there is a certain circularity about it all. For having been told of a mid-life transition, for example, it would not be surprising if we can discern one as a result. This is not to deny the value of such an idea, but it is to suggest that the ways in which we both create and make sense of our lives will be based within the patterns offered by our culture.

The theories encountered in this unit are best not taken as statements about the way all adults develop, but are to be mined for what inspiration they may provide in creating your own life pattern. Use the analyses they provide as a tool for discussing patterns and possibilities in your own biography, and for coming to terms with the paradoxes and contradictions you may find. They may be of some value in encouraging self-determination within a framework of reflectiveness and understanding.

ACTIVITY 5   (optional)

Notes for an autobiography

If you have the time and interest, you might like to consider assembling materials and notes for an identity or autobiographical project.

1   Collect together any evidence of feelings, thoughts or actions from your earlier life (photos, letters, school reports, old toys may all help reawaken the feel of your personal world at different stages of your life).

2   You might encourage relatives or people who knew you in the past to talk about how they saw you.

3   If you have friends prepared to cooperate, ask them to jot down notes about how they perceive you now – the kind of person they see you as.

4   Put these together, along with the chronology of your life pattern which you created for Activity 1.

5   Sketch out the evolution of your own personal world to the present time.

6   How do you see your world developing into the future? How would you like to create it?

PROGRESS BOX 5   Further perspectives on adult development

1   *Continuity* is a key feature of the experience of living.

(i)   One way to conceptualize the life course is as an interacting set of *contours*, e.g. historical background, social context, biological functioning, autonomous actions, etc.

(ii)   Plath suggests *self, convoy* and *pathways* as core concepts in understanding the life course.

2   Any account of a life course is inevitably a *construction* influenced by 'cultural archetypes' and personal needs and values.

3   Some approaches to understanding the life course focus on periods of *transition and crisis*. Crises can be a source of personal growth and transformation.

4   *Unscheduled crises:*

(i)   The significance of *coping strategies*.

(ii)   Fryer and Payne's study of strategies used by the 'creatively unemployed' emphasizes the importance of autonomous behaviour.

(iii)   *Pearlin's* study of *stress situations* suggests:

   (a)   two key *ways of coping with crisis* are the manipulation of meaning and selective commitment.

   (b)   stress is *age-related* (there is more occupational stress for younger people: more permanent problems for older people).

   (c)   stress is *class-related* (there is more stress and fewer resources for coping among lower socioeconomic groups).

   (d)   life development patterns vary depending on the *social situation* of the people concerned.

5   *Normative crises and transitions:* most attention has been given to the mid-life transition.

(i)   *Jung* – the task of the second half of life is self-realization: individuation as a process at mid-life (cf. Levinson).

(ii)   *Jaques* – the source of mid-life crisis is heightened awareness of eventual death.

(iii)   *Vaillant* – emphasis on the liberation which can occur at mid-life.

(iv)   All studies agree that there is likely to be increased reflectiveness and *'turning inward'* at mid-life.

(v)   There is some *disagreement* about the time of onset of 'crisis' and mid-life, whether this is culture-bound or whether it exists at all.

6   *Existential issues:*

(i)   They become more prominent during times of *transition*.

(ii)   *Time* is regulated by the social clock as well as by biological functioning. Reversal of directionality with age.

(iii)   *Identity* has continuity but evolves with changes in body functioning and in how others see and react to us.

(iv)   The need for *meaningfulness* and the kinds of meaning sought vary with age.

(v)   *Autonomous* action is involved in constructing our own lives, particularly in the context of contemporary society. Humanistic psychologists suggest that people strive for self-acceptance, self-actualization and increasing their competence.

(vi)   The enterprise of living is both a *moral* and *social* affair.

7   *Life-course theories* are best regarded not as definitive accounts of adult development but as sources of ideas for encouraging reflectiveness and self-determination.

PART 2: BLOCK CONCLUSION: MAKING SENSE OF AND MANAGING OUR LIVES

The purpose of this conclusion is to look back over the Block and to pick up some of the implications which the ideas and approaches discussed there have, in particular for:

(a) the kind of understanding of personal worlds which is possible;

(b) the relevance of psychology to the ways in which we live our lives.

1 SUMMARY AND REVIEW

Before reading further, you might like to take a few moments to think back to the content of each of the three units which comprise this Block. Make notes about what was dealt with and the main points in each. You may need to look again at the text but it is suggested that before doing so you spend a little time trying to recollect what you can.

A brief synopsis of the material in each unit is given below. This provides little more than an outline, however, and you may want to supplement it with your own revision notes and comments. If you come across any statements or concepts which you are not sure about it might be worth checking by referring to the relevant part of the text. Prompting questions are also given which you might like to see if you can answer (look them up in the unit concerned if you prefer).

Unit 12: The experience of being a person

We began by exploring the nature of personal worlds – the subjective experience of being a person. With the help of analyses of accounts of the personal worlds of four different people (Liv, Christopher, Leonard and Roland) thirteen key features of personal worlds were proposed.

Can you remember what these were?

Three methodological problems were noted: that all personal worlds are inevitably constructions; that they are therefore partial and selective; and that the only access we have to other people's experience is by inference.

The unit then went on to discuss four existential issues.

How would you define an 'existential issue'?

1 *Time and finiteness:* Various factors which can influence our experience of time were discussed (e.g. the nature of activities engaged in, physiological states, age and, in particular, social context and the impact of technology and capitalism). The focus of this section was on the awareness of finiteness and eventual death, ways of coping with this and the importance for authentic existence of confronting their reality.

2 *Choice:* After discussing how the concept of autonomy can be reconciled with the evidence that so much of human behaviour is determined, the notions of commitment, responsibility and accountability were considered. Because choice is often irrevocable and may have to be made ultimately without grounds, people are often reluctant to exert the potential freedom which they possess. Existentialists again argue that, for authentic living, it is necessary to choose and to accept responsibility for the consequences of one's choices. The possibility of fostering the exercise of choice and will was explored. Analysing the determinants of our behaviour, for example, paradoxically may help us to increase our ability to act autonomously.

3 *Meaningfulness:* By examining the nature of meaningfulness and its origins in biological need and cultural socialization, it was argued that the development of science and the complexity of contemporary, technological society has undermined the power of such traditional bases to give clear and meaningful structure to people's lives. The paradox of meaningfulness is that although a sense of direction is important for living, we have no sound rational basis for constructing one. The different kinds of meaning found in life and the way these change as we grow older were also discussed.

4 *Identity and existential isolation:* The nature of identity and its psychosocial nature were explored. Not only are its roots partly in group memberships, but a sense of individual identity may be intensified by the fact that we participate in many social sub-worlds. Gender and the labelling-theory account of the construction of a deviant identity were used to illustrate the psychosocial basis of identity. The related problem of existential isolation and different ways of escaping this were then considered. For an existentialist, to be authentic requires that we do not deny our fundamental isolation but accept its reality.

The unit concluded by briefly opening up discussion as to how far personal worlds can be considered to be socially constructed and how far they reflect the fundamental experience of existence as human beings.

Unit 13: Making sense of subjective experience

The aim of Unit 13 was to show some of the ways in which psychologists have conceptualized subjective experience.

Can you recall the main theories discussed and their basic propositions?

---

1 A brief account was given of William James's conception of *consciousness* as an ever-changing, *continuous stream* involving sub-worlds of experience and active selection from simultaneous possibilities.

2 Goffman's *frame analysis* explores something of the different kinds of framework we use in making sense of the world. He emphasizes the multiplicity of experience, how it is socially constructed and how it can be both fluid and yet stable.

3 In looking at the ideas of both Jaynes and Romanyshyn on consciousness, we came to grips with the elusive but important idea of consciousness as a *metaphorical* reality. The use of metaphor in scientific theorizing was discussed and the difficulty of finding adequate metaphors to deepen our understanding of consciousness because of its unique nature. Metaphor itself was suggested as the

best metaphor for consciousness. Like a metaphor, consciousness is capable both of representing experience and transforming it. If our experience of the world is metaphor-like, then it resides neither in consciousness nor in the external world but in the reflection of one through the other. This can explain how people's experience of the same situation may vary but yet consistency and communication are possible. The usefulness of this conception and its implications for psychology were discussed. Romanyshyn has also made the point that to understand someone's action is not to give the causes of the action but rather to set it in a narrative of reasons and events leading up to the action in question, i.e. to 'set them in a story'.

4 *Personal construct theory* is the most influential of psychological theories which try to make sense of subjective experience. Its consistency with the analysis of personal worlds given in the Block was noted. It was suggested that it might be helpful to think of constructs as metaphors. Kelly's methods of self-characterization and fixed role therapy were seen as similar to the idea of making sense of someone by setting him or her in a story, and to the proposition that a major function of psychology is 'imaginal reconstruction'.

5 The important place of *daydreaming* and *imagination* in subjective experience and the role of the unconscious were then discussed.

Can you recall the different categories of fantasy which were suggested?

In what ways may unconscious factors assert themselves in subjective experience?

The mythology of a culture is a rich source of personal myths and metaphors and may have a powerful influence on the behaviour of individuals. Jung suggests that archetypes in the collective unconscious also play a role. The problem of finding myths appropriate to our time was noted.

6 The final three areas discussed concerned the origins of consciousness in evolution, history and culture.

The ideas of two theorists were put forward about the adaptive function of consciousness and why it developed in the form that it did. Who were they? What are the key points which each makes and what implications, if any, do they carry for the practice of psychology?

Jaynes describes consciousness as originating in the 'breakdown of the bicameral mind'. What does he mean by this? With what evidence and/or arguments does he support his thesis? What are the limitations and value of his ideas?

Ways in which society may influence consciousness were illustrated by Berger *et al.*'s theory about the ways in which technological and bureaucratic developments have influenced contemporary consciousness.

Can you remember:

1 The features which characterize technological production?

2 Ways in which these writers assert that it has influenced 'cognitive style'?

It was also suggested that the 'pluralization' of life-worlds in contemporary society may serve to strengthen a sense of individual identity.

Can you recollect how it might do this?

The influence which a person's occupation may have on his or her subjective experience and the effects of technological society on the nature of our thinking about the world were also discussed.

Finally, it was suggested that the theories presented should not necessarily be taken as competing or contradictory but rather that they throw light on different aspects of subjective experience.

Unit 14: Development and change in personal life

1 This unit was concerned with the ways in which personal worlds change over time. Adult life is a problematic area to investigate because so many aspects are involved and most of the research has been relatively recent.

2 Erikson's theory of the eight ages of life was presented.

Can you remember the four stages of adult development which he proposes?

In what sense are they conceived in a dialectical fashion?

What does he mean by describing ego development as an epigenetic process?

Erikson sees personal development as a function of the interaction between biological changes and the reactions and influences of the social context in which a person lives. Although his theory has been criticized as ethnocentric and male-oriented, it has been influential and is useful as a tool to think with. It suggests, for example, different ways in which existential needs may change as we grow older.

Can you recollect some of the changes of this kind which were suggested?

3 The development of *research* on the life cycle was introduced by brief reference to the work of Bühler and Neugarten.

What were the main features of their research and findings?

A detailed account was then given of the phase theory put forward by Levinson and his associates.

Into how many *eras* did Levinson divide the life cycle?

What are the periods of early and middle adulthood?

What does Levinson mean by the Dream, the mentor, the special woman/man?

Can you describe what he regards as the primary tasks of the Mid-life Transition?

Levinson's theory offers a schedule of the typical phases of development in early and middle adulthood. He claims that although these are closely age-linked, there is considerable scope for individual variation in the precise form which development takes. It is questionable how far his theory can be considered to be empirically based, as is the extent to which it can be applied to men in other cultures and to women in general. Some possible sources of difference between the typical life cycles of men and women were discussed.

Can you remember what these were?

Although there is some consistency between the findings of different research studies on the life cycle, there are problems in comparing them because of their different ways of conceptualizing development and interpreting data. Such studies are primarily useful as 'anticipatory socialization' and because they get us to think about the way experience may differ at different stages of life.

4   Approaches to conceptualizing the life course other than phase theories were then discussed such as the idea of life *contours* which emphasize the continuity of development, and theories which focus on the role of crisis or particular transitions.

What two kinds of crisis were distinguished?

Can you recall the strategies which were suggested as useful for coping with stressful situations?

Pearlin's work suggests that both stress and coping resources are unequally distributed in the population and that typical life course patterns will therefore vary according to socioeconomic situation.

Mid-life is the transitional stage which has received most attention. Jung sees it as a turning point in life towards inner concerns and self-realization. After discussing the views of Jaques, Vaillant and others about the mid-life transition, the Unit concluded by focusing on change in existential needs through life and the moral and social nature of the enterprise of living.

2   THE USE OF THEORY

You might like to make a list of some of the primary perspectives and theories used in the Block.

The different approaches and theories drawn on in the Block, as well as connections to other parts of the course, are discussed in some detail in the *Vade Mecum* (Metablock Part 2, pp. 30–4). It should therefore suffice to list here (in no particular order), with examples, the main theoretical perspectives discussed.

Theoretical position	Examples in Block 4
Phenomenological (focus on or appeal to direct experience).	James, Jaynes (consciousness as metaphor), Romanyshyn, personal construct theory, analysis of types of fantasy.

Existential (focus on issues stemming from the experience of human existence).	Discussions of time, choice, meaning and identity. Fromm.
Psychoanalytic (focus on the unconscious).	Freud, Erikson, Jung, Gould, Jaques.
Symbolic interactionist (focus on the way people communicate and make sense of their experience and how this is a function of social process).	Goffman.
Social constructivist (focus on the influence of social structures on behaviour and experience).	Berger et al., Labelling theory, Jaynes (bicameral mind).
Sociobiological (focus on evolutionary analysis).	Humphrey, Crook, Jaynes (bicameral mind).
Eclectic/empirical (empirically based focus on analysis of interview or other data).	Levinson et al., Neugarten, Bühler, Nicholson, Pearlin.

Compiling a chart of this kind brings home a point made in the Metablock – the difficulty of classifying research and theory. Fromm, for example, is normally considered as a psychoanalyst and yet those aspects of his work which we have focused on in the Block come more appropriately under the label existential, given the categories used here and how they have been defined. Jaynes's theory about the origins of consciousness appears under two headings because it draws on both evolutionary and social construction type explanations.

3   UNDERSTANDING PERSONAL WORLDS

I would now like to round off our consideration of personal worlds by briefly looking at two kinds of implications which it raises. This section will be concerned with *epistemological* issues: i.e. what our examination of personal worlds indicates about the nature of such a subject-matter. What kind of understanding is possible here? How best might it be studied? Then, in section 4, we shall look at the *ethical* implications (in the broadest sense of that term): in other words, what relevance might psychology of this kind have for the way in which we lead our lives?

At least three features of personal worlds which emerge from the analysis presented in this Block make them difficult to investigate in an orthodox scientific way:

1   Personal worlds are constituted by *meanings*.

2   They depend on the complex *integration* over time of many factors – biological, social and personal.

3   Although much of any personal world is determined by factors outside that individual's control, paradoxically it also seems to have the quality of being an open and autonomous system. (This 'Janus face' of human nature is discussed in *Freud and Psychoanalysis*, pp. 135–8). A personal world is always open to change,

and individual awareness and autonomous action play some part in creating what it is and will be like.

Let us consider each of these three features in turn.

1 The centrality of meaning in human behaviour and experience and the problems related to studying it are discussed in some detail in Metablock Paper 5 and in Chapter 11 of the Set Book *Freud and Psychoanalysis*, both of which were set reading for week 10. At some stage, you might like to refresh your memory about the major points made there and consider them in relation to the approach and the material presented in this Block.

One feature of a meaning system is that it forms a *Gestalt* where one part takes meaning from the others and the whole is more than the sum of its parts, and this is difficult to investigate in a reductionist way which involves analysing the component elements of the phenomenon in question. A major point made in the readings is that, because of the significance of meaning, the positivist assumption that investigation should be confined to a subject matter which can be rendered in operational form is inappropriate for the study of subjective experience. Rather than the search for cause-effect laws by experimental testing of hypotheses, it is argued, what is required is a *hermeneutic* approach. This involves the interpretation and unpacking of meanings (see also Metablock Paper 8 for further discussion of the hermeneutic perspective). In line with this, much of the approach of this Block has been descriptive and exploratory, attempting to dig into and differentiate the nature and meaning of personal experience.

Such an approach has an interesting possible implication for the practice of psychology. Making sense of meaning is an act of imaginative reconstruction. As was suggested earlier in discussing the work of Humphrey (Unit 13, section 5.1.3), psychologists' capacity to do this may well be facilitated by extending their personal experience (either vicariously through reading and clinical work, for example, or in actuality) so that they possess a richer fund of possibilities and 'scripts' available to them for this reconstruction task. At the moment, this is not considered as an important or even relevant dimension of the training of psychologists: perhaps, though, consideration should be given to the possibility that it might be.

2 The second problematic aspect arises because of the *holistic* nature of our subject matter. In looking at theories of development through adult life, we noted that one of the difficulties of such research is the breadth of subject matter it has to encompass. As almost all the theorists acknowledge, development is the outcome of the interaction of multiple contours from biological growth to different social situations and historical change. The issue of integration is outlined in Chapter 1 of *Freud and Psychoanalysis* which was optional reading for Unit 13. It is also taken up in the final chapter of that book which is the set reading for Part 2 of this Unit. It is suggested there (see p. 144) that the fundamental problem here is finding a way of relating the essentially different concept languages of the various perspectives and developing a superordinate framework which can effectively integrate them. This Block has not been able to provide that but it has tried to present a variety of perspectives on subjective experience (see especially Unit 13) to illustrate its multiple aspects and the different factors which underlie and influence it.

3 The third problematic property of personal worlds – *autonomy* – was discussed in some detail in Unit 12, section 3, and it is examined further in Metablock Paper 9, which is part of your work for the study weeks immediately following this Block.

Human autonomy derives both from the power to confer meaning and the capacity to initiate actions. One consequence is that in studying personal worlds we are dealing with an active construction which is continuously open to change. A further consequence is that, as consciousness has the power, like metaphor, not just to represent but to transform experience (see Unit 13, Section 3.2), so too does theory. As we saw in the case of a concept such as the mid-life crisis, and as is also exemplified by psychoanalytic theory (see Chapter 13 of *Freud and Psychoanalysis*), psychological statements may be self-fulfilling. They may result in behaviour and experience being created in their own image. In the study of an area like personal worlds, analysis and subject-matter may be linked in a curiously circular way. For our theories reflect our background and the kind of persons we are (see Metablock Paper 7). But the concepts we assimilate can help determine the ways in which we experience, behave and make sense of ourselves. In investigating personal worlds, we need to be alert to the possibility that the accounts people give of themselves are likely to reflect current 'myths' of their time.

Both as psychological theorists or as persons making sense of their own lives, it is important to be reflexive about one's assumptions.

Have you detected any particular assumptions underlying the kind of analysis of personal worlds presented in this Block? Can you specify what some of these might be?

Like any other construction of reality (see Metablock Paper 7), the analysis put forward here has been based on certain implicit assumptions. It presumes, for example, that the best mode of making sense of personal worlds is to adopt a rational and phenomenological approach. It also works from the premises that life, as we experience it, is finite and that persons have some capacity for agency and choice. Although there may be good grounds for such existential assumptions, each is open to question and depends on an act of assertion and appeal to the reader's experience of what existence is like. There is no way of avoiding assumptions of some kind. We can only try to be aware as far as possible of what these may be.

The curious feature of personal worlds and the meanings we attribute to ourselves and the world about us is that we can make sense of them in so many different ways. They have potentially something of a chameleon-like nature. Although they may possess continuity and stability, they are always capable of change. They can be modified radically as we progress through life, or by the act of reflecting upon them, or as we assimilate new ways of conceptualizing. Perhaps at the end of this course your personal worlds will not be quite the same as when you commenced. This fluid quality of personal worlds was one implication of Prather's remark quoted at the beginning of Unit 13 about the problem of trying to figure out how things 'really are' when all the time 'they weren't'.

All this suggests that in the study of personal worlds the goal becomes not so much definitive analysis as to offer ideas, ways of looking at things, scenarios to test against experience and to stimulate thought. Heightening consciousness in this way may help to increase the power a person has to transcend and transform the ways in which he or she experiences and behaves.

But what kind of understanding is this? Wilber (1982), following Habermas, has distinguished between different kinds of knowing. For example, when we are interested in understanding the physical and sensory world, the mode is empirical-analytic: when we are concerned with understanding other minds, the mode is 'hermeneutic, phenomenological, rational or historic' (a similar distinction is made in Chapter 11 of *Freud and Psychoanalysis*). An effective scientific method must be geared to the nature of the subject-matter with which it deals. Traditionally, much of psychology has been dominated by the positivist emphasis on the empirical-analytic mode. This, it can be argued, provides methods and metaphors more appropriate to the study of the physical world. One reason for this emphasis may be, as noted earlier in Unit 13 (see section 5.3.4), the prevailing technological images and consciousness of our time. The effect has often been, as Heather observed, to reify the subject-matter of psychology and thus to obscure its essence.

In a somewhat long-winded fashion, Sarason makes an analogous point in the final article in the Course Reader (pp. 314–30), which is optional reading for Part 2 of this unit. He emphasizes that social action is of a fundamentally different nature to the physical world. The problem-solving analytic techniques of orthodox science are simply inappropriate for dealing with many of the issues which confront us in social science and, we might add, in the study of personal worlds. Problems are often intractable and, as with existential issues, do not admit of definitive solution. Because subjective experience is a construction where the meaning of any one aspect is given by its relation to other aspects and is always open to transformation, there is inherent ambiguity. As Pirsig has aptly expressed it: 'In the high country of the mind one has to become adjusted to the thinner air of uncertainty' (1974, p. 127).

Set reading

Chapter 14 of *Freud and Psychoanalysis* takes up a number of the issues raised in this Conclusion and should be read at some stage during your work on this Unit. It touches, for example, on the possibility that the 'mechanistic' type concepts often applied in the study of behaviour may be a function of the technological society in which we live. It suggests that what the author calls a 'dialectical' approach might more usefully take the place of the positivist, empirical-analytic mode in studying personal worlds. (You may remember that Erikson's eight ages of life was one example of a dialectical approach). Although this is hardly more than a sketch of some of the factors which need to be taken into account, it may help your thinking about alternative approaches and the limits and nature of understanding which is possible in an area such as this.

Theories and analyses of personal worlds, then, are not statements of 'truth' or accounts of 'reality' but ways of conceptualizing experience and behaviour. They help to provide metaphors which direct our attention and give shape to our understanding. As Chapter 14 suggests though, there are criteria which can be used in evaluating analyses of personal worlds, such as *differentiation* (the extent to which they sensitize us to different aspects of the phenomenon in question of which we were unaware) and *consistency* (the effectiveness with which the various aspects of the picture presented by a particular metaphor or theory hang together and the degree to which it is possible to test or establish that). Taken together, these two criteria are related to how *plausible* an account is in making sense of the subject-matter we seek to understand. Criteria for evaluating analyses of personal worlds are discussed further in Metablock Paper 2 (section 5) and in Paper 10 (see in particular Box 1).

4 LESSONS FOR LIVING

The aims attributed in the previous section to a psychology of personal worlds suggest that such a psychology might well be a source of guidance in the way we construct our lives. Traditionally, psychologists have shied away from articulating the ethical implications of their theories and research. In part this has been because of their positivist empirical-analytic perspective. This assumes that people's behaviour is essentially determined rather than autonomous. It was also due to the belief that a researcher should be neutral and 'objective'. Trying to keep a check on the influence of presuppositions and values on one's research and theorizing is admirable but this is, however, quite different from and in no way precludes exploring the value implications which arise from the findings. In any case, if we accept the argument for the potentially self-fulfilling nature of psychological theories, there is no way in which psychologists, in the study of areas like personal worlds at least, can avoid the possibility that their ideas may influence the ways in which people think and behave. Whether psychologists like it or not, psychology is in this sense a 'moral science'.

But what sort of ethical implications can psychological theories have? An idea which emerges through the Block is the possibility of self-directed evolution: that, both as individuals and societies, we are capable to a considerable extent of directing our own development and what we shall become. This opens up an issue raised in several places in the Block (see for example Unit 13, sections 3.4 and Epilogue) – the question of psychoethics. Given the alternative possibilities open to us as individuals and societies in terms of ways of living, styles of consciousness, ways of making sense of the world and building our social structures, can guidance be given in terms of what is 'psychologically desirable', rather as a dietician can recommend some diets as more conducive to health than others? Although almost all psychologists avoid doing this in any explicit way, 'recommendations' are often conveyed by their writings, if only by implication. Is not the effect of Erikson's scheme, for example, even though he may deny the intention, to hint as to what kind of development is desirable for us to aspire to – to be generative and not stagnate, to attain ego integrity and not despair? Levinson's analysis also implicitly suggests the best courses to take through the stormy waters of our life transitions, in order to arrive at calmer and happier havens in later life.

But psychologists are unwilling to confront directly the possibility of criteria for a psychological 'good life': I believe rightly so. They are aware of the constructed nature of their own formulations. The different theoretical standpoints they offer represent psychological life as a reality of reflection through the mirror of metaphors which each provides. Each theory acts like a superordinate metaphor. It deepens our understanding by directing and shaping our attention. Each is capable of revealing some facets, while in so doing obscuring others that a different metaphor might throw into relief: hence the need for the multiple perspective approach which has been adopted. A metaphor which is useful for one person may not necessarily be so for others. To present pat definitive solutions to the tasks we face in creating our life would be to undermine our power and fate to be the autonomous agents of our own futures.

However, through the analyses and ideas it provides, psychology has a potentially transforming power. One theme which comes through the Block, for example, is the problem that confronts us in accepting and taking responsibility for the potential choices which we have. We have looked at possible reasons for this reluctance, our need for authorization and the avoiding tactics which may be adopted to avoid responsibility for choice. We have also been alerted to the paradox of meaningfulness and direction. We require these to engage in life with vitality, and yet ultimately (in a world where there are only metaphorical realities of reflection) we have no rational basis for creating them. No definitive solutions emerge from analysis of this kind, but it may play a part in increasing our awareness of our own position in terms of such issues. It may help to stir the imagination, offer us metaphors to try on for size, show us what might have been or yet could be. Enriching our awareness of possibility is a sustenance we need in the task that each of us confronts in helping to create the personal worlds of ourselves and others.

Further reading

If you are interested in the issues raised in the Block, you may like to look at the following books.

Unit 12

YALOM, I. D. (1980) *Existential Psychotherapy*, New York, Basic Books.

Unit 13

GOFFMAN, E. (1975) *Frame Analysis*, Harmondsworth, Penguin Books.

JAYNES, J. (1979) *The Origin of Consciousness in the Breakdown of the Bicameral Mind*, London, Allen Lane.

BERGER, P. L., BERGER, B. and KELLNER, H. (1974) *The Homeless Mind*, Harmondsworth, Penguin Books.

FROMM, E. (1960) *Fear of Freedom*, London, Routledge and Kegan Paul.

Unit 14

LEVINSON, D. J. *et al.* (1978) *The Seasons of a Man's Life*, New York, Knopf.

ERIKSON, E. H. (1950) *Childhood and Society*, New York, Norton, Reprinted in paperback (1977) by Triad/Paladin.

STEVENS, R. (1983) *Erik Erikson: An Introduction*, Milton Keynes, The Open University Press.

KIMMEL, D. C. (1980) *Adulthood and Aging* (2nd edn), New York, Wiley.

References

BARDWICK, J. M. (1971) *Psychology of Women*, New York, Harper and Row.

BEAUVOIR, S. DE (1972) *Old Age* (trans. by P. O'Brian), London, André Deutsch and Weidenfeld and Nicolson.

BÜHLER, C. (1968) 'The developmental structure of goal setting in group and individual studies', in Bühler, C. and Massarik, F. (eds) *The Course of Human Life*, New York, Springer.

BUSS, A. R. (1979) *A Dialectical Psychology*, New York, Wiley.

ERIKSON, E. H. (1950) *Childhood and Society*, New York, Norton, Reprinted in paperback (1977) by Triad/Paladin.

ERIKSON, E. H. (1959) *Young Man Luther: A Study in Psychoanalysis and History*, London, Faber.

ERIKSON, E. H. (1964) *Insight and Responsibility*, London, Faber.

ERIKSON, E. H. (1968) *Identity: Youth and Crisis*, London, Faber.

ERIKSON, E. H. (1969) *Gandhi's Truth*, London, Faber.

ERICKSON, E. H. (1976) 'Reflections on Dr Borg's life cycle', *Daedalus*, No. 105, pp. 1–28.

ERIKSON, E. H. (1980) *Identity and the Life Cycle*, New York, International Universities Press.

FARRELL, M. P. and ROSENBERG, S. D. (1981) *Men at Mid-life*, Boston, Auburn House.

FERGUSON, M. (1980) *The Aquarian Conspiracy: Personal and Social Transformation in the 1980s*, Los Angeles, Tarcher.

FRYER, D. M. and PAYNE, R. L. (1984) 'Proactive behaviour in the unemployed: findings and implications', *Leisure Studies*, Vol. 3, pp. 273–95.

GILLIGAN, C. (1982) *In a Different Voice: Psychological Theory and Women's Development*, Cambridge, Massachusetts, Harvard University Press.

GOULD, R. L. (1978) *Transformations: Growth and Change in Adult Life*, New York, Simon and Schuster.

GUTTMANN, D. (1977) 'The cross-cultural perspective: notes towards a comparative psychology of ageing', in Birren, J. E. and Schaie, K. W. (eds) *Handbook of the Psychology of Aging*, New York, Van Nostrand Reinhold.

HORNER, M. S. (1972) 'Toward an understanding of achievement-related conflicts in women', *Journal of Social Issues*, Vol. 28, pp. 157–75.

JAQUES, E. (1965) 'Death and the mid-life crisis', *International Journal of Psychoanalysis*, Vol. 46, pp. 502–13.

JUNG, C. G. (1969) 'The stages of life' (trans. by R. F. C. Hull), in *Collected Works* (2nd edn), Vol. 8: *The Structure and Dynamics of the Psyche*, London, Routledge and Kegan Paul.

JUNG. C.G. (1973) *Letters*, Princeton, Princeton University Press.

JUNG, C. G. (1977) *Memories, Dreams, Reflections* (recorded and edited by A. Jaffe, trans. by R. and C. Winston), London, Collins.

KIMMEL, D. C. (1980) *Adulthood and Aging*, (2nd edn.), New York, Wiley.

LEVINSON, D. J. *et al.* (1978) *The Seasons of a Man's Life*, New York, Knopf.

LEVINSON, D. J. (1980) 'Toward a conception of the adult life course', in Smelser, N. J. and Erikson, E. H. (eds) *Themes of Work and Love in Adulthood*, London, Grant McIntyre.

LIVSON, F. B. (1976) 'Patterns of personality development in middle-aged women: a longitudinal study', *International Journal of Aging and Human Development*, Vol. 7, No. 2, pp. 107–15.

LOWENTHAL, M. F. (1977) 'Toward a socio-psychological theory of change in adulthood and old age', in Birren, J. E. and Scaie, K. W. (eds) *Handbook of the Psychology of Aging*, New York, Van Nostrand Reinhold.

LOWENTHAL, M. F. and CHIRIBOGA, D. (1972) 'Transition to the empty nest: crisis, challenge or relief?', *Archives of General Psychiatry*, Vol. 26, pp. 8–14.

MURPHY, J., JOHN, M. and BROWN, H. (eds) (1984) *Dialogues and Debates in Social Psychology*, Lawrence Erlbaum (Course Reader).

NEUGARTEN, B. L. (1967) 'A new look at menopause', *Psychology Today*, December 1967, pp. 42–5, 67–9.

NEUGARTEN, B. L. (1968) 'The awareness of middle age', in Neugarten, B. L. (ed.) *Middle-age and Aging*, Chicago, University of Chicago Press.

NEUGARTEN, B. L. *et al.* (1964) *Personality in Middle and Late Life*, New York, Atherton Press.

NEUGARTEN, B. L. and GUTTMAN, D. (1958) 'Age-sex roles and personality in middle age: a thematic apperception study', *Psychological Monographs*, Vol. 72, No. 17.

NICHOLSON, J. (1980) *Seven Ages*, London, Collins.

PEARLIN, L. I. (1980) 'Life strains and psychological distress among adults', in Smelser, N. J. and Erikson, E. H. (eds) *Themes of Work and Love in Adulthood*, London, Grant McIntyre.

PIRSIG, R. M. (1974) *Zen and the Art of Motorcycle Maintenance: An Inquiry into Values*, London, The Bodley Head.

PLATH, D. W. (1982) 'Resistance at forty-eight: old-age brinkmanship and Japanese life course pathways', in Hareven, T. K. and Adams, K. J. (eds) *Ageing and Life Course Transitions: An Interdisciplinary Perspective*, London, Tavistock.

RIEGEL, K. S. (1975) 'Adult life crises: a dialectic interpretation of development', in Datan, N. and Ginsberg, L. H. (eds) *Life-span Developmental Psychology: Normative Life Crises*, New York, Academic Press.

SHEEHY, G. (1976) *Passages: Predictable Crises of Adult Life*, New York, Dutton.

SMELSER, N. J. (1980) 'Issues in the study of work and love in adulthood', in Smelser, N. J. and Erikson, E. H. (eds) *Themes of Work and Love in Adulthood*, London, Grant McIntyre.

SONTAG, S. (1982) 'The double standard of aging', in Allmann, L. R. and Jaffe, D. T. (eds) *Readings in Adult Psychology: Contemporary Perspectives* (2nd edn), New York, Harper and Row.

STEVENS, R. (1983a) *Erik Erikson: An Introduction*, Milton Keynes, The Open University Press.

STEVENS, R. (1983b) *Freud and Psychoanalysis*, Milton Keynes, The Open University Press (Set Book).

STEVENS-LONG, J. (1983) *Adult Life: Development Processes* (2nd edn), Palo Alto, California, Mayfield Publishing Co.

VAILLANT, G. E. (1977) *Adaptation to Life*, Boston, Little, Brown and Co.

WILBER, K. (1982) 'Reflections on the new-age paradigm', in Wilber, K. (ed.) *The Holographic Paradigm and Other Paradoxes: Exploring the Leading Edge of Science*, Boulder and London, Shambhala.

Acknowledgements

Grateful acknowledgement is made to the following sources for the material used in this Unit:

Figure 1 reproduced by permission of *Daedalus*, journal of the American Academy of Arts and Sciences, E. H. Erikson, 'Reflections on Dr Borg's life cycle', Vol. 105, p. 26, Boston, MA., 1976; *Figure 2 and extracts* from D. J. Levinson *et. al., The Seasons of a Man's Life*, copyright © 1978 by David J. Levinson, reprinted by permission of Alfred A. Knopf Inc., and The Sterling Lord Agency, Inc.

Index of concepts